COMING HOME TO MYSELF

COMING HOME TO MYSELF

WYNONNA JUDD

with

PATSI BALE COX

A SIGNET BOOK

SIGNET
Published by New American Library, a division of
Penguin Group (USA) Inc., 375 Hudson Street,
New York, New York 10014, USA
Penguin Group (Canada), 90 Eglinton Avenue East, Suite 700, Toronto,
Ontario M4P 2Y3, Canada (a division of Pearson Penguin Canada Inc.)
Penguin Books Ltd., 80 Strand, London WC2R 0RL, England
Penguin Ireland, 25 St. Stephen's Green, Dublin 2,
Ireland (a division of Penguin Books Ltd.)
Penguin Group (Australia), 250 Camberwell Road, Camberwell, Victoria 3124,
Australia (a division of Pearson Australia Group Pty. Ltd.)
Penguin Books India Pvt. Ltd., 11 Community Centre, Panchsheel Park,
New Delhi - 110 017, India
Penguin Group (NZ), 67 Apollo Drive, Rosedale, North Shore,
Auckland 1311, New Zealand (a division of Pearson New Zealand Ltd.)
Penguin Books (South Africa) (Pty.) Ltd., 24 Sturdee Avenue,
Rosebank, Johannesburg 2196, South Africa

Penguin Books Ltd., Registered Offices: 80 Strand, London WC2R 0RL, England

Published by Signet, an imprint of New American Library, a division of Penguin Group
(USA) Inc. Previously published in a New American Library hardcover edition.

First Signet Printing, June 2007
10 9 8 7 6 5 4 3 2 1

PHILIPPIANS 4:13—I can do all things through Christ, who strengthens me.

This book is dedicated to my Lord and Savior for His grace and mercy and for loving me as much on my worst day as He does on my best!!

I believe!!!

Acknowledgments

I would like to express my love and gratitude to . . .

My husband, Roach, my soul mate–I can't imagine being on this journey without you.

My daughter, Grace, my sons, Elijah and Zac–Being your mother is the hardest job I've ever loved. You are my heart.

My little sister, Ashley, and her husband, Dario–Please take good care of each other.

My Mom and Pop–There's always hope!

My Mamaw and Papaw Ciminella and my Papaw Judd–I miss you.

My Nana–Thank you for always seeing the good in me.

Each Judd, Ciminella, Roach, Mandell, Franchitti and Strickland family member–God bless you all!

My brother, Michael–I hope to meet you and the rest of the Jordan family one day.

My cowriter, Patsi Bale Cox–I can't wait to write another book just so I can hang out with you. I love your colorful spirit!

My dearest friend and personal manager, Kerry Hansen–We've come a long way together in ten years!

Rondal Richardson–You're my favorite!

Jennifer Lowry and Tami Olin at Wynonna, Inc.–You are both such amazing women!

The rest of the Wynonna, Inc., family–Jim Baber, Robert Bailey, Steve Cox, Ken Craig, Curtis Flatt, Randy Flowers,

Mike Frogge, Vicki Hampton, Steve Mackey, Tony Obrohta, Steve Potts, Harry Sharpe, Tom Spaulding, Ashley Swann, Mark Thomas and Linda Bram Wilbourn.

Penguin/NAL–Kara Welsh, Tracy Bernstein, Leslie Gelbman, Liz Perl, Craig Burke and Alex Gigante for publishing my very first book!

The William Morris Agency–Mel Berger, Greg Oswald, Julie Colbert, Richard Rosenberg, Gayle Holcomb and all of the other hardworking agents and assistants. Thank you for seven wonderful years!

Linda Carbone and everyone at KSA–I know you've got my back.

My financial advisors: MaryAnn McCready, President, and Jamie Cheek, Business Manager–What a difference you both have made in my family's life.

Diane King and the rest of the FBMM team–Thank you for your constant efforts each day.

My legal team: Rose Palermo, my second mother, and Denty Cheatham–Thank you for always being there when I need you.

John Frankenheimer and Denise McIntosh Stevens at Loeb & Loeb–Thank you for looking out for me.

J. D. Holt–Thank you for helping me find out the truth.

Gary Wood–Thank you for standing in the gap.

Oprah–You've encouraged me from the very beginning. Thank you for believing in the human spirit the way you do.

My Musical Team: Mike Curb and the Curb Records Family–Twenty years and counting!

My producers–Brent Maher, Tony Brown, James Stroud, Narada Michael Walden, Dann Huff and Keith Thomas.

All of the songwriters in my musical life–You give me a reason to sing.

All of the musicians who have performed on my records–Your gifts are awe-inspiring.

To all my friends at radio–Thank you for being a part of my career for twenty years now!

The Judd-Roach Ranch Team: Bill Cannon, Jane Newcome, Cathy Lewis, Darla Delancey, Mary (Ya-Ya) Eller–Thank you for taking such good care of us. God bless you and your families.

Dominick and the DiVito Family–Thank you for your loyalty and support these past four years.

Don and Christine Potter–Thank you for intercessory prayer and unconditional friendship.

Dr. Lee Tucker, Dr. Mona Lisa Schultz, Dr. Craig Farrell, Dr. Janice Christianson, Dr. Cutsinger, Dr. Xiao, Dr. Jill Hargrove, Dr. Barbara Nylander, Dr. Carl Wingo, Dr. Michael Miller, Dr. Lee Meehan, Dr. Gary Owens–Thank you for your alternative and conventional medical wisdom. You are my teachers.

My Life Coaches: Ted Klontz, Marjorie Zugich, Rich Kahler, Ms. Jennie, Warren Brent, Louise Strang–You've changed the way our family loves and communicates.

Trish Dean, Charlotte Trainer, Adie Gray, Davita Hungate and Suzanne McLemore–Thank you for your healing hands.

My Glam Squad: Robert Vetica, Billy B., Eric Barnard, Gordon Robinson, Angela Hall, Susanne Shepherd, Kathleen Marr, Houri Barahimi, Pasquale Di Fabrizio, Mary Freeman, Renee Layher and Robert Warner.

Randi Lesnick and Hospitality Consultants–Thank you for such an awesome wedding!

My church families: Bellevue Community Church, Grace Chapel and Christ Church–Thank you for a place to just "be."

My friends and their families: Bryce Edgar, Lisa Ramsey, Jennifer Grisham, Angelique and Christopher Pitney, Dolly Gillespie, Ira Parker, Anthony and Karen Thomas, Lucia and Mark Davidson, Bart and Lydia Butler, Mike McGrath, Peggy Claude Pierre, Scott and Donna Calder-head, Lark Foster, Chuck and Gena Norris, Big D. and Margaret Darnell, Art McCloud, Gabrielle Belkin and Mariska Hargitay.

Bono–Thank you for opening my eyes to the AIDS pandemic.

Kate Roberts–Thank you for opening my heart. To my friends at PSI–working with you has inspired my life. For more information about YouthAIDS, log on to www.youth-aids.org.

My dear fans–I could not have made it this far without you!

To anyone else who has helped me along the way–Thank you for your love and prayers.

Preface

My pop once told me, "If you don't make a decision in life, life will make the decision for you." It was the fall of 2003, and my doctor had told me that my cholesterol and triglyceride levels were dangerously high. I was at great risk for a heart attack, a walking time bomb. I was terrified that if people found out about it, everyone would focus on my health instead of my music. But as much as I wanted to hide my health scare, I was spent—physically, mentally and spiritually. I felt like my body was giving out, and knew that if I didn't make a life change soon, I would surely die. It seemed like I was working myself half to death, yet not getting ahead financially. I was still reeling from the secrets that had been kept from me all my life. And while I needed to take some time off to take care of myself, I was crushingly aware that I supported a great many families. It seemed overwhelming. Looking back, I now realize that the decision I made to call my manager, Kerry Hansen, about my concerns was the beginning of *Coming Home to Myself*.

"Kerry Hansen," I said. "We need to talk!"

Kerry says when I'm really upset about something, I always use her first and last name.

"Wy, what's wrong?" Kerry asked. "Are you okay?"

"No. I'm not. I'm not okay at all," I answered in a calm, matter-of-fact tone. "I'm at an end. I don't think I can keep going anymore. I feel like I'm starting to lose it."

"What do you mean?"

I didn't answer.

"Tell me what you're talking about, Wy," she said. "You're scaring me!"

"I've hit a big wall. I'm so tired. I don't know if I can bounce back this time."

"Where are you? Do you want me to come be with you?"

"No," I said. "I'm alone but you don't need to come all the way out here."

"What can I do to help?" Kerry asked. "What do you need right now?"

"I'm not sure," I said, and began to cry.

"Do you need some time? Do you need to go somewhere and get help? Do you want me to make some phone calls to clear your schedule? If you want me to, I can cancel some tour dates—we still have time before we finalize the contracts."

"I don't have an answer right now. But I am not canceling. It's not an option for me!" I choked out.

At this point Kerry sounded really concerned. "Wy, if there's something seriously wrong, your fans will understand. We have to do what's right for you."

The words *your fans will understand* repeated over and over in my head. I had only canceled a few times in my career. I had never let anything or anyone get me down for long. I knew I couldn't give up. So much had been planned. Everyone had been working so hard. They were counting on me. I kept hearing my mom's voice whispering in my ear: *Judd women always land on their feet!*

I struggled for composure. "Uh, I guess—I think I'm just exhausted and feeling a little overwhelmed right now. I'm sure a good night's sleep will help me feel better tomorrow. Just talking about it has made me feel better. I appreciate you listening. I'll call you in the morning."

We said goodbye and hung up. I was up most of the night, thinking about my situation. I had been telling myself for the past few years that even though my body was getting weaker, my spirit was still strong. It was that determined spirit, that Judd work ethic that I had learned from my mother, the want and need to be loved, that kept me working so hard for almost twenty years. I agonized about it all night.

I had tried for so long to keep everyone and everything going. I felt I couldn't let the people around me down. Deep in my heart I knew that I couldn't continue to let myself down either, but I just didn't have the strength to make a change. There was a world out there that was already signed, sealed and delivered. For me to make the change would be to call a halt to the party, and I didn't have the ability to do that. In the studio I knew how to say, "That doesn't work for me." But in my personal life I couldn't stand up for myself.

I found myself thinking, I will either make it through this crisis—or—*well, if I do have a heart attack, I'll have to stop*. I now stood at the crossroads in a struggle between selfless and selfish.

When I woke up the next morning, the sun was shining, thank God! Even though I had not slept much, I was thankful for the new day. I called Kerry's direct line at the office to check in.

"How are you today?" she asked.

"I feel so much better!" I said, trying to sound enthusiastic. "I just needed someone to talk to. Thanks for being there."

"Are you really okay?" Kerry asked. "Are you sure you don't need me to do anything for you?"

She still sounded worried, so I tried to reassure her. "I'm fine," I said confidently. "I'm just anxious about the album and the tour and the wedding. But like I always say, 'The show must go on.' "

And so it did. Less than a week later, I was going about my life as if nothing was wrong. On the surface, things seemed to be going *very* right. So much was happening! My sixth solo album, *What the World Needs Now Is Love*, had been out for two months, and the first single was flying up the charts. Calls flooded into the office daily and the calendar was filling up fast. I was already booked far into 2004, and through the next few months, I was scheduled to travel from New York to Los Angeles to visit radio stations and perform on television shows, gearing up for the concert tour beginning in January.

I was also busy putting the final touches on my wedding in November to D. R. Roach, who had been my road manager for eleven years. Immediately after the wedding, Roach and his thirteen-year-old son, Zac, were moving in with my eight-year-old son, Elijah, my seven-year-old daughter, Grace, and me. I was preparing for the big merge, going full steam ahead.

But that call to Kerry could not be taken back. Just that one short phone conversation was the beginning of *acceptance* for me. I admitted that I had a problem. And the call continued to weigh on Kerry's mind, despite my trying to put up a good front. It was the beginning of a chain reaction that would end in a life-changing—live*saving*—year. When Julie Colbert, my agent at William Morris, called to ask Kerry if I might consider allowing Oprah to film my wedding, Kerry relayed her concerns about my schedule, mentioning my phone call. Then, during a "girl-talk" call to Oprah's producers, Julie passed along the information.

Wynonna feels she's hit a wall.

And so I received a call from Oprah saying that she wanted me to come to Chicago to talk with her about everything that was going on in my world. She had learned, she said, that I was worried about my health and that I truly wanted to do something about it. I wondered if my visit with Oprah might mean I would get some advice from someone who had been there, who might inspire me to begin the process of making a change in my life. I accepted the invitation.

On October 29, I boarded a flight to Chicago. I had butterflies in my stomach all day long, and by the time I buckled myself in the seat on the plane, the butterflies had turned to knots. Roach sat next to me and took my hand for our usual takeoff prayer. He could tell that I was emotional, and so he continued to hold my hand as we sat quietly waiting as the plane took off. I leaned forward and looked over at Kerry, who sat nearby. She smiled at me. Tears filled my eyes and I smiled back. I felt truly blessed to have two of my best friends going with me. What would my visit with Oprah bring?

I always feel closer to heaven when I fly. It's comforting to me. And as we approached thirty thousand feet, I sat looking out my window at the blanket of clouds below me. I realized that it had only been a few months since I had received the bad news from my doctor about my health, and now, here I was, about to sit face-to-face with one of my (s)heroes to tell her my story. It was going to be difficult, because my truth was—even though I was still going strong professionally after twenty years—behind all the success was a woman in crisis. I was scared to death. I knew that I needed help, but I didn't know where to begin.

As I continued to look out the window, I wondered what it would feel like to die. I thought about my father and wondered if I would meet him in heaven. Will I ever get to meet my guardian angel? I thought about Roach and the children. I thought about family and friends and what an incredible journey I'd had so far in life. I thought about my career. I'd been on the road half my life. What would I do if I didn't have my music and fans? I also thought about Mom and what our relationship might have been if we hadn't sung together.

I miss Ashley, I thought. I wondered what she was doing. Where was she at that very moment? Was she having a good day? My thoughts were so scattered. What would I order for lunch at the Ritz Hotel? They have twenty-four-hour room service! Am I going to cry when Oprah walks in the room?

We began our descent into the Chicago airport, and I felt a wave of panic wash over me. What in the world was I going to say to Oprah when we sat together in her office?

"Hi, Oprah! I'm afraid that I could die if I don't lose weight. I'm depressed and I feel like a complete failure when I look at myself in the mirror. Other than that, everything is just terrific! How about you?"

I had not talked openly about my deepest feelings and insecurities about myself and my body, or about how chaotic my lifestyle had become. But was I ready to tell Oprah the absolute truth? Was I willing to talk about what was going on behind the music? That I was working too hard and couldn't seem to slow down long enough to take care of my own health. I had become the very thing I tell my fans not to become—*a martyr*! I had struggled alone and in silence. I had continued to put my personal problems on hold for the sake of family and career. Day after day I convinced myself that I could take care of all my professional and personal responsibilities, determined that I could have it all! But trying to have it all was costing too much—maybe even my own life. It was time to surrender to my absolute truth, that I had lost myself. I had forgotten to put myself on the list.

I looked at Roach and he leaned over and kissed me. Good timing!

No one said much on the ride to Oprah's Harpo Studios. I could feel that Kerry and Roach were nervous for me. My heart was racing as our limo pulled into the entrance of Harpo. I thought, *It's too late to turn around and go home now, country girl.*

We got out of the limo, and several women from Oprah's staff greeted us. I had been here many times before, but this visit was very different. I wasn't here to talk about singing or show business. I was not here about a celebration. I was here to speak from the heart about my real life. As I began walking up the stairs to Oprah's office, I asked myself:

How in the world did I get to this place in my life?

A LITTLE BIT OF LOVE
(GOES A LONG WAY)

I was born into chaos.

At the end of summer 1963, my mother, Diana Ellen Judd, was seventeen years old and beginning her senior year of high school when she found out she was pregnant with me. She was a beautiful, smart, popular girl. She played piano in the church and made good grades. She was a good girl. She could have gone anywhere and accomplished anything. I can only imagine how she felt living in the small Southern town of Ashland, Kentucky, being pregnant and unmarried.

On the night I was conceived, Polly and Glenn Judd, my mother's parents, had left her alone in the house to go visit their firstborn son, Brian, in the hospital. He was dying. It was Mom who had found the lump on Brian's back one evening while the family sat at the supper table. That discovery led to Brian being examined and diagnosed with Hodgkin's disease.

When Mom told my dad, Michael Ciminella, that she was pregnant, he agreed to marry her. They wed at the Baptist church in Parisburg, Virginia, on January 3, 1964.

They didn't have much of a wedding, certainly not one that families dream about. Five months pregnant and beginning to show, Mom wore one of her mother's suits. Her daddy bought her a little corsage and recorded 8 mm home movies. The Judds and Ciminellas did the best they could to help Mom and Dad do the right thing. Mom and Dad lived with his parents, Mike (Papaw) and Billie (Mamaw) Ciminella at 1515 Morningside Drive. Mom finished school with a home tutor, who also tutored her brother Brian until he died at age seventeen.

I was born Christina Claire Ciminella on May 30, 1964. Some of Mom's graduating classmates came to visit her at the King's Daughter Hospital. They showed her their new diplomas, and she showed them her new baby daughter.

The day that Mom brought me home to 1515 Morningside Drive, the battle between the Judds and the Ciminellas began. Mom, an inexperienced new mother, and Mamaw, an experienced grandmother, both had very different ideas about how to care for me. Two strong-willed women in one household with one baby could mean trouble. Mom said Mamaw Ciminella was a perfectionist. Mamaw said she was trying to teach a young girl how to keep house and take care of a family. Mom said Mamaw was obsessed with ironing shirts and keeping the house perfect. Mom nearly went crazy because of Mamaw's "germ warfare." According to Mom, Mamaw was fanatical about keeping everything I touched perfectly sanitized. When Dad married Mom, Mamaw was excited about the idea of having a daughter she could be close to. Mom said she felt stuck. Mamaw taught Mom everything she knew! (Mom *still* talks about it today!) And Mom must have been a good pupil, because she soon became very picky herself about how she wanted household chores done. (It's being passed down generation to generation, too, because I'm already teaching Naomi Judd's Towel Folding 101 to my daughter, Grace!)

We lived in Kentucky until I was three years old. In 1967 Dad took a job as a salesman in California and we moved to a little house in the San Fernando Valley. Ashley was born on April 19, 1968. I'll never forget the day Mom brought Ashley home. I thought she was a gift for me. I absolutely adored her! But I quickly discovered that she didn't do much more than eat, sleep and poop. How many times I'd look at her and think, *You're really cute, but you stink*!

I know that Mom loved being a mother, and that she did everything she could to make our house a home. But we only had one car, which Dad took to work. So Mom, Ashley and I ended up alone together day after day. Mom must have felt stranded at times, and on some level, I think I knew it. I missed my Mamaw and Papaw so much; theirs was the first home I'd ever known. Several months after my baby sister was born, Mamaw and Papaw sent money so that I could come back to Kentucky for a visit.

And so, in the summer of 1968, Mom took me to the TWA terminal and left me in the hands of a stewardess (that's what they called them back then). The stewardess was young, pretty and, in her uniform, seemed very important. I felt like such a big girl when she bent down and pinned the little TWA wings on my dress. She then escorted me to my seat in one of the front rows, and buckled me in. Even though it was the first time I had ever flown, I wasn't afraid. As the engines roared and the gigantic plane taxied down the runway, all I could think about was 1515 Morningside Drive.

By the time the plane landed, I was so excited I had butterflies in my stomach. I looked out of the window and there Mamaw and Papaw stood, waiting for me. I could feel the love even from that distance. I rushed down the steps to where Mamaw and Papaw stood with open arms on the tarmac. Papaw picked me up, and off we went to the terminal to collect my baggage. We got to the car, and Mamaw and I got in the huge backseat of their Lincoln Continental. Mamaw had my favorite pillow and blanket waiting for me, and a large cooler sitting on the floorboards.

"Since it's such a long drive, I brought something for the trip," she said. "Would you like a snack, Chrissy?"

A snack? The cooler was overflowing with treats! There were cookies, seedless grapes, little sandwiches with the crusts cut off wrapped in plastic wrap, and individual bottles of different kinds of fruit juices. It took about an hour and a half to drive from the Cincinnati, Ohio, airport to Ashland, Kentucky, and I snacked off and on the whole way.

The house looked huge to me. Of course, everything always appears bigger when you're four years old. The minute we arrived, I ran through the house, just to make sure everything was still the same. My playroom was exactly as I had left it. Mamaw always kept my toys and favorite things for me in the very last place I had played with them. She even kept my little handprints on the wall until she died.

That night, as we did every night after supper, Mamaw and I took a long walk. She loved to show me off to her friends. We held hands and sang silly little songs that we made up together. I was in heaven! Now I keep Mamaw close to me by re-creating those memories on long walks with my children.

Later, Mamaw bathed me and dressed me in a brand-new nightgown. We always had a nightly snack, a big bowl of Cheerios topped with sugar. Mamaw rubbed my feet until I felt sleepy. Then I curled up beside her in bed, we said our prayers and I fell asleep.

I woke up the next morning to the smell of coffee and bacon. I knew Mamaw had cut each piece of bacon in half so that when it cooked, it curled up. I raced downstairs still in my nightgown to find my favorite breakfast: scrambled eggs, curly bacon, wheat toast with red raspberry jelly and cranberry juice. Mamaw always sat next to Papaw in the booth across from me in the breakfast nook. He read his paper and drank his coffee. And at those moments, all was right in my world. I now realize that my love for food began with Mamaw and Papaw. Each day I was with them, everything revolved around what, when and where we would eat the next meal. *Food was love, love was food.* (Of course, it didn't help that the hospital had sent Mom home with a baby formula recipe made with Karo syrup and Carnation evaporated milk!)

Over the years, as I grew up, the trips to 1515 Morningside Drive remained much the same as that first one. Going to visit Mamaw always meant shopping for new dresses, shoes, stockings and swim clothes. She saved her grocery money all year for these shopping trips! Mamaw loved to dress me up like a little doll, and if I loved something that didn't quite fit, we simply went to the alteration lady. How grand I felt standing on the platform as the woman pinned up a hem.

"Turn a little this way, darling. My, you've got an awfully pretty granddaughter, Mrs. Ciminella!"

Mamaw would beam. "Yes, I do!"

In the afternoons we always went to "the club." Papaw had worked long and hard to afford to belong to the local country club. Built in the 1940s, it was filled with Southern charm, from the green awnings surrounding the redbrick building to the bloodred leather wingback chairs in the lobby. To me it was the most exciting place on the planet!

We always started out a day at the club the same way. After breakfast I put on a new and fashionable swimsuit, and packed my favorite swim towel and goggles in my new swim bag, another gift from Mamaw. It was see-through plastic, with white patent leather handles and high-fashion models wearing bathing costumes and big hats stenciled on the sides. Mamaw sat patiently while I swam all afternoon. When I got hungry or thirsty, I went to the snack bar and ordered anything I wanted. I didn't even need any money! I just signed the Ciminella membership number, 67. I felt like the luckiest girl in the world.

After swimming until I was waterlogged, I would go to the women's locker room, where town ladies sat in the lounge, playing cards, smoking cigarettes and drinking gin and tonics. When the women came in wearing golfing shoes, their cleats made a swishing sound on the green indoor-outdoor carpeting. I thought that the ladies' lounge was very high-class. It had bamboo furniture, card tables and a long dressing table with trays filled with amenities. Everything was free of charge, too, all the little bottles of shampoo, miniature soaps and hand lotion. I couldn't believe my good fortune. I would sit at the dressing table, look into the mirror and pretend that I was a woman of luxury, just like the card players. I had never experienced anything like it—this was like being in a movie.

Sometimes we ate dinner upstairs in the formal dining room, where men had to wear ties and dinner jackets. *Very* fancy. The waiters and waitresses all wore white coats that matched the white linen tablecloths. The flatware was sterling silver. When you sat down a waiter brought a big basket of bread, accompanied by a refrigerated glass dish containing thick slices of butter with the letter "B" stamped on each one. ("B" for Bellfonte Country Club.) I would sit up tall in my seat and order my usual Shirley Temple with extra cherries. It was truly grand.

Most afternoons, after Mamaw helped me shower and dress, we met Papaw for lunch at a downstairs restaurant called "the Grill," where you could sit beside big picture windows and watch the golfers tee off. After their game, ladies (usually in pairs) drove their carts from the club-house and parked right beside the entrance to the Grill. I loved watching them! They'd wander in laughing and joking, all tanned and sweaty, wearing bright shades of summer lipstick, matching golf shirts and visors. Then they'd begin to visit with other players, who were already seated and having lunch. Some of Mamaw's friends would stop and visit me at our table. I felt included in this exclusive club where you signed for food and got free hand lotion in the ladies' lounge!

They were women of leisure. I couldn't get over the fact that they could spend their whole day playing golf and playing cards. My mom had to work every day— sometimes two jobs at a time. There were no golf dates or card parties for her. It was such a contrast. And as I grew older, my perception of how the women of the Bellfonte Country Club and Mamaw Ciminella lived compared to Nana Judd and Mother became even more striking.

So it's not surprising that I preferred to be at 1515 Morningside to the San Fernando Valley. I remember once calling Mom when I was very small, and telling her:

"Mommy, I can't come home. Mamaw has spoiled me *rotted*!"

In my mind Mamaw and Papaw lived just for Ashley and me. Kids learn very early whether they are their parents' priority or not, whether their mother and father are there to meet their emotional needs or vice versa. Right or wrong, from a very early age, I believed that my mom needed me as much as I needed her. As far back as I can remember, I was her sidekick. She has often said that from the moment she found out she was pregnant with me it was the two of us against the world. And I believe that the dynamics of our sometimes codependent relationship exist to this day.

When I was with Mamaw and Papaw, I felt like they had planned all year for me to come visit. They were so happy to see me that they set everything aside just to play with me. Mom has told me that my birth brought a new energy into Mamaw and Papaw's marriage. Their only son, Michael, had been born sickly and Mamaw's constant worrying and attention smothered him. He became independent very early. I think it broke Mamaw's heart. He was their only child and she had a hard time letting him go. As he got older, he became even more aloof. They did not ever have a close relationship.

Looking back, I think it was sometimes a concern for Mom and Dad that Mamaw and Papaw were so demonstrative with me. But don't you think it is the grandparents' job to completely adore the grandchild? It's a second chance at parenting and at love.

Growing up, both our parents were dreamers. They lived creatively and taught Ashley and me a great deal about thinking outside the box. Mom and Dad both had high expectations of us. Dad wouldn't allow us to use the word "bored." If we did, we had to do extra chores and read. And for as long as I can remember, Mom was a true visionary, always painting the picture of what life would be like *when we made it*. No one knew what "it" was—but I knew it involved being rich and famous. Mom was always into fantasy, into dreams about fame. I think she wanted to be famous her whole life. In California, Mom got in the sixties spirit. She got a pixie haircut and wore miniskirts and boots. She campaigned for the antiwar presidential candidate, Eugene McCarthy. She checked into a variety of religions.

Dad and I have always had philosophical conversations about our beliefs. I think he was coming from the place of *prove to me there is a God*. I would challenge him: *prove there isn't*. I felt that he often saw my sensitivity as a weakness. Throughout my childhood, both before Mom and Dad's divorce and after, I felt he connected to Ashley more than he did me. They seemed to have so much more in common. She was much more like him. I was more like Mom. Ashley was quiet and bookish. I was restless and unable to sit still or concentrate for long periods of time.

Mom and Dad chalked up my constant daydreaming to a lack of initiative and laziness. The truth was, I got bored easily. It was hard for me to focus on my lessons. I was easily distracted. What I've come to understand through much work and reading is that my brain just works differently than some. We all process information differently. I probably should have been put in some alternative classes, ones that supported my creative spirit, since conventional classrooms didn't support my individuality.

I did go to some open schools when I was young and we lived in California. There, I was able to work at my own pace. I was promoted because I thrived having the freedom to move faster in several subjects. I tell parents who struggle with their children that all brains are not alike! Because I'm more of a right-brainer, I respond well to the arts, but didn't do well in math. I'm drawn to the visual, to poetry and to the heart. Words inspire me, numbers exhaust me. Give me a stage and a place to dance! Put me in a small space without a window and ask me to sit still and I become depressed. I had a difficult time trying to understand what was wrong. I thought it must be me.

In 1971, when I was seven years old, we were a two-car family living in a two-story house in West Hollywood. By then Mom and Dad's marriage had begun to fall apart. Fighting. Arguing. *Chaos*. I watched them fight. I could *feel* every fight, hear every accusation. I knew it was hopeless. By September, when Dad left, I had developed asthma and it was getting worse every day in the L.A. smog.

I believed two things at this point: that I had contributed to Mom's unhappiness at being trapped in the marriage, and that I was responsible for them getting a divorce. I'm not sure how I knew that my being born had been a large part of the problem. I do recall someone telling me once that I was born at a bad time. And I know that children of divorce frequently feel responsible for their parents splitting up. It's a tremendous loss for everyone. Too often children are expected to assume adult roles and they end up carrying much of the burdens themselves, in their bodies and spirits. I was a divorced single mother until 2003, so I feel very free to express how I feel about single parents.

One bright spot during the California years was my friendship with two girls, Mariska Hargitay and Angelique L'Amour. We were best friends from kindergarten until the third grade. Mariska is a Golden Globe–winning star on *Law & Order: Special Victims Unit*, but back then I knew her as the daughter of the late Jayne Mansfield and Mickey Hargitay. Mariska lived with her dad, and it always seemed strange—and mysterious—that her famous mother had died in such a horrific car accident. Angelique is now a successful actress, married with two beautiful daughters. But I first knew her as the daughter of the legendary Western writer Louis L'Amour.

It was pretty funny, because these two girls seemed so wealthy and glamorous, especially compared to our hand-to-mouth existence. The L'Amour house in particular was like a castle to me. Angelique had the most beautiful long blond hair, and she wore brand-new clean white Keds, and pretty blouses with lace collars and matching sweaters. I used to watch her mother roll her hair at night. I remember thinking: *This is what royalty does!* You could tell early on that Angelique would become an actress; she began practicing as a young girl. Either that or she'd inherited her father's vivid imagination and ability to tell a tale. She once told me in all seriousness that her parents had arranged for her to marry a prince. I believed her. Anyone who lived in a castle probably had a prince stashed away somewhere. And she certainly seemed like a princess! Angelique had such beautiful porcelain skin that I sometimes wondered if she ever sweated. She *glistened*.

I was in absolute awe of Angelique's parents. Louis was often in his library writing, and I was aware that he was famous for it. Her mother, Kathy, is a strikingly beautiful woman, with coal black hair, and the whitest, most perfect skin. She wore ruby red lipstick and designer clothes. Sometimes I worried about the fact that our place had been furnished with secondhand furniture, but Mariska and Angelique never played into those feelings of being "less than." The three of us were equals. Angelique and Mariska made no distinctions between my life and theirs. And though I didn't have the money, I definitely had the energy and personality to keep up.

I think it was with those two girls that I developed my ability to use a sense of humor and personality to cover up feelings of insecurity. I had to be creative. When Mom and Dad divorced, I began hiding my sadness, loneliness or fear by being witty and clever. I think this time marks the beginning of me as an entertainer. I had to keep up with my two best friends.

The three of us had plenty of sass, and people to this day say they remember us from grade school. Mariska and I were more the tomboys. Angelique was more feminine. We took turns being the leader. I love them both and to this day we've continued to stay in contact.

I think if there's a lesson I learned during my time in Hollywood, it's this: children are not by nature prejudiced or discriminating. It is taught. Ashley and I were raised to believe that we are all equal. Mom and Dad set wonderful examples and taught Ashley and me that it didn't matter if you lived in Appalachia in a shack or in a Hollywood mansion. We are all souls having a physical experience.

Separated from Dad, Mom started taking one job after another, everything from secretarial work to modeling to becoming a game show contestant on *Hollywood Squares* and *Password*. Such is life in Hollywood. Nana has said that she always thought Mom would go to Hollywood and become a soap star or a soap opera writer. She never thought that her daughter would *live* a soap opera.

Mom went through several image transformations. First, there was the Mod look, that early sixties London/Twiggy thing with a lot of false eyelashes and mascara, with plastic go-go boots. Next had come a forties Film Noir style. She wore dresses with tight waists and padded shoulders and lots of bright red lipstick, a style I later adopted while living in Marin County in the seventies, and again while attending high school in Tennessee in the early eighties. Finally she settled on a kind of Native American/mountain woman image. She let her hair grow out and then stopped coloring it. She wore to-the-ankle skirts with her Indian-style belts made of leather, turquoise and beaded jewelry, and moccasins laced to the knee. Mom as Earth Mother.

When he left, Dad asked Mom how she planned on supporting Ashley and me. She did it by working any job she could find. Ashley and I became latchkey kids. I wore a necklace with a key that hung around my neck. It's hard for me to believe now, but at the age of seven I came home after school and stayed alone all afternoon until Mom picked up Ashley at the next-door neighbor's. It was a lonely time, and I spent many hours snacking on Ding Dongs and watching *The Brady Bunch* and *Gilligan's Island*.

I attended West Hollywood Elementary. I walked down Sunset Boulevard every day, past the Whiskey A Go-Go, a famous rock club, and the Classic Cat, a "gentleman's club." I often walked to school with a friend and his grandmother. But sometimes I walked alone.

One day, while I was walking home alone from school, past the playgrounds, a man pulled up beside me in a blue car. He leaned over and rolled down his window and asked me to come over to his car. Mom had given me "the talk." You know the one: *don't talk to strangers*. I put my head down and began walking faster.

"I'm looking for a friend," he said, driving alongside of me.

"What?" I said, confused.

"Do you know where Dick lives?" he asked.

I couldn't understand what he was talking about.

"Do you know where Dick lives?" he repeated, and looked down.

I was standing close enough to the car that I could see inside. I looked down, too. He had his penis in his hand. It was the first time I'd ever seen an erect penis. My heart began to race!

I took off, running as fast as I could go to a nearby

house, screaming at the top of my lungs every step of the way. I will never forget the police coming to the house and asking for a description. I was so nervous that I couldn't remember seeing anything but the man's penis. I learned a terrible reality that day. *I was no longer safe*. From that day on, I kept up my guard, waiting for another situation to happen again where I wouldn't feel safe.

When people are violated, emotionally, physically or spiritually—however big or small—one of two things happens. They retreat inward or they act out. They become silent or they become loud. Some children become listeners, never saying much; others become physical: biting, hitting, screaming and throwing temper tantrums. I developed a sense of sarcasm, which is anger with a twist of humor. I was emotional and verbal, aggressive and tough. I started to understand that I needed a thick skin. I felt insecure, but acted sure of myself. I was a walking contradiction.

Children often sense when someone or something is unsafe. I listen carefully when my children say they don't want to be around someone. They know intuitively when something is wrong. Listen to your gut instinct. Your gut gets it before your head does. Sometimes we try to justify things because we don't want to believe that something bad could or would happen. But it does, each and every second of each and every day.

Every person in the world has had inappropriate things happen to him or her, from childhood to adulthood. Maybe it's still going on. Abuse, violations are not always sexual. What I didn't realize for years was how even the smallest violation affected my sense of self. Because I wanted love and attention I allowed others to come in without knocking—emotionally, spiritually or physically— whether it was a man putting his hand on my body or a fan touching my hair when I came offstage at a show or my manager telling me in front of other people that I looked like I was putting on weight. Until recently I wanted to be loved so badly that I set few boundaries. I'm changing all that now!

I was physically and emotionally violated several times in my childhood. The violations involved inappropriate touching by people who are not in my immediate family. I have forgiven them and set myself free from blaming them. I was never raped or penetrated. However, just because I wasn't actually raped doesn't mean that it did not have a huge effect on me.

When I was around twelve, there was an incident that involved a boy of around sixteen. I had spent the night after a family gathering at his parents' house. I woke up one morning and there he stood in the doorway of the guest bedroom. I thought he was coming to wake me up for breakfast. He walked over to the bed and lay down beside me. His teenage hormones must have been raging because within moments, he'd rolled over on top of me and started kissing me and touching me in an inappropriate way. I was too shocked to react at first and I shut down; then I felt traumatized. I had known this boy my whole life. We'd grown up together and I couldn't believe this was happening. I'd trusted him, and he'd molested me. I carried this shame for years, worrying that I had done something wrong, or something to encourage him. That and other situations with men when I was a young girl have affected me my whole life, from the way I interacted with the opposite sex to my early preferences for less revealing stage clothes.

When I was ten years old, after six years in Hollywood, Mom finally packed it up and decided that we were going back to Kentucky. Ashley and I would live with Dad while Mom took some time to find herself. So we went to Lexington, where Dad was working as a leather craftsman. I think Dad craved a simple existence. He'd had all sorts of jobs, in offices and in the horse business. But now what he wanted was to get away, to get back to a carefree, less stressful lifestyle. I don't even think he owned a suit during that time. He was ready to get back to the country.

Meanwhile, Mom drove home by way of Texas. She made two important discoveries in Austin. First, she discovered that she loved the blues, Western swing and country music and, second, that she wanted to get a nursing degree. And so, in the winter of 1974, just as Dad was getting ready to move us to a new home, he agreed to let Mom move in with him so she could pursue a nursing degree at Eastern Kentucky University in Richmond. I was stunned and began to dream about us as a family again.

WHAT THE WORLD
NEEDS NOW IS LOVE

"We'll be river rats!" Dad said, excitedly, pulling his MG convertible up to the little house. That's what the city folks called people who lived along the Kentucky River, *river rats*. It was winter, and bitterly cold. The place Dad rented was named Camp Wig. It was located between a cow pasture and a concrete block church where the congregation often sang and praised all night long.

It was an unheated summer fishing retreat, so he purchased one of those black coal-and-wood-burning stoves, and put up sheets of metallic protectors on the kitchen wall to keep the house from catching fire. We all took turns waking up through the night to keep adding wood. If Mom and Dad were gone, it was my job to keep the home fires burning. We wore clothes on top of clothes and rubbed our hands a lot. Mom, Ashley and I often slept together under piles of blankets, quilts and coats. Our pipes froze a lot in the winter, so we always seemed to be out of water.

We had to get up early at Camp Wig. Mom left before dawn for her nursing classes, driving her red VW through the back roads to the ferry across the river, and finally to the highway bound for Richmond, Kentucky. Ashley and I got up before dawn, too. We'd warm ourselves by the wood-burning stove each morning. I have vivid memories of standing and looking out the window, watching Mom bust up coal outside the kitchen door at five a.m. to warm us all up for breakfast. Afterward, Ashley and I would walk up the long driveway to the main road to catch the school bus. It was over an hour's ride to town.

The small village around Camp Wig was poverty-stricken. Many of the other river rats lived without electricity or plumbing. A few of my friends used coffee cans for toilets. Some families lived up to eight in a three-room shack, curtains hung across the room to separate the kitchen from the sleeping areas. Many of the children had never been out of the county.

Yet with all that poverty, these people were the friendliest you could imagine. They were family out there. It reminds me of a story I was told about a woman who was asked which she thought would be worse, to be too rich or too poor. She thought about it and said, "Too rich, because being too rich can be lonely. If you're poor, you may not have much but at least you know who your friends are."

As spring replaced winter, Ashley and I discovered the real magic of Camp Wig. We fell asleep each night to the sounds of crickets and frogs, and awakened each morning to the birds singing. Flowers bloomed, and finally that summer, the blackberries ripened! Dad, Ashley and I would pick the berries, then sit on the back porch and eat them until our faces were stained blue-black. Camp Wig was where I came to love the four seasons. There was always something to look forward to, even if you did have to put up with frozen pipes.

Our house was so far off the beaten path that there were days that we never saw a single soul or made it into a town.

We seldom ate in restaurants or went to movies. But Dad was happier than I'd ever seen him, and it made me happy just to see him content. He'd run a trot fishing line across the river and bait twenty or more hooks to catch fish. At night Ashley and I swam out to check them. He'd watch as we'd swing from vines into the river. We'd take bars of soap and go out in the huge front yard that filled with water in places during a thunderstorm and take baths. Sometimes we'd play in the rain. I find myself going out into the rain with my children, just to feel that same joy from such a wonderful time in my life.

There was something about living at Camp Wig that was defining for me. As harsh as the conditions were at times, it was also peaceful. We had very little, but we relied on one another. It felt natural for me to be there. The lifestyle was simple and the people were real. We had lots of gatherings with neighbors where people played musical instruments and sang. Dad loved the Stones, Warren Zevon and Frank Zappa, so this was where I developed a real passion for rock 'n' roll. I also discovered my first "(s)hero," Joni Mitchell. Mom, Dad, Ashley and I were together. And we were family.

We were happy until an unusually wet season upped the ante for living along the river. Camp Wig flooded and kept right on flooding until almost all of our belongings were ruined. Mamaw and Papaw Ciminella were never happy about us living along the river anyway. After the worst of the floods, they drove out often to try and convince Dad that it was no place to raise children. By that time, Mom and Dad agreed.

Dad finally moved back to town, and Ashley and I stayed with him until we finished school. Mom—in true Judd fashion—grew restless, packed up and went searching for a new adventure. She had moved to a little one-room bungalow in nearby Berea, Kentucky. The town is home to Berea College, where low-income students can work their way through school using their talents doing various jobs in the community. The entire area reflects an artisan spirit, with homage paid to its Appalachian roots. Berea is filled with arts and crafts stores and classes everywhere, as well as some of the most beautiful handwork in America. There is a hotel called Boone Tavern that is run by students in the heart of the town. When Ashley and I were with Mom, and Mamaw and Papaw Ciminella came to visit, they stayed at Boone Tavern and took us to eat in the restaurant.

The day our lives changed—at least for a while—started out with another of those hard Kentucky rains. Ashley and I were in Berea visiting Mom, and we were driving home from the grocery store in the pouring rain. Mom was having a difficult time seeing the road, when she suddenly slammed on the brakes. Despite the downpour, we could see that an elderly woman had slipped off of the curb, and fallen into the street.

"We almost hit that woman!" Mom shouted as she jumped from the car.

Mom rushed over to help her up. We got the woman into our car, and rushed her to the hospital's emergency room. We stayed at the hospital with the woman, Caroline Hovey, waiting for her husband, a professor at Berea College, to arrive. Once Mr. Hovey got to the hospital and his wife was being treated, Mom introduced us, and explained that she was a nursing student at Eastern Kentucky, and that the three of us were in Berea looking for a place to live. Because of Mom's kind deed, the Hoveys called a professor at Berea College, Margaret Allen, and told her about a single mother with two children who needed an affordable place to live.

Margaret Allen called and said she wanted to meet with us at her home in Morrill, a forty-five-minute drive from Berea. Even though we'd lived along the river and seen poverty up close, we were unprepared for the sight when we turned off the main highway and onto the long gravel road leading to Mrs. Allen's. We passed old outbuildings and run-down trailers with farm animals running loose. Malnourished dogs with their ribs showing were tied up to old tires. There were junked cars on cinder blocks.

"Mom, are we lost?" I asked.

"No," Mom answered with a frown. "This is the road."

I looked at Ashley and shrugged. Surely a professor at Berea College didn't live here.

Then suddenly, the gravel road ended and there was a huge red gate. It was open, as if we were expected. So we entered the property and drove up the paved road. It was like a scene from a movie. There on a hill sat a lovely, cared-for house as different from what we'd just driven by as could be. Mrs. Allen came out and greeted us.

"Welcome to Chanticleer," she said with a big smile.

Her estate had two homes: Windswept, where she lived, and the house she called Chanticleer, named after one of her favorite children's stories. Mrs. Allen explained that she was a music teacher, and along with the two homes, she had cabins on the property, where students stayed each year for her music camps.

Chanticleer was magical! It was completely furnished, with beautiful hardwood floors and hand-hooked rugs throughout. We each got our own bedroom, with a hand-made quilt on every bed. Most of the furniture was antique, and all the furnishings seemed to match. In the kitchen, beautiful china filled the knotty pine cabinets. In the living room there was a Steinway piano beside the huge picture window overlooking the front porch. There were apple trees in the front yard, and berry bushes in back. When Mrs. Allen offered to rent Chanticleer to us for a hundred dollars a month, Mom could barely speak.

That summer we raised a garden and Mom taught Ashley and me how to can. Those are things I *promise* that I will make time to do with my own children. Chanticleer was where my lifelong love for animals began. We had kittens being born in the barn and homeless dogs wandering into our lives. I learned how to shear sheep, spin the yarn and weave tapestries on a loom. There was no television and no telephone. We relied entirely on our own creativity for entertainment. I loved to visit my best friend, Ramona Van Winkle, down the road. We'd go to the main road and sing Loretta Lynn songs at the top of our lungs to passing motorists. This was my first experience singing as a duo. I guess I was in training and didn't realize it!

If Camp Wig had opened my heart to nature, it was Chanticleer that opened my soul to music. It was during this time that I discovered the guitar. Someone had given one to Mom as a going-away gift when she left California. Dad had already shown me a few chords on his guitar, so that was enough to inspire me. I started singing and playing around the house. I'd sit on the porch and practice for hours. And so my life as an artist began.

Dad's love of music and my desire to play was one of the first true connections I felt with him. He often brought his leatherwork to Berea's art fairs, and I'd stay with him in a tent while he sold his wares. We'd sell by day, play and listen to music by night. It's one of my happiest memories! The big tents, the lights, the people singing and playing— it was there that I discovered jamming with other musicians. I began to play by ear. The guitar became an appendage. It was the first time I remember feeling as though I had a purpose in life.

Mrs. Allen started giving me piano lessons that summer. The lessons taught me discipline, but while I liked the piano, I was more drawn to the guitar. Still, Mrs. Allen had faith in me and even allowed me to attend her music camp free of charge. It is one of the most magical memories of my life. Mrs. Allen was so gifted. She taught us about the passion of music, the rise and fall of notes. She was the first person to show me the difference between playing technically and playing from the heart. She had such a musical style, and such a big heart. (The camp took in children from all walks of life.) At the end of music camp, the students always put on a show on her elaborate patio. That year it was *Porgy & Bess*. It was my first performance. A milestone!

I was starting to get *really* excited. Music was becoming more than an interest—it became my passion. By the end of the summer it was just that guitar and me. I'm glad I wasn't a Top 40 kid. It was because we shopped in used record stores that I discovered Rounder Records, and the label's great collection of authentic music. I also discovered Emmylou Harris, Doc Watson, Ralph Stanley, Merle Haggard, Bill Monroe, Dolly Parton and Hazel and Alice—the Boswell Sisters. I got hooked on hillbilly music—bluegrass and the old mountain folk songs. By the end of summer I was addicted to the way that Doc Watson played the guitar. I started to learn the Autoharp, and when my uncle Mark, Mom's brother, brought me a banjo, I started learning to finger pick.

Mom loved the way Hazel and Alice harmonized and started trying to work up harmonies to my lead. Even though she had never done that before, it somehow felt natural there in the mountains, with so many singers, writers and musicians around.

One of my great influences was the Yancey family, Minnie and her four children. Minnie is the one who taught Mom to make lye soap, which would later cause television host Ralph Emery to start calling us the Soap Sisters. The Yanceys were like family to us. Minnie's daughter Sonja Bird sang and played dulcimer as well as guitar. Sonja Bird was very important in my own musical journey, since she was my first real guitar and vocal teacher.

The Yanceys lived in Berea, which Mom thought had the best school in the area, so we enrolled there. She drove Ashley and me into town each morning to the Yancey house so that we could catch a ride to school with Minnie's sons, Toddie and Garrett. We had to get up very early to be in the car by five a.m. I remember once, when I woke up to use the bathroom at about two a.m., I went ahead and got dressed for school.

After school I'd walk to the Berea College Student Center to hustle pool. I became a pretty sharp pool player, so I ended up winning money most days. Then I'd take my winnings to Mama Mia's and play pinball for hours, just killing time before Mom got out of nursing school and came to pick us up at the Yancey house. I wore the same sort of clothes every day: blue jean overalls, flannel shirts and hiking boots. All I cared about was music, pool and pinball.

I could have lived at Chanticleer forever. But Mom, being the gypsy she is, decided to move us back to California and continue nursing school at the College of Marin, north of San Francisco. She packed us up in a U-Haul and off we went. Uncle Mark came along to help. I was terribly sad to be leaving a life that had meant so much to me, to leave a place that had nurtured me and inspired me to begin taking the first steps on my journey as an artist. Living on that mountaintop gave me a sense of self and purpose that I don't think I'd had before. We had little financially, but a wealth of joy and a connection to the earth, to one another.

Since we didn't have much money for the trip back to California, we took along a mattress for Uncle Mark to sleep on when we stopped at motels for the night. Ashley and I rode in the back of the U-Haul with the furniture. Mom rigged the sliding door so it would stay open just a little and we'd have fresh air. Deeply unhappy and left to my own devices, I acted out. Ashley was lying down on the mattress when I jumped off of the chest of drawers and on top of her. I held her down and pinned her so she couldn't get up. Then I licked her face until she peed her pants.

When Ashley finally got away from me, she jerked off her T-shirt and frantically waved it out the back, hoping somebody would see it and save her. Suddenly I heard a siren. We pulled off to the side of the road. The back of the U-Haul was rolled open and there stood a highway patrolman next to Mom and Uncle Mark. The cop chewed out Mom for putting us in the back of the U-Haul. Mom chewed me out for taking out my frustration on my sister, and Uncle Mark spanked me in the bathroom of a truck stop. I'll never forget that feeling of humiliation. I worshipped my uncle Mark.

When we got to Marin County, we moved into a small one-bedroom apartment. Mom put the mattress on the floor in the corner of the living room, and she and Ashley slept there. I got the one bedroom. Mom worked as a waitress while attending school, and also as a private nurse for an older man named Skipper, who lived next door. He adopted us as his only family, and helped Mom out financially to pay some of our bills. What a change in environment! From Chanticleer to that small apartment next door to a bar.

Between school and jobs, Mom worked all day and most of the night. There's a scene in Ashley's first major movie, *Ruby in Paradise*, where her character has tried and tried to find work. She gets turned down during all her job interviews and ends up working in a Laundromat. I remember seeing that film with Mom, and watching her weep as she sat in the theater.

Mom drove by an Arabian horse farm every day when she went to work as a waitress at a restaurant named Rancho Nicasio in Nicasio, California. She says that she was concerned that I take on more responsibilities, so she got me a job cleaning tack a couple of days a week, after school. I rode my bike to and from my job. I was fourteen, and didn't mind the hard work because I got to be with horses and out in the open. The barn had a radio that played country music constantly and I found myself listening to it. Soon I was singing along, memorizing every song I heard. Merle Haggard became one of my favorites.

Mom picked me up one day when I'd finished mucking stalls, and I immediately tuned to KNEW radio. They were giving away tickets:

"KNEW is bringing you Merle Haggard and the Strangers, live and in concert at Oakland Coliseum! Be caller number ten and be a winner!"

I wasn't caller number ten.

"Mom, if I save the money for the tickets, would you take me?" I asked.

"Sure," she said. Mom loved Merle's music, too.

On the day of the show, we left Ashley at a friend's house, and off we went, country music blaring all the way. When we pulled into the parking lot, Mom just leaned out, smiled and asked to park in the backstage area, where all the buses and trucks parked. It was so like Mom to park in back, right next to the tour buses. Mom was so beautiful that she always seemed to get a backstage pass whenever she needed it. Plus, back in those days, they didn't have the security issues they have today. Just as we pulled up next to Merle Haggard's bus, he was coming out to walk his little dog, Tuffy.

"Well, hello," Merle Haggard said. I was in awe!

What he must have thought of Mom and me! We wore our best dresses, me in lace anklets, Mom in seamed hose. Mom was *such* a hottie and she had that Southern accent! She must have made quite an impression on Merle because he immediately invited us to come on his Silver Eagle.

Getting on that tour bus was a defining moment, my first taste of a star's world. That bus seemed to me like the mobile home of life. It had the leather seats, the kitchenette. I could *see* myself on this bus! I could picture myself driving down the highway on my way to the next show. I was ready to hit the road.

Merle invited us to watch the show from the side of the stage. What I remember most is the audience's reaction when the lights came down. And when I saw Merle's band in matching stage outfits, that, too, was a defining moment. I could visualize myself on that stage with my own band.

When Merle invited us to go on the road with him for a few days, Mom didn't hesitate. We just left the car right there in the parking lot and we left with him. Merle introduced me to his sons, Noel and Marty. I got such a crush on Noel! After a few days, Mom and I flew home. I was heartbroken when Noel kissed me goodbye. It was back to reality and that crummy apartment in Lagunitas.

That road trip was the beginning of our adventure of going backstage at concerts. It became Mom's hobby. We heard Emmylou Harris and met her opening act, Ricky Skaggs. We went to a Dolly Parton show, and I was mesmerized by her opening act, Doc Watson. I was also into Huey Lewis and the News, as well as the Little River Band, BIG time. I discovered Tower of Power, and it was because of them that years later I added a horn section to my band when I toured. I was in love with Doc Kupka's showmanship.

Mom began to play harmonica and we started jamming some with local musicians. And although I didn't understand it at the time, the duo that would later be The Judds was being born. She started thinking that maybe—just maybe—we could put together a family act. After the divorce, Mom had gone back to her maiden name, Judd. Now she changed her first name from Diana to Naomi. She was determined to reinvent herself and a name change was a start. She bought a '57 candy apple red Chevy with "Red-Hot" on the license plate. She always said she felt like she was at the front of the parade when she drove it. And that is a little like I always felt, that Ashley and I followed along in Mom's parade.

Mom and I started singing together in small area clubs. We sang at Rancho Nicasio with a group called Susie McKee and the Cowpokes. We did charity events. We sang in church. We recorded a few songs at a local studio that a friend of Mom's owned. And we invested in a reel-to-reel recording machine, a mixing board and a couple of microphones.

In 1978, Mom decided that it was time to get serious. After a trip back to Kentucky for Christmas, Mom packed up again, and headed back to Austin, Texas. This time, I went with her. Ashley stayed in Kentucky.

In Austin, Mom started dating the harmonica player from Asleep at the Wheel. We hung out with Jimmie Vaughn and the guys in the Fabulous Thunderbirds. It's funny. I didn't have any idea who Stevie Ray Vaughn was when I first heard him jam in the kitchen of one of the band members. I just thought they were all great guitar players.

While we were in Austin I decided to change my name, just as Mom had done. I did it for the same reason Mom had—to create a new identity. I was following Mom's lead and looking for something entirely new. Ray Benson, the lead singer of Asleep at the Wheel, chose my name from one of their songs, "Route 66." The line goes: ". . . don't forget Winonna." I could change the "i" to a "y"— Christina Claire Ciminella becomes Wynonna Ellen Judd. I took the "Ellen" because it's Mom's middle name. I just remember thinking that with Naomi, Wynonna sounded better than Christina.

Wynonna and Naomi were beginning to be an act.

I felt like I was playing a part in a movie! I started pulling my hair back with rhinestone barrettes, and wearing mascara and bloodred lipstick—very forties. In a way I was mimicking Jimmie Vaughn's girlfriend, who I thought was the bomb. She wore bright red lipstick and mascara, too. I was fourteen years old, on the road and caught up in a fantasy world of being part of the backstage scene.

I loved the music, but sometimes the boys who hung out with bands made me uncomfortable. The guys were much older. I was always the youngest one in the room, and it would be many years before I felt comfortable around guys.

However, I did learn early how to fit in in a man's world. I had to come up with a lot of clever anecdotes and comebacks. I learned about jockeying for position and holding my own. I found a way to survive. The blessing was that this experience on the road prepared me for what was to come. The burden was that I should have been at home going to school, hanging out with high school friends and cruising the town square on Friday nights.

That I should have been in school, studying, having a normal life—that's all hindsight. Back then, the fact that I was missing school didn't concern me. I was living in my own fantasy world. I put feelings of school and home behind me. There was no turning back. I was ready to go out on tour!

Mom had wanted "something more" since she was a child, and was so caught up in her fantasies that she really had little choice. She had to follow her dreams. She was starting to write songs, and to sing harmonies. Still, I can imagine leaving Ashley behind to pursue music then, and later when we had a record deal, was something that continued to haunt her. Mom has said that the fact that Ashley was with Nana was comforting, and very helpful in easing the pain of the separation. But Ashley had to have felt on some deep level that she was abandoned. Mom and I were starting to make music together, and I think Ashley sometimes felt that she was in the way. I have such clear memories of Ashley coming into Mom's room to say something when we were practicing our music, and Mom holding up her hand to stop her from interrupting.

"What do you want?"

Ashley would silently turn and leave the room. She definitely was not getting what she needed. I've often said that parents too often want their children to fit into *their* agendas. It doesn't mean that they don't love their children or make them terrible parents, but it can't do a child a lot of good to know that *she* has to be the one who fits in. Ashley fit in by turning inside, by being quiet and self-sufficient. She created her own reality to survive, discovering that she could travel anywhere in the universe when she read books. Her imagination and ability to survive on her own has made her the champion that she is today.

I know I took up a lot of the energy in our family dynamic. When we really got serious about music, I was a young teen, desperate for Mom's approval. I had music fever. For so many years, Ashley was there for us, and I still grieve because I was so caught up in my own success. I was trying to live up to expectations, to keep it together, and didn't take the time to nurture my relationship with my only sister. If I attend an awards show or something that is Ashley's event, I try to walk behind her so I don't crowd her light. I feel it's necessary to celebrate her—it's Ashley's turn.

After a few months in Texas, our journey took us back to California. Once in Los Angeles, Mom bought us matching letter jackets with *Hillbilly Women* embroidered on the front and our names on the back. "The Judds" were already being promoted. It was just that nobody but us knew it. We were having our own party and it was just a matter of time before more people wanted an invitation!

It was through my curiosity about Hollywood and superstars like John Travolta that Mom met the man who would become the great love of her life. I was sitting in a back booth, waiting on Mom to finish her shift at the Howard Johnson's in Studio City, where she worked as a waitress, when in walked a very recognizable country music star—Mickey Gilley. His entourage sat down at one of Mom's tables. She told Mickey all about "The Judds—Hillbilly Women"—and he seemed nice. So when they called me to come meet him, I didn't hesitate to ask about one of my favorite stars.

"What's John Travolta like?" I asked.

"Would you like to meet him?" Mickey responded.

I couldn't believe it. I'd recently seen *Urban Cowboy* and loved John Travolta! Of course I'd like to meet him!

"I'm going to be on *Merv Griffin* today, and John's supposed to stop by. Want to come along?"

Did the pipes break at Camp Wig? Of course I wanted to come along! It just meant convincing Mom, who didn't think our clothes were nice enough to go to a television studio. Only after I threatened to never clean my room again in my life did she agree. Off we went, following Mickey's limo in our Chevy, heading to the NBC Studios in Burbank. Mom spent her time talking to Mickey, while I patrolled the backstage area in search of John Travolta. He never showed. Instead, we were introduced to Sly Stallone's brother, Frank. Nothing against Frank, but I was *very* disappointed!

After the show Mickey took us out for Chinese food, then on to the Palomino Club, where J. D. Sumner and the Stamps Quartet were playing. That was exciting, because J. D. Sumner and the Stamps' amazing harmonies were famous for having backed Elvis Presley.

Mom didn't get to spend any time with the band's bass singer that night but he made quite an impression on her. Larry Strickland would become a major figure in our lives, bringing us food when we were down and out in Nashville, giving Mom some of her best and worst times, and managing me when I went solo. He would become my pop.

We continued going back to the Palomino Club and even entered one of their talent contests. We didn't win, but we did meet the man who was responsible for our decision to move to Nashville. Jeff Thornton was a Nashville promoter working on a television project and he offered Mom a job. So in March of 1979, despite the fact that Ashley was missing us more and more, and the Ciminellas were infuriated that I wasn't in school, off we headed to Las Vegas, where Jeff's company was deep in production of a Lola Falana special. Since we were "with the band," so to speak, we were put up in a suite at the Aladdin Hotel. I spent my time playing guitar in the suite, playing pinball in the employee cafeteria in the afternoon, and roller-skating on the weekends. Nights I went to the Aladdin's showroom to hear Loretta Lynn.

I was instantly in love with Loretta. I think I connected to her because she reminded me of my people in Kentucky. And I loved the way she dressed—I had never seen so many ruffles in my life! There was nobody like her. Also, Loretta had backup singers—something I'd never seen before! It fascinated me. One of her backup singers was a beautiful black man with a powerful bass voice that resonated with every fiber of my being. It's like when a tuning fork is struck and everything in the room in the same key vibrates. That's how I felt. I was vibrating to his voice. He soon learned that I was a fan, and took Mom and me to church there in Las Vegas. It was my introduction to an all-black church and it profoundly influenced my music and my life. I also was impressed with the Gatlin Brothers show, because of their blood harmonies.

It was because of women like Loretta—and Dolly Parton and Tammy Wynette—that I dedicated my life to music. You couldn't have forced me into any other profession, even though I did learn quickly how fast you can go from a suite at the Aladdin to the streets of L.A, because the trip to Las Vegas ended abruptly.

"Pack your bags!" Mom said, rushing into the room.

I put down my guitar and stared at her.

"Jeff's project is history!"

"So?" It still hadn't hit home.

"We're in this suite because of Jeff's show! If the show doesn't go on, we may have to pay our bill!"

That hit home. The show tickets. The room service. The *suite*! We threw our clothes in bags like we were crazy women, and maybe we were! Down the back stairs of the Aladdin we ran, out the back and into the red Chevy. I felt like Tatum O'Neal on the lam in *Paper Moon*. Mom and me, sneaking out the back of the Aladdin one step ahead of management.

Mom said all was not lost, though. Jeff was still optimistic about our career, and promised to help relocate us to Nashville, which was where he said we'd have to be if we wanted a career in country music. Mom and I returned to Los Angeles for a very short time, staying with our dear friends Nancy and Gabriele Balaz, then soon heading to Nashville. We lived in a motel until Mom got on her feet and could bring Ashley to Tennessee. Then we moved to an old house on Del Rio Pike, just outside of Franklin. The place needed a lot of work, but Mom did her best to fix it up. She's always had a gift for taking old used things and making them look new again.

Mom went to work in Jeff's office. She continued to plan and organize. When she wasn't writing scripts to pitch to production companies or coming up with ideas for the Country Music Foundation, she was talking to people about filming artists singing their hits, a precursor to the video.

As it turned out, one of the first acts Jeff signed back in Nashville was J. D. Sumner and the Stamps. Within days of their meeting, Larry Strickland and Mom began a whirlwind romance that continues today. It must have been providence that Jeff signed J. D. Sumner and the Stamps so soon after Mom started working there, because she started nursing as soon as she got her Tennessee credentials in the mail!

Mom said it was love at first sight. From the time they went on their first date, they were inseparable. The only problem was, Larry's connection to Elvis had helped create quite a mystique around him. He sang with "The King" from 1974 until Elvis' death in 1977. Larry even had clothes in boxes under the bed that Elvis had given him when he gained weight! Larry had been on the road for years, and had developed quite a fan club among the girls. It almost drove Mom insane, but they were addicted to each other.

Ashley and I soon began to call him Pop. There was always a real sweetness to Pop, but it was like he was two people. At home he was a family man. Then he would put on those gold chains, unbutton his shirt and climb into his Corvette to go to Music Row in Nashville. I was fascinated by the dueling personalities. He'd come home and hang his stage clothes in the closet, and he was Pop again. He formed his own band, Memphis, and when he parked his tour bus in the drive, I'd sit on it for hours and fantasize about being on tour.

Life with Mom and Pop was always either really good or really bad. There was no in-between. He'd come home from the road and they'd fight; then Mom would throw him out. She'd pack all his stuff, and I'd sometimes help Pop carry his suitcases to the car. He'd leave. Eventually she'd let him come back, and we'd resume family life as if nothing had ever happened. One night Mom got mad and pulled her .38 Special on Pop. She fired about four inches above his head, and from that night on, when we ate dinner, I'd stare at that bullet hole in the window and be reminded that things could always change quickly. I guess that's when I started becoming secure with insecurity.

I started high school, a semester behind, at Franklin High. Starting late and living so far out in the country left me feeling somewhat disconnected from the kids at school. I looked older than most of the girls, and I never wore jeans to school. My clothes were often Mom's forties-style dresses, hair was pulled back with combs, and wedge shoes with ankle straps and anklet socks. On the first day I arrived, some students thought I was a teacher.

When I enrolled, I put my name down as "Wynonna" even though I was sure it was illegal! I didn't think you could just "decide" to change your name! (As it turned out, I was right. I legally changed my name when I was eighteen and we got a record deal!)

I often drove the red '57 Chevy to school. Some of the kids started calling me "Hollywood" because, they said, I looked like a movie star. I liked having my own style, but I still wanted to fit in so badly. I didn't have much in common with the popular middle-class kids with nice clothes and parents with money. I felt that I could relate more to the misfits. Some of my friends were kids who'd been excluded from the popular cliques. Yet I went to most of the parties. I think part of it was the fact that people wanted to ride in Mom's car! I also became the designated driver, since I didn't drink back then. I wasn't a Goody Two-shoes. I just liked helping people out.

One of the times I went out to a party turned into a nightmare. I had gone to a country music club with a girlfriend who met an older guy who invited us to a party at someone's house. The guy had a friend. I was going to get into a car with two strangers—not one of my best decisions. But because of my girlfriend, I went along with her plan.

Once inside the party, I realized that I had forgotten my purse and went back out to the car to get it. One of the boys followed me. *What a gentleman*, I thought. But the minute we got to the car, he shoved me into the backseat, got in and locked the door. Then he held me down, and started taking off his belt. He pressed his hand over my mouth so hard that my braces cut the whole inside of my mouth. When he demanded oral sex and I declined, he slugged me.

I agreed to do whatever he wanted; then, when he calmed down and was off his guard, I punched him in the face as hard as I could. I shoved the driver's seat forward, unlocked the door and opened it. Thank God the car was old and the locks were manual. I ran inside, got my girlfriend, and we called the police. By the time a patrol car arrived, the two boys we'd come to the party with had already left, so nobody was arrested. The police drove us back to my girlfriend's car. It was a terrible experience that could have been much worse.

Because of experiences like this one, I was a late bloomer. I was a senior in high school before I had my first real boyfriend. His name was Stephen McCord, and I met him at a party at a friend's house.

We couldn't have been more different. He liked the all-American blond babe types, and I was a redhead with a guitar. He wore blue jeans and T-shirts, and drove a truck. I wore dresses and heels, and drove a '57 Chevy. He drank beer, smoked cigarettes and liked to party. I liked to hang out, listen to music and practice my guitar.

I'd been around enough beer and cigarettes when Mom and I were hanging out with musicians in Austin. I didn't think it was so cool. I guess hanging out with older people who partied a lot allowed me to see the reality of what drugs and alcohol do to people. The biggest change I saw alcohol make in those musicians had to do with the way they treated women. (And I'm certainly not talking about *all* of them!) Some guys were gentlemen until about the third beer; then they would come on to anyone—even an underage girl like me. It seemed to me that "alcohol" promoted "disrespect."

I made a decision when I was a teenager that cigarette smoke would damage my voice, and I was not going to allow that to happen. I challenged Stephen one night when we were sitting at a stoplight, telling him to put out the cigarette or I'd walk home. He did put that one out, but he didn't stop smoking.

Stephen was one of the best-looking guys at Franklin High School. He was pure Southern good ole boy—ran with the popular crowd, had the body of a Greek god, was a bit of a hell-raiser, yet loved his mama and went to church with her every Sunday. He treated her with respect.

Stephen's mother was one of the most important influences in my teenage life. I'm not sure who I was more in love with, Stephen or his family, so much so that when Stephen and I finally broke up I felt like I lost five people instead of one. The very first time I met Mrs. McCord, I was enthralled with her faith and dedication to her family. Her husband and children meant everything to her—she lived for them. (I wanted her to be my mom!) I did feel like I was a part of the family. I went fishing with Stephen and his dad. Mr. McCord was a real "man's man." He was always working on his boat, wearing his signature ball cap.

I loved the fact that the McCord home had "Mom and Dad" reclining chairs. I loved the fact that Mrs. McCord baked and canned and served up supper every Sunday after church. She prepared great feasts of roast beef, mashed potatoes and gravy, corn, green beans, homegrown tomatoes, cornbread and lemon ice box pie. The whole family ate together, and they stayed together.

The McCord house was full of love and laughter. Everywhere you looked there were reminders that they were believers. There were calendars with daily words of encouragement, little boxes with pages of Scripture for each day of the year. Mrs. McCord's Bible was always on the dining room table, where she sat every single morning to have her devotional time. I had never witnessed someone who had daily devotionals, who had a Bible with so many notes on each page. She even had a prayer list with names written on it, people she believed needed her prayers. She had *Guidepost* magazines—a kind of Christian *Reader's Digest*—in the bathroom. This was all new to me.

Mrs. McCord was always spreading the faith! Yet she was one of the first highly religious people I ever met who didn't preach. Her way was to teach. And she did it with a smile on her face. She knew that her husband and her son both drank. She made them keep liquor in the garage. But while she didn't like them drinking it, she didn't give them a hard time. Her attitude was "I'm just going to hoe my own row." She is the woman who taught me about grace and forgiveness. She definitely had a light. I think she knew that her prayers covered everyone so she became a prayer warrior for all of us.

Stephen was wild as a buck, but he had a good heart. He was sweet, one of the good guys. He was never disrespectful to me on any level. He had a good, solid family foundation, and you could feel it in everything he did. I was madly in love with him *and* his family. I thought that I would marry him one day—it was all worked out in my mind.

Although he was the first love of my life, our relationship remained chaste for a long time. Usually the most we ever did was sit on the love seat and put our arms around each other. That's about as intimate as we were for a long, long time.

One night Stephen and I did go up to his bedroom, where the door was supposed to be open at *all* times. This time we closed it without thinking. Then we fell asleep on top of the covers on his bed. When Mrs. McCord walked in the room, she did what a lot of mothers would do—she assumed a lot. She woke us up and asked me to leave. I was mortified. I knew that I had *really* crossed the line. I went home and wrote her a long letter, explaining what had—and had not—happened. After she read it, she asked us to meet with her.

"We have rules," she said. "I can't have you two up in Stephen's room with the door closed. But I believe Wynonna when she says nothing happened between the two of you, and I believe you can be trusted to act responsibly. I love you both, and want the best for you."

I was stunned. Instead of busting in the door and screaming that we were headed straight to hell, she set a boundary, and talked to us about being responsible to ourselves. I'd never had such a loving talk when I had made a mistake. There was no shame or guilt. Just love. Mrs. McCord still drops me a note from time to time or sends me a card on my birthday. I will always remember her and be thankful that she was such a blessing to me at a time when I needed one. And to this day, when I drive by their street on Sundays, I have the urge to stop by and ask, "What's for supper?"

I fell in love with another family, and that, too, was tied to food! Dolly Gillespie was the daughter of a wealthy family. Her dad was a builder, and they lived in a big, beautiful home. As it was with Stephen McCord, Dolly and I could not have been more different. She wore designer jeans and ostrich boots. She had spiked hair and wore several earrings in each ear. She smoked and cussed. She was a rebel, and my best friend.

Dolly had a fake ID, which I thought *rocked*! We'd go to clubs in Nashville to dance to punk rock music. She liked me because I was quirky, and I liked to cruise with her. I liked going to her house because her mom was always home. I was fed such wonderful dinners at Dolly's house!

The refrigerator was always full and Mr. and Mrs. Gillespie were always cooking.

I think Dolly liked coming to my house because she was fascinated with our lifestyle. (It sure wasn't because the refrigerator was always full!) But whereas Dolly's mom represented "home," my mom represented "hip." Actually, a lot of kids liked coming to our house. The boys thought Mom was a real babe! And our house had a creative, funky vibe. The kitchen had a tiny refrigerator with a freezer that had room for just two ice trays and one package of food. We had an antique pie safe. Our stove was old, with one of those big drawers in the bottom to store your pots and pans in.

Because our refrigerator was one of those small old-fashioned ones with a pull-down handle, I had to shop for food every day or so. Over time, I figured out a way to pocket some extra spending money for the weekend. On Fridays I'd return boxed and canned goods to the Franklin Kroger and get the cash refund. The folks there knew me well. *So* well, as it turned out, that when I was busted for grand-theft lipstick, they called me by name.

One night, while shopping, I decided I wanted some lipstick. Since I didn't have the money, I stuck a tube of pink and a tube of red into my pocket. I guess I thought I needed both colors to go with my wardrobe. I paid for the groceries, and as I walked back out to the car, an undercover security guard approached me.

"Hey, Miss Judd. I need to talk to you for a minute."

I felt like my heart was pounding out of my chest.

He took me back inside and walked upstairs to the office, where I signed what I guess was a police report or admission of guilt. I was so horrified and scared I don't remember all the details. Then I was taken to the Williamson County jail, where they called my mom. She wanted to teach me a lesson, and left me there. Mom must have been scared to death for me, worried something very serious was going wrong with her daughter.

Franklin is a small town. As it turned out, the guy who signed me in at the jail was my school bus driver. Actually I had never been able to get away with much while I was growing up. The first time I skipped school I even got caught! Ask my mother.

I sat there traumatized for what seemed like forever. They assigned me a counselor and put me on probation for six months. I had to check in once a week, and looking back on it now, I realize that it was a lifesaver. Shoplifting was an obvious call for help, and I'm sorry to say that I'd taken some things before that. I think part of it was because we never had the money to buy things like some of my friends.

The counselor quickly saw how conflicted I was. I wanted a career, and wanted out of school to pursue it. I took musician magazines to school and hid them behind my books in class. I wanted a band! Instead I had chores and the responsibility for Ashley. I've seen my counselor, Betsy Jewel, several times since I made it in country music. The first time we met after I was an adult was such a strange moment for me, talking to her about that dark time in my youth. She said she knew I was a good kid all along.

I wanted so badly to be a good kid. But I also wanted to be independent of Mom. Maybe shoplifting was my way of breaking out. I hadn't been ready for the role of being in charge of so much, so young. I remember day in and day out putting my chores off on Ashley while I sat in my room and listened to music. My fantasy was that I'd go on the road with Bonnie Raitt. I was R.T.G.—ready to go! But my reality was that my mom was a single parent working double shifts at the hospital. That left me in charge of my little sister.

I often stood in the gap between Mom and Ashley. I not only was required to do a lot for Mom, I was also expected to be there for Ashley. I became her "Sister-Mommy." I drove her everywhere. At times I was all she had, when I'm sure she would have preferred Mom.

Sometimes I still drive by the house on Del Rio Pike, pull in our old drive and sit there. It was the last place where I was as connected to my sister. Sometimes I cry. Sometimes I laugh. What memories! Sometimes I can still hear the eighties rock 'n' roll blasting from that old house, the place I sometimes called *Ashley's Party Palace.*

All her friends liked coming to our house because we had no neighbors, and they wouldn't get caught if they drank beer. I never did figure out how, if twenty kids were invited, fifty would know to show up. Ashley would wait until Mom had to work a double shift at the hospital, then put the word out. She had a lot of guts! For a long time she got away with it, and I helped her! I lived vicariously through my sister and her popularity.

Unfortunately for Ashley, we took some photos at one of the parties, and dropped them off at the local Moto Photo. Mom stopped by and a clerk gave Mom our photos in addition to her own. That was the end of Ashley's gatherings for quite a while. I'd give anything to go back and watch my funny, smart, popular little sister holding court at the Party Palace. Yet at the time when I went out on the road, I didn't think much about what it might do to her. I was too caught up in my own world.

We were forced to be together so much as children that I longed to get away. Now I long to have my sister to myself like I did back then. Besides my husband and children, my love for Ashley is the deepest I've ever experienced. I have this tender, sweet place in my heart that is reserved for her. I have so much respect for her in what she went through, and how she survived it. She thrived and flourished in spite of all she had to endure. Mom raised two high-spirited daughters under tough circumstances.

I wrote a song for Ashley, called "You Are." It's not just about her physical beauty, but the freedom and beauty of her spirit. Someday I hope to write *the* song for her, a song that celebrates how I feel about the two of us growing up together. I don't care how rich and famous she becomes—she'll always be my baby sister. I'm amazed that people still ask me if there was competition between us. It's all I can do not to choke them. I am very protective of our relationship.

My music success is sometimes bittersweet. I've been blessed with a life full of excitement. I've traveled the world. But I also know that success is what took me away from the sister that I love so dearly.

· 3 ·

DREAMCHASER

"Here they are, folks—Wyoming and Nairobi— The Judds!"

Television host Ralph Emery had just announced us, right after the Farm Report, of all things! I almost died. This was going to be even cornier than I thought.

"Is that how you pronounce your names?" Ralph chuckled.

"Wynonna and Naomi," Mom said.

Ralph looked over his notes. "It says here you make soap."

"Homemade lye soap. I'll bring you some, Ralph," Mom promised.

"Okay, if you don't want to be Wyoming and Nairobi, we'll call you the Soap Sisters."

I groaned inside, thinking, *I'll never live this down*. We had gotten up at three in the morning to perform on our first television show. Mom looked so prissy, dressed up in her thrift store forties-style dress, doing her hillbilly accent. Later we started wearing clothes from the Alamo, a Western-wear store down on Nashville's lower Broadway. But that day we were dressed more like the Andrews Sisters.

Somehow, Mom had booked us on Ralph Emery's five to seven a.m. Nashville show. I knew a lot of people who watched it while they got ready for work. Kids watched it, too, because Ralph announced weather alerts and school closings. It wasn't exactly how I had planned to make my debut. I feared that some of the kids at Franklin High would watch us and then tease me mercilessly. Then, the minute Ralph started pronouncing our names as Wyoming and Nairobi, the Soap Sisters, I was *certain* I'd hear about it at school. I was embarrassed at the thought of people whispering behind my back that I was some country music hick wannabe. On the other hand, we became semiregulars on the show and I earned twenty-five dollars for each appearance!

As it turned out, some students did kid me about being a "soap sister" at school, but I started to understand that people weren't really making fun of me. Some of them liked my singing. There's a great deal of irony in the fact that while I knew the girl at Franklin High who would ultimately help Mom and me get a record deal, I had no idea she knew me. Diana Maher was a year ahead of me at Franklin High. She was every parent's dream. She made good grades. She was outgoing. She had big, beautiful eyes and a sweet disposition. She was popular, and she was a cheerleader. I wouldn't have had the first idea how to try and strike up a conversation with her. She ran with the beautiful people, *way* out of my class. But she not only knew who I was—both she and her mother were fans and had been trying to get her producer father to listen to Mom and me sing.

Mom was working at the Williamson County Hospital in Franklin when Diana was brought in after a bad car crash. When Diana mentioned that she was a regular viewer of the *Ralph Emery Show*, and wanted her father to listen to Mom and me sing, Mom's ears perked up. She didn't do anything right away though, but waited until Diana was well on the road to recovery. Then she gave Brent Maher a demo that we'd recorded on a thirty-dollar Kmart tape recorder. We didn't hear anything back. Music City hopefuls seldom understand that producers get *hundreds* of unsolicited tapes.

As time went by, Mom and I began to struggle more than ever before. Our ideas of how things should be with regards to our career dreams were very different.

I wanted to be in a band. She wanted the two of us to be a duo.

I wanted to play at clubs around town and enjoy being a musician. She wanted us to wait until we had a record deal and a hit on the radio before we sang in front of a crowd.

She choreographed stage moves in front of her mirror at home while I pictured myself jamming with the band.

She loved painting her nails and I had calluses on my hands from practicing the guitar.

She wore Jungle Gardenia perfume, and it gave me a headache. I wore patchouli oil.

I can laugh now, but the more I think about it, the crazier it seems—some of our most passionate conversations out on Del Rio Pike involved what our stage costumes would look like when we "made it." Mom wanted matching outfits and I wanted a style of my own, separate from hers.

Mom did have great ideas. She also had an attitude that said, *I'm not going to give up until we make it.* She would work a double shift at the hospital, come home and change clothes to go down to Music Row. I knew all along that I needed and depended on her, and I sometimes resented it. I had the passion for music and she had the ambition. Moreover, as a teenager, I had all the time in the world. In her mid-thirties, Mom didn't.

It took me years to fully appreciate and understand how much Mom had gone through to make it. She had struggled to make her dreams come true for all of her adult life. She was a single parent raising two children at home with a boyfriend who was gone a lot playing shows out on the road. It must have been so frustrating for her to see that her young daughter had so much talent, but lacked the ambition she had. I think she worried a great deal that I wouldn't take it as seriously as she did. I needed to have my own identity, and in Mom's vision, our identities were joined. Our realities were very different. It's really a wonder that we even made it to our first audition, when I think about it. I certainly never saw myself getting a record deal and ending up on a bus with Mom for ten years.

Weeks later Brent Maher listened to our tape, and when he stopped by the house and we sang live for him, he loved what he heard! I thought that might be the end of our search, but Brent said it was just the beginning. From that day on, it was practice, learn songs, jam and hope we'd find the magic.

Part of the magic found us when Brent brought musician and singer Don Potter to Del Rio Pike. Don became my spiritual father. He was then and continues to be a light in my life. Certain people seem to get mentioned as crucial to The Judds' career: Brent Maher first worked with us. Our manager, Ken Stilts, became a father figure for me. Dick Whitehouse got us to Curb Records. And Joe Galante signed us to a recording contract with RCA. But if it had not been for Don Potter, The Judds would not have made it or survived—I'm certain of it. We would have imploded at some point.

Don had no idea what he was about to get himself into! It started out innocently enough. The producer and the guitarist began coming to a farmhouse to meet two Kentucky natives, a mother and daughter who respected traditional music and sang harmony. A family of skunks lived underneath the porch. We often lit the house with kerosene lamps. A wringer washer sat out on the back porch. And in that rustic setting, each person had a role. I was the lead singer, Don was the instrumentation, Brent was the producer and Mom was the songwriter and harmony singer. Together, we made up a complete family.

But what neither Don nor Brent knew at first was what was happening between the mother and daughter before and after those magical get-togethers. The arguing that started back then and continued into our career already had a pattern. We'd fight right up until Brent and Don arrived to jam. Then we'd make our music. Later, Mom and I would fight right up to the point at which we walked out onstage. We'd step into the light, hear the audience cheer, and everything would be fine while we sang. But when the show ended every night onstage so did the harmony.

Don and I bonded instantly, both personally and musically. When he came by the house, we jammed for hours. I'd play rhythm and Don would play rhythm and lead. (He is a master at his craft. When you hear him play, you realize just how anointed he is.) When we started going places to perform, Don always covered for me. If I forgot my capo (which was often), he always seemed to have an extra one to lend me. He even carried my guitar for me sometimes. I didn't feel quite so distracted when Don was around because he was always watching my back, helping me focus.

He began to teach me about God and spirituality. Mom had introduced Ashley and me to many kinds of religions. We had attended many kinds of churches, from Unitarian to Holy Roller Pentecostal. But it was Don's loving spirit and his gentle way of teaching that made me see that in God's eyes I was loved just the way I was.

Don took all the negative things I said about myself and turned them into something good. I had a hard time being organized and showing up on time. He'd say, *Pick one thing and do it well. Work on your strengths, not your weaknesses.* I worried that I was incapable and scattered, flying all over the universe. He reminded me that God loves spontaneity. I often felt embarrassed about my sensitivity. Don said, *God loves you to show up with an open heart.*

I opened up to Don, explaining that I'd always felt less competent than Mom, that I didn't have her discipline, her ability to organize and plan every move. I felt like something was wrong with me. Later I would accept that my brain simply works differently than Mom's, and Ashley's, too. I have different gifts, different knowledge. Through Don I came to understand that marvelous, beautiful things happen in your life when you open yourself up to them. He showed me that you don't always have to have a script or an agenda, that though Mom's way worked for her, it didn't have to be my way. He taught me to keep it real.

As Mom and I continued to work together, and later, when we got our record deal and went on the road, many times Don stood in the "gap" between Mom and me. He stood there figuratively and literally. People listened to Don because of his talent and his experience, having been on the road for such a long time performing with people like Chuck Mangione.

During our jam sessions, it was Don who drew me out, who encouraged my input and ideas. In my heart, I think Don was one of the first people I ever truly felt understood me. Don never looked down on me. He looked straight at me. He didn't walk in front of me or behind me. He walked beside me. If others didn't pay attention to what I said, he listened. He respected me as a musician and a singer, and became my interpreter in the studio and on the road.

One of the reasons Don became so influential was because Mom respected him so much. She listened to him, and he was able to become a mediator. He could take my ideas and explain them to Mom in a nonthreatening way. He never "took sides." He stayed neutral. The way he communicated, we both felt it was a win-win. To this day I marvel at Don's ability to make the person he is talking to feel that they are the most important person in the world and that he has all the time in the world to listen to what they have to say.

He was one of the people in my spiritual life who became a teacher, not a preacher. He readily admitted he'd made many mistakes in the past, and in a way, his having made those mistakes drew me to him. He was open and honest about his imperfections. Throughout my life I'd felt dangled over hell many times in the church. Through Don's story I started to feel that God did love me the same on my best and worst day. And believe me, we had the best and worst of times back then. The best of times were when we sang together.

And we had the worst of times. One of them was when Mom was out on the road with Pop, and I stayed at home on Del Rio Pike to take care of Ashley. Then I got a call from a friend of mine.

"Hey, Wy—I want to go down to Atlanta for a couple of days. Can you drive me?"

I thought it over. This was one of the many times that my on-again, off-again relationship with Stephen McCord was off-again.

"I think so," I said, wondering whether the car Mamaw and Papaw Ciminella had bought me on my sixteenth birthday was in good enough shape to make the trip.

"Come on, Wynonna—it'll be fun!"

And the more I thought about it, the more fun it sounded. So Ashley went to stay at a friend's house and I packed a bag. We took off out of Nashville in my Honda Accord. I justified going off to Atlanta because Mom was out on the road.

She'll never know, I thought.

Our first problem didn't involve my mom, though. It involved my friend's parents. We had only been in Atlanta a few hours when he called home, and they threatened to send him to boarding school if he wasn't home by midnight that night. He went to the airport and caught a flight to Nashville. Things promptly went downhill from there, because the brakes on my car went out and I was stranded. Finally I called a guy I had met when he sang at the Stockyards earlier that year. This guy was a pretty good singer, and *very* good looking. And—he lived in Atlanta.

When I phoned to tell Mom where I was, she told me not to bother coming home.

The singer I'd called took me to his mother's house, and she welcomed me in. Very quickly I realized that she saw me as "the *nice* girl" her son needed. Of course, he already *had* a girlfriend—or an ex-girlfriend—and *that* became a problem. As soon as this girl found out I was staying with the family, she started driving by the house late at night, honking her horn and yelling out threats.

"I'm gonna kill you!"

Then the guy would run out on the porch and shout back at the girl, telling her to go home. I was the one who should have been running—right back to Nashville! But, feeling that I wasn't wanted there, I became yet another teenage girl ripe for indoctrination. If you've ever wondered how young kids get mixed up in cults, look no further than this story. There I was, upset, feeling like no one wanted me at home, and someone—an adult woman—started telling me what the Lord wanted for me. Or didn't! The Lord, she said, didn't want me to be mixed up in the music business because those people were evil. And, she said, my own mother didn't want me around! I was so gullible! The seeds of doubt that she planted in my mind confused me and I mistook brainwashing for concern.

"You can stay with us," she said. *Us* meant her and her bipolar son.

I ended up staying with them about a month, helping her clean houses to earn money. The guy's condition worsened when he got off his lithium, which was about any time he decided to go out to an Atlanta club and sing. He'd have a beer and get a little crazy. I hadn't even kissed this guy and some girl wanted to kill me and his mother wanted me for a daughter-in-law and he—well, I think what he wanted more than anything was to be a country music star.

What did I want? Somebody to love me. I wanted my mom, or somebody, to *demand* I come home, to *make* me come home. For a while it looked like that was never going to happen.

Now that I have a daughter, I understand how scared Mom must have been. I know she was trying to teach me a lesson, but I felt abandoned. As a parent, I know we often think we are teaching our child a "good lesson." It depends on what day it is whether I believe that Mom was just so mad at me that she was punishing me, or whether she was testing me to see if I'd come running home. The longer I stayed away, the more I was unable to make that decision for myself. Somebody was going to have to step in, and somebody did.

When Mom fully realized what was happening to me, she got Papaw Ciminella involved. He came to Atlanta and contacted the FBI because he thought the family might really *be* a cult. Papaw took charge. He got my car fixed.

Then Dad flew to Atlanta, picked me up, and together he and I drove to Ocala, Florida, where he was working in the horse-breeding business. Dad rented a little guesthouse on a horse farm in what seemed like the middle of nowhere. The land was very flat, with miles and miles of fenced horse pastures.

I stayed with Dad for quite a while, feeling worse by the day, feeling cut off from Mom and Ashley. It was one of the lowest points of my life. Mom was so mad at me, I was so mad at Mom, and Dad was mad at Mom. Dad tried to rescue me in the best way he knew how, by giving me what he thought I most needed: tough love, discipline and a makeover. He asked me to cut my hair short, to stop coloring it red. I wasn't allowed to wear makeup. Dad's focus was on what he saw as the most important thing for me to do—to get an education. And so he started talking to me about going to college. One of the gifts Dad gave me that trip was the encouragement to listen to classical music and to read. In doing so, he introduced me to another world. But more than anything, I still wanted to sing, and it seemed to me that going to college meant giving up that dream.

One night I decided to call and check in with Mom. But before I could say much, she explained that Pop was playing a show near Ocala.

"Your clothes are packed up in trash bags, and on Pop's bus," she said. "You can go see him and pick them up this weekend."

Our talk was brief because neither of us knew what to say. I didn't ask to come home, and she didn't offer. When we hung up, I sat in Dad's house and cried for a long time. Mom had given up on me. I felt hopeless. I started wondering if that's how it felt to be a juvenile delinquent. I felt like I had been sentenced.

Dad was staying home that night, so I took his car and

drove the twenty miles to town. I went to a sports bar and ordered a drink. What I still can't figure out is how I ever got served. I guess I looked older than I was, because the bartender never carded me. I was a teenager, and didn't even know what drink to order. I started sampling various drinks from the menu. After a couple of drinks, I discovered something I liked—something that didn't taste like alcohol. A Long Island Iced Tea! I drank several, trying to distract myself from the pain I was feeling. I started thinking about how completely finished everything was.

"You live around here?" the bartender asked. It was a weeknight, and almost no one was at the restaurant.

"I'm visiting my dad," I said.

"Where are you from?"

"Nashville," I said, choking on the word.

I wouldn't be going back to Nashville. I was going to college, and my musical dreams were over. I had never planned to end up with Dad. I wasn't even sure he wanted me there. He had his own life. I never planned on going to college. I was going to be a rock star. Bonnie Raitt. Joni Mitchell. Now I belonged nowhere.

By the time I left the bar, my head was spinning. It was pitch-black outside, and I didn't know exactly where I was. The horse farms around Ocala are hundreds of acres in size, and at night the roads are lonely and confusing. And so I just drove around drunk, lost and crying. What you are feeling when you start to drink is amplified a hundred times when you get drunk. Suddenly it hit me, *If I can't do music, I don't want to live*. At that moment, in my mind, there was nowhere to go but straight into a telephone pole and kill myself. I sped up and headed for the pole, but then at the last moment I turned the wheel and spun a three-sixty.

It had been a spontaneous act. I hadn't really planned on

killing myself that night. But young people make tragic mistakes in a moment of despair. I sat there in front of a tree sobbing. I was completely freaked out at what I'd almost done. I finally sobered up enough to get back to the house, and never said a word about it to Dad. He almost had to know that I'd been drunk though, because I was sick for about three days. On Saturday morning, I pulled myself back together and got on a Greyhound bus to travel to Pop's show. I brought a couple of empty suitcases, and kept wondering what I'd do if my clothes wouldn't fit in them.

I now think that Pop believed there was still a chance that Mom and I could make it together in the music business, because this was one of the first times that he stepped in between us on behalf of our career. Before that, I felt I had been the one stepping in between Mom and Pop on behalf of their relationship. Now the roles were reversed.

Pop's music group, Memphis, was playing at a hotel lounge. I sat at a table up front. When the show was over, Pop took me upstairs to his hotel room and sat me down. The room was kind of run-down, with threadbare carpeting and the smell of stale cigarette smoke in the curtains. But, on that night, the shabby room became transformed into the Church of Pop. It felt like divine intervention.

"Your mom loves you very much," he said.

"Obviously not," I said. "She won't let me come home."

"You know how your mom is, Wynonna. She has a lot of pride. But if you come home, I believe you'll work it out. You belong home with your mom, and you belong onstage singing."

Tears started falling down my face.

"You're gifted, Wynonna," he went on. "Come home and make this work."

"What if it doesn't work, living with Mom?"

"We'll work it out when we get there. If nothing else, I'll help you get your own place. *Come back to Nashville.*"

I sat there for a while, thinking about Mom and our music. "Take the clothes on back to Nashville," I said. "I'll pick up my things at Dad's and come home."

I came back to Tennessee pretty broken but determined to play music. Mom and I barely mentioned all that had just happened. We just resumed working with Brent and Don.

In June of 1982, another component fell into place when Mom met a public relations agent named Woody Bowles. Woody listened to our tapes and was determined to help us find both a record label and management. And he soon brought us to the attention of Dick Whitehouse at Curb Records, and to the man who would become our manager, Ken Stilts.

Ken was a successful manufacturer who loved the music business so much he had started a little record label. He wore expensive suits, dark sunglasses and drove expensive cars. He looked like a Mafioso Don, the Godfather. The first time I saw him, he pulled into a parking lot in a big car with tinted windows. He seemed very mysterious, and he radiated power. He had so much charisma that we used to say he could even get God to change His mind.

Things happened pretty fast after Dick Whitehouse and Ken Stilts got involved. Joe Galante at RCA agreed to let us play live for him and his executive staff. (I'm not sure why Dick Whitehouse isn't mentioned more in the stories about The Judds' musical journey. He was the first label executive who showed interest, and was a crucial part of our Curb/RCA signing.)

I know you are going to be truly shocked to read this, but on March 2, 1983, the day of our RCA audition, Mom and I were fighting. I don't even remember what the fight was about. I was scared to death of the audition. I've tried to imagine what Mom was feeling, but I can't know. I know that I wasn't prepared for the experience. I'm not sure that Mom was either. We had thought that the audition might be canceled, because just prior to that day, Ken Stilts had a heart attack. But he insisted we go on as planned. Even a heart attack couldn't stop the show.

We met Brent and drove to the label in his Volvo. Tony Brown was an RCA executive at that time. I later heard that he had been told this big story about a Kentucky mother/daughter duo with Appalachian roots and fine-tuned mountain harmonies. He had heard about the '57 candy apple red Chevy. Then when he looked down in the parking lot, he saw us get out of a Volvo, and he thought, *Yeah, right!* It was hard for anyone to believe our story.

We arrived at the label at six p.m. It was after office hours and the building seemed nearly deserted. Only a few people were working in the offices we passed, and it was deathly quiet in the halls. We immediately went into the bathroom. I leaned up against the wall to watch Mom primp. She checked her makeup and puffed up her hair. Then she sprayed so much Jungle Gardenia on herself that I could taste it. I was so mad because Mom knew that Jungle Gardenia perfume gave me headaches! I was already diarrhea-nervous and trying to decide whether I needed to throw up or look for the nearest exit.

When we finally walked into Joe Galante's office, I was struck by the fact that his office had a fireplace. *Wow*, I thought, *he must really be rich.* I guess I thought that record executives were all big, tough, powerful-looking men who smoked cigars. But Joe was quietly well dressed, and didn't fit the stereotypes. I went over and sat down next to the fireplace. We sang Mom's song "Change of

Heart," then "Mama He's Crazy." The entire audition seemed to last just minutes. The men in the room thanked us for coming, and I couldn't wait to get out of there!

Woody told us to go to a nearby O'Charley's restaurant and wait because the men wanted to talk. Mom and I sat at the restaurant and waited for Woody to show up and give us the news. I don't think we could have been any more nervous! I wondered if the men might decide that I was too young, and tell us to come back later when I had a little more experience. How could I get a record contract when I hadn't even been to Music Row?

When Woody walked into O'Charley's, it was with a big grin on his face. I'll NEVER forget him saying:

"Congratulations. You are now RCA artists."

I felt like we'd won the lottery. Mom jumped up and ran to the pay phone. The first person she called was Larry, who wasn't in his motel room. Next she called Papaw Judd, who said, "Don't quit your day job."

And to understand Mom, you have to understand the implications of that day. After experiencing such an important event in her life, Mom had turned to the two most important men in her life and found one was missing and the other didn't get it. Mom had me beside her, but I can imagine that she felt very much alone in her moment of victory.

You're gonna get too big for your britches. From the beginning I can imagine it was one of Mom's biggest concerns, that I would get above my raising. But she needn't have worried. When I was thrust into the spotlight at age eighteen I felt like Jodie Foster in the movie *Nell*. Like her character, I felt like a backwoods recluse dragged by strangers into an unknown world, terrified by the elements and speaking a completely different language. I didn't have a clue what I was getting into.

It would be an understatement to say that I was challenged by show business. Nothing but the singing came naturally to me, nothing. Not meeting deejays or journalists, not picking out wardrobe, not photo shoots, and not award shows. When you saw The Judds win any of our awards, you could be assured of two things: I was unprepared and scared to death. On the way to the stage, I would often "check out." I'd feel like I wasn't even real. It's like when Annie Lennox sings in one of her songs "Dying Is Easy." It's living that scares me to death. It was so hard for me, so unnatural, that I felt like I didn't take a single deep breath during those early years. In success, some things changed and some things didn't. I had just signed a record deal with RCA Records. Yet I felt like I worked for Mom.

RCA decided that our first album would be a six-song mini disc. Don Potter, Brent Maher, Mom and I spent months in the studio, working on the songs, the harmonies, simply creating. It was as if we had all the time in the world to play. (Years later our record label decided that our demos were so unique and of good quality they ended up putting them out as a Judds music box set. There was no other sound like it.)

We recorded at a small studio outside Nashville in a residential area, a laid-back atmosphere perfect for our kind of music. Don started each session by leading us in prayer. We recorded as if we were playing live—all the musicians played at once and I sang along. The players would then fix any mistakes they made, but for the most part we left the spirit of the live recording alone. I love the way we made records then. It's different today! Now there is so much technology that a producer can take a singer's voice and fix the quality, make the voice sound stronger by adding additional voices to thicken the sound. They often take two different singers and have them sing the same line, and then blend them together to make them sound better. We didn't have that stuff back then. If my voice sounded imperfect here and there, Brent cared more that the emotion—the feeling—was right. The vibe was the most important thing when we made Judd records—not perfection.

Mom's harmony was so like her personality. She colored outside the lines. She thought outside the box. Sometimes she sang her harmony to fit my voice perfectly. At other times, Don would say, "Okay, Naomi, try singing it this way." She would try, but end up singing it the way she heard the line in her head. Don developed a unique way of training her to try new ideas.

Don became a master at his signature guitar licks like on "Grandpa" and "Why Not Me." We continued looking for material, and the song that was to become our first single came from an unexpected source.

When we first heard "Had a Dream," Mom thought she'd heard it somewhere.

"It's on an old Elvis record," Brent admitted. "It's on the B side of 'Hunka, Hunka Burnin' Love.'"

Brent wasn't sure about doing an old Elvis song, but after talking to Pop, we realized that the harmony parts made it perfect for us. So perfect, in fact, that after we finished recording all six songs for the mini disc, "Had a Dream" was chosen as the first single.

When "Had a Dream" was released on November 16, 1983, RCA sent Mom and me out for a radio promotional tour. I can still remember vividly where I was the first time we heard ourselves on the radio. We were on Nolensville Road in Nashville, heading for an interview at WSM. I heard that guitar strum, and my voice!

"Had a dream about you, baby. Had a dream 'bout me and you."

I flipped out! It was really us! We were on the radio! Maybe that's the first time it felt true, like it was really happening. We couldn't sit still! You can record and listen to yourself on a tape player all you want, but when your voice comes out of that radio and you know that hundreds, maybe thousands, of people are hearing it, it's *real*. Mom and I both cried. Our moment had finally arrived. All our hard work had paid off. Brent's production along with Don's exquisite guitar work had allowed our voices to shine. It was a fresh new sound. People everywhere stopped and listened.

The critics seemed impressed from the beginning. With country music coming off the pop-flavored urban-cowboy years, our timing could not have been more perfect. Our lyrics were positive, the themes traditional, and our blood harmonies pleasing to the ear. Judd music was hip. Our musical presentation, the way we looked, and the way we talked set us apart from the rest of the artists. We somehow bridged the gap between traditional and contemporary. When people read our bio, they'd call the office and say, "Who did you pay to write this story? It can't be for real." Well, it was for real. We had lived it!

We were lucky to have the creative team we had, and to have a record label so supportive of us. The career launch that RCA put together for us was one of those rare magical events that seldom happens in today's entertainment industry. Mom and I embarked upon a yearlong radio and media tour. We would fly into major cities, where a regional rep from the label would meet us in a rented car and drive us to three or four radio stations a day. We'd do an on-air interview, and then sing live. I always brought my guitar. We met every person at the station and signed autographs for everybody. A lot of staff members often brought their friends and family to meet us.

After our day of radio visits, we would then go to a hotel suite that night to sing again for station music directors and program directors as well as other industry people. Mom and I also visited the retail warehouses for "meet & greets" with hundreds of workers. They brought in pizzas, gave everyone a lunch break, and we'd sing for all of the people who helped distribute our records. Times are so different now; the business is far less personable. I don't think it's possible anymore to do it the way we did. Technology often takes the place of a handshake. It reminds me of a line in "Grandpa"—*We call it progress, but I just don't know*.

From the very beginning there was no doubt that Mom was the spokesperson, the cheerleader of The Judds. She had such charisma, as well as those magical *stories*. I loved watching people's faces as she started telling her tales of her homemade lye soap, doing laundry on a Maytag wringer washer, chopping wood, bustin' coal and livin' in the hills. I think it was hard for a lot of people to believe her, but they loved hearing the stories regardless.

She was so beautiful—like a painting. She looked so young! No one could believe she was the mother. I wish I had a nickel for every time I heard someone ask, "Which one is the mother and which one is the daughter?" I'd be a billionaire! She had a tiny waist and a big bosom, small delicate hands and peaches-and-cream skin. She worked hard to keep her hair and makeup perfect. I used to love watching her do her lips. She would line them perfectly, then fill in the top and bottom lip with the same color lipstick, and finally put a dab of undereye concealer in the very center of her bottom lip. She said it gave her a "pouty" look. It's one of the tricks she learned back when she was working as a model in California.

I liked it that Mom did most of the talking during our

performances because I was more comfortable when I had my guitar strapped on and was behind the mike singing. She loved working a room. She was a natural when it came to wowing deejays and industry types, as well as making fans feel so special and so loved. Mom did most of the talking in interviews, too. Of course, I make jokes now about how I had a reputation for interrupting Mom because it was the only chance I had to get a word in edgewise. In the beginning I was so shy and introverted that I didn't mind. By the end of our radio tour, we had our timing down. Mom would launch into a story, making it just as charming and funny as the first fifty times she'd told it. She had code words that would cue me to begin playing my guitar. We timed it so that her last word was said a few beats before I started singing the first verse. By the end of our radio tour, we were ready for the stage. Or so I thought.

In March of 1984—a year after our original RCA audition—we got our first gig. Marshall Grant, the Statler Brothers' manager, called and asked RCA if we'd open a show for the legendary group. It happened so quickly that we had no time to put together a band, so Brent called some of the studio musicians who had played on the album. Mom dubbed them "the Emergency Band." (Mom later named our touring band the Judd Boys.) Don Potter was bandleader, of course. I probably couldn't have made it through that night without Don onstage with us.

We flew into Omaha, Nebraska, for the concert at the Aksarben Event Center. (Which is Nebraska spelled backward.) The first thrill was learning that Mom and I would have separate hotel rooms! Brent Maher and his wife, Janel, also flew in for the show. Neither Mom nor I had stage clothes at that point. I wore a leotard, a jacket I had bought at the mall and pants from Wal-Mart. I didn't care what I wore anyway, because my huge Guild guitar was my best asset. That's the way I have always liked it. Mom also wore pants. That was one of the last times she would dress so casual. From that point on, she wore those famous Naomi "Prissy-Butt" dresses.

Most of the details of that night are a blur to me. However, I do have a vivid memory of Mom and me standing backstage behind the big curtain, listening to a prerecorded version of the Statler Brothers singing "The Star Spangled Banner." The audience went crazy!

My God, I thought. *They are playing the national anthem! We've only had two real rehearsals! I'm not ready!*

Having a patriotic song playing while we waited there just intensified my fears of failure. I panicked and started looking around for an exit sign. The crowd went crazy when "The Star Spangled Banner" finished, and as the curtain started to rise, I turned to Mom and said, "I want to go home."

"It's going to be all right, Wy! I'm right here," Mom said.

"You girls are going to do just fine," Don called, just as the curtain rose high enough for me to see ten thousand people sitting there applauding. *Ten thousand!* The closest I'd come to performing for a crowd was at the Franklin High Talent Show! *This is too much,* I thought. *There are too many people out there!* I seriously thought I was going to puke.

My mind must have turned off at that point. I think it's like being in an automobile accident, where everything happens in slow motion. You never quite remember the point of impact. I felt like my spirit slowly rose up out of my body and I watched these two women from above the stage. I remember this: the lights were too bright and I couldn't really see the audience past the first five rows. They looked like a blurred mass of faces. I could only hear them—the applause and excitement. I'm told that I never moved once from the spot where I was standing when the curtain went up. We forgot to talk, forgot to thank the audience. We didn't fully introduce the band but despite those mess-ups—we did great.

After the show, Mom and I ran back to the dressing room. We cried and hugged each other. Then we hung out talking with the musicians, listening to the Statlers' show, and I must have jumped up and down a hundred times.

That was the second thrill: when it was over!

The next morning, Mom went to breakfast dressed in full stage makeup just in case somebody recognized her. And someone did—an elderly woman asked her if she was the mother or the daughter. But the real excitement came when she went to buy a copy of the Omaha *World Herald*, who compared us to both the Andrews Sisters and Bonnie Raitt. My (s)hero's name and mine were in the same article!

With that success behind us, RCA booked some more dates. Since we wouldn't be making enough money to pay a full band, we had to send them home. Then Don Potter, Mom and I started the first Judds Tour in a Winnebago. It was hilarious. There The Judds were, running up and down the road in a motor home, too broke to pay a band or get a bus, but still the subject of Nashville's latest buzz! The Winnebago broke down right away. We sat on the side of the road waiting for help, then ended up having to catch a plane to the last date in Cleveland, Ohio. I didn't care, 'cuz we were in the big time!

The funny thing is, when we hit it big, in some ways my world started to shrink. Mom loved being in the public, being recognized and talking to a crowd of fans. That intimidated me. I became so afraid of saying the wrong thing that I avoided talking as much as possible. I stayed away from hotel lobbies and restaurants—lived in my hotel room. Room service waiters were my confidants and housekeeping was my pal. I would tell them about my day and ask them about theirs. I craved intimacy. It was Mom who loved the crowds.

It would've been so much better if Mom and I had seriously talked about what was really going on behind the scenes. I was warned just how fast things could move very early in our career. When I met my sisterfriend Bonnie Raitt, she told me, "Get ready for the roller-coaster ride of your life! Just hold on." It's true. I just tried to hang on and sing with everything I had.

To this day, when I sit in my living room and see these young talents make it on *American Idol*, I literally holler at the television! I understand their passion and want them to succeed.

I say, "Get a good lawyer and save your money!"

Sometimes I close my eyes and pray, "God be with them, because their lives are about to completely change forever for good and bad." Every decision they make will be in public. It's like winning the lottery. Too many people will try to tell you who you are.

Personally, I wrestled with our success from the day we had our first hit record. It was hard for me to understand how I could be so young and so blessed. Making it so fast. People talk about overnight success. Ours was *over-a-coffee-break* success. I went from high school to having an accountant. We went from secondhand clothes from local thrift shops to stage clothes and stylists. We went from years of worrying that we might run out of food before Mom got her next paycheck, to having a $250 food allowance at Caesars Palace each day when we opened for Merle Haggard. We went from welfare to millionaire in a matter of months. For me it was too much too soon.

I can imagine what a relief it was for Mom. The day our

song "Mama He's Crazy" went #1, she drove to her job at the hospital for the last time. She traded in her nurse's uniform for designer skirts with peplons that she lifted up and shook when she danced and twirled on stage. Mom was thirty-six when she made it, and she had lived through hard times. I felt she deserved it.

I wasn't sure if I did. It's very strange, but I felt that I was somehow going into battle. There were giant forces taking over my life. Even though Judd music was getting bigger and bigger, I felt like I was getting smaller and smaller.

· 4 ·

CHANGE THE WORLD

I quickly saw how a fast-moving career affects your personal life. The first harsh reality was, of course, separating from Ashley for long periods of time. How many times was I out on the road, too busy to talk when my "Sweet Pea" called, needing to talk to her big sister? I'd be in the hotel suite, putting on my makeup, trying to make it to an interview or a meet & greet, and the phone would ring.

"Wy?"

"Hi! How are ya doin'?"

"Well . . ." Sometimes Ashley would sound so sad, so far away. I can only imagine how many times she really needed me when there was something significant going on in her life. But too many times I could only listen for a short while, and then I'd have to go.

"Ashley, honey—let's talk later. I'm already late!"

It makes me feel heartsick to even write those words—words that re-create so many feelings of being separated from and missing my only sister. It's so ironic. Now I call her and she's traveling most of the time or on a movie location or at the races with her husband, race driver Dario Franchitti.

Then, in the summer of 1984, Papaw Judd died. We flew home to Kentucky, went to his funeral service and then flew back to open for Lee Greenwood in Memphis that same night. I never felt I had time to properly grieve for him, and I'm wondering if Mom did, either. I know there are other people who have shared in that same experience. You rush to a funeral, cry for someone you love, then take your show right back on the road.

There was little time to grieve for loved ones, and even less time to nourish a loving relationship. I still thought Stephen McCord and I would get married one day after my career got established. When we first went out on the road, I talked with him several times on the phone every day and night. Of course, I usually shared a hotel room with Mom and sometimes I would ask her to go into the bathroom, so I could talk to him. She once picked up the phone and flushed the toilet when she couldn't take it anymore. But as time went by, the calls were less frequent. My life was changing, and Stephen and I were moving in different directions. I guess in some ways it's like when childhood sweethearts go off to different colleges. We were both growing up and growing apart.

Still, I was sure that our relationship could survive my career. Why did it have to be a conflict? Mom saw that I was being torn between my teenage life and life on the road. She didn't think it was going to work out. But I honestly don't think Mom would have liked anyone I dated then. I was pursuing a dream with her, and she didn't want a boy bringing me down or standing in the way of our career.

Stephen and I kept going together until 1984, when "Mama He's Crazy" caused an increase in our bookings, our televised appearances and our popularity. Everything just seemed to go crazy, right along with the song title. When our relationship finally ended, I think I felt worse about the loss of Mr. and Mrs. McCord than Stephen! I felt like calling and saying, "Even if I don't marry your son, can I still be part of the family?"

Sadly, Mom and Pop broke up while "Mama He's Crazy" was on the charts, too. With both of them out on the road, and Mom's continuing concerns about Pop's female fans, the relationship came to a sudden halt. Pop had a hard time letting Mom go out on that road he knew so well—he knew how hard it was going to be.

A lot more was unraveling. Mom and I fought more than ever after we got the record contract. We argued about everything from attitude to outfits. Eventually, I couldn't take it anymore. One night I left the house and showed up on Woody Bowles' doorstep. Woody and his wife, television personality Elaine Gannick, took me in, and I lived with the Bowles family for nearly a year. When I moved in, Elaine was pregnant with twins. Their nursery was right next to my room. What an education!

I will always be thankful for Woody and Elaine's generosity. And it must have been stressful for Woody. He was trying to support me and teach me how to become more independent. And on the other hand, he worried that Mom thought he was trying to come between us. It was a hectic time. He spent a lot of time on the phone with Mom, trying to mediate. But there were so many layers of differences. He did understand that my opinion of myself was frighteningly poor. In an interview, Woody said that he believed that around the time we got a record deal, I would have had to work my way up to low self-esteem. He was right.

Much has been made of what has long been labeled the *contentious relationship* Mom and I shared. Well, we had fought before we ever had a record deal, and living in a goldfish bowl magnified our differences. I think the roles we assumed were set early in the career, just as The Judds were becoming what the press dubbed *America's Sweethearts*.

One of the first things that RCA asked us to do after we got signed was to go to media school. Early on, it was apparent that I was easily distracted and didn't know how to talk in interviews. I had severe performer's anxiety, and some very annoying quirks. It's as if whatever I was feeling showed up on my face without any kind of warning. If I was upset, it showed. If I was sad, it was hard for me to look excited. I wore my heart on my sleeve. I have finally accepted this today, but back then it was very frustrating to a lot of people. I was so used to being with Mom that I would forget we were on camera, and because I felt so comfortable in giving her my opinion, I often came across as too opinionated or harsh.

The media coach working with us showed us some early Ralph Emery shows. It was really obvious that when Mom was talking I was looking around the room. It looked as if I wasn't interested in what was going on. Part of it was that I was also very shy. But mostly these nervous tics—shifting in my chair, rolling my eyes, looking away—were coping mechanisms that helped keep me from blurting out what happened to be on my mind at that moment. It could have been a disaster for our career, because I had a tendency to say the things that other people were thinking, and my reactions to Mom were not always appropriate. We all act differently with family than we do with strangers. We're often not as polite!

Sometimes—hearing about the lye soap for the hundredth time—I *had* to roll my eyes! I *knew* her Southern accent wasn't normally that thick! I also knew that she had a tendency to linger and embellish, as many storytellers do. I felt it was *my* job to keep her honest and to bring her back to the original question. And remember, Mom and I had even worked out routines where it was important that I interrupt and start playing the guitar to get into the next song. Truth of it was, I just wanted to get on with the music, but it came across as though I was very disrespectful.

Everyone wanted to help, especially our manager. The music was really taking off and it was just a matter of time before we were on all the major TV talk shows. Ken reminded me that soon we would be doing *The Tonight Show* and embarking upon a national campaign. I had to come across as professional in an interview as I did onstage.

I was so creative and so right-brained that it was really hard for me to focus. Mom was very organized and, at least on the surface, seemed to be the left brain. (In reality, Mom has that right-brained creativity as well.) Jay Leno once said that together the two of us made up a whole brain. I wasn't sure how to take that.

I feel that it was unfortunate that the answer to our public persona problem was put at my doorstep. It was up to me to change the way I related to Mom, not the other way around. This was especially frustrating because I was the lead singer, the "front man." In rock 'n' roll, the lead singer leads. He or she is the spokesperson on- and offstage. But working with Mom, that was not the case. And because many times I didn't feel heard, or given the chance to offer my opinion, I began resenting the protocol. I simply wanted to be free to be myself, to sing.

Some people thought that I had developed a diva attitude. Others thought that I had an anger problem or that I was ungrateful for all the fame and fortune. And I suppose it must have looked that way from the outside. I was young and didn't have the experience or wisdom Mom had about life. I didn't like doing interviews as much as Mom did. It was hard to contain me. I still tended to say what was on my mind. (It wasn't until I was in my late thirties that I could finally accept the fact that it felt awesome to be spontaneous.) I didn't like sitting still and being asked so many questions. It was hard to suck it up when I was feeling emotional and in need of a break! I tried to stay on my best behavior, but everyone seemed to always find out about every mistake I made. How many times was I called into my manager's office to have *the talk*?

"Wynonna, you are in the public eye. You've got to stop interrupting your mother!" Ken would say.

I'd usually start out by trying to tell him about something that had happened between us.

"I don't care what the dynamic of your home life is. You have to become more professional in the way that you react to Naomi. It's not just the two of you on that mountaintop anymore."

"I know but—"

"Country isn't pop, Wynonna! You *cannot* get away with having a bad attitude. Music Row is a very small community—and I promise you that you'll see the same people on the way down that you saw on the way up!"

"I'm not trying to act—"

"And you can't look at your mother that way and say, '*Oh, yeah, right.*'"

"Well, what if she—"

"If you're not careful, you'll learn this too late and your public image will be 'What a talent, but what a *smart aleck.*'"

"Ken, Mom and I—"

"People want biscuits and gravy. Mother and daughter. Country music is about family. You have to work together."

I didn't feel like I had the chance to explain myself during these meetings. *The talk* would work for a while, but before you knew it, I'd leave a television studio so mad over something Mom had said that all I could do was act out. I was still reacting to her like we were at home. She pushed my buttons and I would just go off. And so I did. I started spending money and drowning my emotions with food, which helped me cope with not having the relationship I wanted with Mom away from show business. I wasn't doing drugs or alcohol, so no one really noticed that I was abusing food to comfort me during my struggle. I did it alone. (I would never overeat in front of others.) I sometimes wonder if I had chosen alcohol or drugs if I'd even be alive today. But food is just a slower form of suicide.

A pattern was repeating. When I was a child coming home from school alone, I ate and watched television. As a star, I often came back to my hotel room to eat and watch television. Another concern continued. As a child I had often felt insecure about how I looked. As a star the uncertainty was intensified.

The differences between Mom and me were nowhere more obvious than when it came to wardrobe. Mom made sure that we were never as unprepared for the stage as we had been when we first played that Omaha show with the Statlers. But trust me, when it came to fashion, it was the Naomi Show. (I have to admit—she had a style that no one could match! But I tried!)

Mom loved fittings and only after she decided on an outfit for an album cover or an awards show was I able to pick out something. I always had to coordinate with her. There is an episode of the *Andy Griffith Show* where Aunt Bee is trying to tailor something for Opie and he's twisting and turning and squirming. I relate every time I see it. I always felt like Opie in that scene. I hated wardrobe fittings!

Dressing me presented an additional problem. I often hated the way I looked. I was uncomfortable with my own sexuality. I was painfully modest. The difference between the way Mom and I dressed was pretty obvious. You'll notice that in the early years of The Judds my costumes were pretty provincial. I leaned toward high collars and lace cuffs. I loved an Edwardian jacket that I had made because it reminded me of Bono. I wore it every night for a long time.

When we were nominated for the Country Music Horizon Award for new acts in 1984, Mom planned what she was going to say if we won. She was nervous that I hadn't written anything down and insisted that I start working on a speech. Well, that didn't come naturally for me. As the time for the CMA Awards Show grew closer, Mom questioned me more often—sometimes on the bus, sometimes backstage at a show, sometimes by phone.

"What are you going to say?" she'd ask.

"I don't know, Mom," I would answer. "I'm just going to play off you like I always do."

I had done it a million times, but this was unacceptable to Mom. It seemed unprofessional and I'm sure she fretted and worried about what I was going to say in the moment of excitement. But in the beginning I never got the hang of planning like she did.

Our dresses for our first awards show were like something out of a horror film about the Old South—Mom called them "movie star ball gowns." Hers was turquoise, mine was bright fuchsia pink. They were tight through the waist and bodice, with sweetheart necklines, and puffed sleeves. We also had matching gloves and little black net stoles that we wrapped around our shoulders. If those dresses had a title it might be *Taste Takes a Holiday*.

We dressed at a hotel suite Ken had reserved for us at

the Opryland Hotel. Then a limo arrived to take Mom, Ashley, Nana and me to the show. I remember thinking it was hilarious that a limousine had been hired to take us such a short distance from the Opryland Hotel right around the corner to the Grand Ole Opry House, where the televised awards were being held. But Ken wanted us to arrive in style, looking like stars. When the awards wardrobe supervisor saw how we were dressed, she asked Mom if she was sure we wanted to wear the dresses in public.

I felt lucky to be going to the awards show and getting to hang out with all of those superstars. It took years before I could stop thinking, *How did I get here?* At the rehearsals I looked at the place cards on the seats where each artist was to sit. Loretta Lynn, Tammy Wynette, George Jones, Alabama, George Strait, the Oak Ridge Boys . . . it seemed surreal to see Wynonna Judd in a seat among them.

Somebody is going to come and tell me I have the wrong seat, I thought. *They're going to make me move to the back of the room, where I belong.*

I didn't know just how strongly I felt that way until I started having recurring nightmares about being escorted from the stage of the Grand Ole Opry House to the exit! I guess it's like the people who have dreams about sleeping through their college finals.

Finally, Tammy Wynette and Ray Stevens came to the podium to announce the Horizon Award.

"And the winner is—The Judds!"

Mom and I just sat there. Everybody looked at us, and finally we got up and headed to the stage. When we took our awards, Tammy congratulated me. I stood there in a trance.

Tammy Wynette just spoke to me!

I was still reeling from my Tammy moment when Mom made her seemingly spontaneous comment, "Well, slap the dog and spit in the fire."

"All I wanted was a pretty dress," I said. What a goofball! I guess it does pay to think about what you might say in case you win an award! As the kids would say, *duh*!

Mom's quote made country music sound bite history. Mine, I'm afraid, was lost to posterity.

I was thrilled to win the Horizon Award but at the same time felt I hadn't really earned it. When I started writing this memoir, I was reminded of just how bizarre my life was at every turn. In 1984 our first full-length album, *Why Not Me,* quickly went platinum. We had found the title cut on the album from the Dean of Country Songwriters, Harlan Howard. It had seemed unbelievable that this legend would come to our house to pitch us a song! We later learned that Brent traded Harlan some fishing lures he'd made himself for driving all the way out to Del Rio Pike. We were worried that the skunks under the house might raise a stink. But they didn't, and Harlan Howard did have a hit song for us. Moreover, while we were recording the album, Ken Stilts presented us with a bus. (I thought we owned it, until someone pointed out that it was actually leased.)

What an amazing time it was. In 1983 Mom had been floating checks to pay the rent. Less than two years later we had won a CMA Horizon Award, a Grammy, ACM Awards for top vocal duet and top single for "Why Not Me" and had four #1 hits: "Mama He's Crazy," "Why Not Me," "Girls Night Out," and "Love Is Alive." When our next album, *Rockin' with the Rhythm,* was released a year later, we had over a half million preorders. We had more chart toppers on this album, "Grandpa," "Have Mercy," and "Rockin' with the Rhythm." And the awards started coming fast. By the time I was in my mid-twenties, we had won five Grammys.

The next thing we knew we were on a plane for New

York to do a round of network shows. Mom will tell you that we were not impressed with our first New York experience. She remembers the extremely high prices and the trash and the crowds. What I remember is that it was Christmastime, and every store in Manhattan had decorated windows and Christmas lights. The combination of lightly falling snow and the sparkling lights went straight to my head. I decided to go Christmas shopping! I had my first credit cards for the trip, and before I was through, I had charged over five thousand dollars' worth of gifts. When he got the bills, Ken promptly cut the cards up.

Bigger success meant bigger pressures and bigger problems. For one thing, we were trying to cover up the fact that our arguing had ended up with me moving in with Woody Bowles and his family. I was being asked questions about my relationship with Mom that really put me on the spot. *What was the worst fight you and Naomi ever had?* I didn't know how to answer. *How are you coping with overnight success?* Another question for which I had no answer.

The one area I felt completely comfortable in and able to cope with was in the studio. It was my home. I could be myself and do what I loved best: sing and create. I felt I had a connection with the musicians and, thanks in part to Don Potter, that they listened to what I said. But on the road, Mom was the head of our family that everyone looked up to. I felt that most of the band and crew often looked at me like their little punk sister. I believe that Mom felt more comfortable and at home with our success. She loved the music business. She had worked in the music industry, on Music Row, and she was the one who had spent the past few years cruising up and down Sixteenth and Seventeenth Avenues looking for someone to listen to us sing. All I had been doing was jamming with Brent and Don.

I still carry some sadness about not having enjoyed the rise to fame more. I seemed to be so busy trying to get to the next gig and simply reacting to the details that I did not comprehend the term "living in the moment." I was booked a year in advance! I was so young and still trying to figure out who I was and what I wanted. What was I going to wear? Would it match Mom's outfit? I was too much of an adolescent to fully embrace that I was living the American Dream—the well-oiled machine was producing it, 24/7!

Even today it's hard for me to admit to my insecurities. I don't want people to think I am a wimp, that I couldn't keep up with Mom or be the life of the party. But for me to get past those insecurities, I have had to learn to embrace them and try to figure out how I got them in the first place. But it was a long time coming. I have tried to explain it to people and I've found that it was difficult for most to understand. People assume that having a gift and being successful in a career make everything in your personal life successful. God, how I wished it worked that way. I often felt like so much was given to me that I had no way to pay it back.

Famous people have as many, and probably more, insecurities and neuroses as anyone else. There is a reason so many of us love the applause. It's because somewhere in our early childhood we learned that being entertaining meant receiving attention and maybe even love. I love singing, but the love it gets me from fans is not the same as having real love in my life. Everyone thinks you are having a huge party somewhere but there have been many times since I got famous that I sat at home alone on my birthday waiting for the phone to ring.

Once Mom and I were established, Ken Stilts presented us with the one thing that I had first equated with stardom—a customized Silver Eagle bus to replace the old leased bus we had been touring in. Mom named the bus Dreamchaser. She had been chasing dreams her whole life, and now they were coming true. Dreamchaser had a living room complete with a kitchen and dining area, three bunks and two bathrooms. My suite had one of those "star mirrors" with lights all around. I could sit there and think back to my first bus experience, Merle Haggard's Silver Eagle. There was only one glitch traveling on the Dreamchaser—no privacy. Mom had to walk through my suite to get to hers, and there were no locks on the doors.

No one seemed to understand that it was just not realistic to put an eighteen-year-old daughter and her thirty-six-year-old mother on a bus together twenty-four hours a day, seven days a week. We slept eight feet apart. She was the first person I saw in the morning, and the last person I saw at night. Even when we stayed in hotels, Mom and I always had adjoining rooms, so I was never able to get away with much. It's hard when your mom smiles and asks a guy, "What are your intentions?" and then laughs. And *that's* before you even give him your phone number. Putting Mom on that bus with me for ten years was in the end a blessing, but it was tough to realize it then.

In my reading since then, I have learned that a child's teenage years are spent figuratively killing off their parents. The young adult begins to separate from his or her parents, because their survival depends on it. And it isn't until they're at least twenty-five (and their brain is fully formed) that they seem to want to come back. Well, I never got the chance to leave and come back.

I have a lot of compassion for Mom now, knowing that it must have been hard for her. She was trying to keep the act together while keeping me in line. My attitude was "Let's have a party and rock!" I wanted more freedom, and she wanted more rehearsals. Her answer was to tell me that I had a curfew—even when I was in my early twenties.

"What are you going to do, ground me from doing shows for a week?" I'd respond. It was incredibly hard for each of us.

No matter how much we fought right before an interview or going onstage, Mom was able to switch from personal to professional in the blink of an eye. She could step into the lights, smile and do her job. It was her Judd work ethic. Unfortunately, I never quite mastered that skill. People were starting to think, "What's wrong with her? *Why isn't Wynonna more cooperative?*"

Yet I don't remember being in meetings and saying flat out no to something that Mom and Ken had decided was best. I don't ever remember being unavailable. Heck, I was seldom if ever asked to the meetings in the first place. They had the meetings and I got the memo. But I never made the effort, either. It was a catch-22. I didn't feel heard, so I didn't bother offering my ideas. By this time, I felt like I worked for Mom *and* the Ken Stilts company. I reacted to whatever they asked of me rather than trying to figure out how to be more of a participant and change the things I didn't like.

I guess the feeling of working *for* Mom instead of working *with* her must have started somewhere around the age when I began doing chores. Mom would leave me a list and I would do the chores. (Well, *almost* all of them!) I guess that method continued into our professional career. I showed up and did my job. When we were just starting out, it would never have occurred to me that Mom and I were equals professionally. There was no separation between personal and professional.

When I started out in the eighties, we did things differently in country music—country was about family, values and tradition. Pop music's indulgences and directness would never have been tolerated in country music. At times, I did have fantasies of saying, *I'm the lead singer and I'm going to do it my way*. But had I said it, my neck would have been jerked so hard back to reality so fast! I could hear my mom saying, *I'm going to kick your butt into next week so I don't have to deal with you this week*.

I know that Mom was just trying to toughen me up. She was trying to raise me to have thicker skin. But our relationship was often confusing. She and Ken both tried their best to raise a champion. However, I now believe that to raise a champion you must never break the spirit. One day recently, I compared how many times I corrected my kids (criticizing them on what they did wrong) and how many times I complimented them (recognized what they did right). I'm so sad to say that it was about three-to-one, corrections over compliments. The difference between the compliments I give now and what I gave then is life-changing!

I think as parents we worry that if we don't constantly guide and direct our children with instruction and discipline, if we don't keep a tight rein on them, they're going to stray or fail. We think that their failure would be a reflection on us. My husband and I learned that the word "discipline" comes from the word "disciple," which means "to teach." We are discovering that if we raise our voices, our children shut down. I'm trying to unlearn some habits and it's hard. But it's been scientifically proven that you can retrain the brain. Roach and I no longer yell in our household. We take a lot of time-outs! The children know I mean business when I take some time for myself to gather together my thoughts and think about a plan. They know a family meeting is probably next.

But, as I said, I was seldom included in meetings with my manager. My relationship with Ken Stilts was almost as complicated as the one I had with my mother. Ken was more than a manager to me. I sought his approval as much personally as I did professionally. My barometer for success was not based on a #1 record, but on Ken's satisfaction. I wasn't good unless Ken (and Mom) thought so. It wasn't enough to please the world. I had to please them. Sometimes I would come offstage thinking I had kicked butt, and Ken would critique the show right away. Since I wasn't able to separate personal from professional yet, I felt as though he was critiquing *who I was* in addition to *what I did*. This business is tough enough even when the people close to you remain positive. A #1 record can take you to the mountaintop and in the very same day a bad review can take you to the valley. *So low.*

Ken Stilts' messages were often conflicting. He'd compliment me in one breath and criticize me in the next. What I heard was, *In the Judds, Wynonna is the voice and Naomi is the brains.* Later, in my solo career, what I heard from Ken was, *Wynonna is the voice and I am the brains.* Language is such a weapon. It's a worse and more lasting weapon than a beating. Mom and I said many things to each other that were hurtful.

"I didn't ask to be born!" I said during one of our worst fights.

"Well, if you had, the answer would have been no," she responded.

I began believing that I was not a lovable person. I didn't feel like I could do anything right but sing. I believed that when I was a new artist and got a manager and signed with a record label, someone was doing me a favor. I think Mom may have felt a little the same. In the beginning, we were both young and naive. In the beginning, we learned many lessons together. But it seemed that the more successful I got, the more gullible I became! I was searching for unconditional love in a conditional career.

Also, I think Mom had a hard time with the fact that when I was in my twenties, I wasn't as ambitious as she was. Or I was ambitious in a different—maybe dreamier—way. It's so odd that people say they value creative spirits, yet they try and stop children from daydreaming or getting lost inside themselves. I've started paying strict attention to what I say to my children. My children are creative, so I build in time for them to be so. If you ask a group of preschoolers which ones are artists, they all raise their hands, but by the third and fourth grade if you ask them, only a few respond. That makes me sad. I don't want to ever lose my ability to play, to laugh, to be childlike.

Einstein once said that imagination is more important than knowledge. When people ask me what my hobbies are, I list daydreaming as one of them. There is value in doing absolutely nothing, because it is in that *nothing* that people are often able to create *something*. And I firmly believe that the proof of that can be found in the music community. The people I have met along the way were almost all daydreamers, creators, dreamchasers.

IT'S NEVER EASY TO SAY
GOODBYE

"Is that what I think it is?" I asked, looking at the little piece of paper so casually displayed on Carl Perkins' wall.

Carl just smiled. "Oh, that. It's the original membership form the Beatles filled out to join my fan club."

"Shouldn't it be in some kind of protective covering or something?" I asked, shocked.

"Oh, I don't know," he said with a little laugh.

That's what I loved about Carl. He was so unassuming, so real. He was the most self-deprecating person I had ever met. I had never met anybody so famous and yet so humble. And when he invited Mom and me to visit him at his home in Jackson, Tennessee, I felt as honored as if it had been to the White House.

I'd first met Carl Perkins when The Judds were playing the Midsouth Coliseum in Memphis, and Carl was in town recording what would become a historic project, *The Class of '55* with Jerry Lee Lewis, Johnny Cash and Roy Orbison. Other musical stars had come to Memphis to be a part of the final session, John Fogerty, Rick Nelson, Dave Edmunds. We were invited to sing on "Big Train from Memphis." Meeting all the stars was thrilling, of course, but I was in complete awe of Carl. He was one of the kindest, most tenderhearted men I ever knew.

He told me about being on his way to the *Ed Sullivan Show* to sing "Blue Suede Shoes" when he was in a car wreck, and couldn't make the show. Elvis, of course, went on to do the show and that was the famous beginning for him. I don't think Carl ever really got over that missed opportunity. We later toured together and I thought about that story every time I watched him sing "Blue Suede Shoes."

I will always regret that Carl died before I got a chance to get back to see him one last time. My backup singers and I sang "How Great Thou Art" at his funeral held in a little church in Jackson, Tennessee. I'd been to many star events before but the outpouring of love and adoration for Carl that came from other artists, like George Harrison and Garth Brooks, was phenomenal. My last memory of Carl is of him in the casket, wearing a suit with his TCB-type glasses on and those famous blue suede boots.

There were many moments in those early years when I thought it just couldn't get any better. Our first appearance on *The Tonight Show* seemed like playing Carnegie Hall. I felt like we had truly made it. We had no idea if Johnny Carson would allow us to sit on the couch and talk. We were told before we went out to sing that Johnny didn't invite the musical guests for conversation very often. But, even though we weren't sure what would happen, Mom and I argued about who would get to sit closer to Johnny in case we did make it to the couch. As it turned out, we were invited and we took turns sitting by his side, switching during commercials. Johnny loved us and we loved him.

But I don't think meeting any artist quite equaled the thrill of getting to know my flame-haired (s)hero, Bonnie

Raitt. In the early days my admiration was all about the passion she had for her music and the way she played her guitar. After I got out on the road and had an opportunity to meet her, it was her heart and her spirit that left the greatest impression on me. She influenced my feelings of womanhood, my dreams of what it meant to be an artist and my desire to be a visionary. When we performed at the Universal Amphitheater in L.A., I called and invited her to be my guest. It was one of the highlights of my life. I dedicated "Love Is Alive" to her, feeling like another sister had entered my life. They say you can't pick your relatives, but you can choose your family. I'm grateful that I was able to find friendship with her along life's highways. As I got closer to her, I realized Bonnie was the big sister that I never had.

When I first met her at a show in Nashville, it was at a time in her career when she was in great transition. It was hard for me to comprehend someone who was so accomplished was having a hard time getting airplay and selling records. *Bonnie Raitt?* I was prepared to follow this woman down any musical road. By the time I was thirteen years old, I was prepared to sing backup. I would have carried her guitar—anything—to be a part of this blues woman's music. It was through meeting and getting to know Bonnie that I would learn success has very little to do with personal fulfillment. I would come to understand that success can be fleeting.

Bonnie's career, while brilliant, wasn't commercially successful at the time. Madonna had just been signed to her label and was the new flavor. Bonnie was still playing clubs and smaller venues instead of the arenas she deserved. I remember spending an evening with Bonnie in Hollywood Hills. Bonnie was talking to me about the differences of opinion between her and her record company.

She taught me a great lesson about artistry and commerciality, and that artists and labels often don't see eye to eye. It was apparent to me that she was frustrated.

I love it that this story has such a happy ending. In 1990 Bonnie won four Grammys, three for *Nick of Time*, and one for her duet with John Lee Hooker on *The Healer*. I could not believe that I had missed the Grammy show that year. It was one of the few times I had not attended. But I had decided to spend some much needed downtime at my manager's Florida home, and watched from there. I remember screaming and jumping up and down each time Bonnie went to the podium to accept yet another award.

I saw Dwight Yoakam's "Honky Tonk Man" video in 1986 and thought he was so cool that I up and invited him to be my date to the ACM Awards. He was so hip and his music was unlike anyone else's. We ended up dating for over a year, and I believe that we could have married if we both hadn't had careers that were so fast paced. To this day he remains a dear family friend.

I couldn't help being fascinated with him because he was unique and *so* passionate about being an artist. I know he deeply cared for me and always treated me with total respect, but it was hard sometimes for me to get his attention. Talk about creative! Dwight is a genius, one of the smartest, most disciplined and eccentric people I've ever known.

He seemed so different from many of the men in the music business. Dwight didn't drink, he didn't smoke, and he lived in Hollywood in an apartment that was so clean I was afraid to sit on the furniture. I loved Dwight's spirit, but in the beginning it was very hard to get close to him. After a while he let me in and I saw the softer side. To this day, some of my fondest memories of Dwight are the times when I washed his jeans. (It's true, girls!) I would put them in the dryer, and then smile as he lay down on the floor to zip them up. He was a trip. I think that throughout Dwight's career, he's been misunderstood in Nashville, where they often mistook passion for arrogance.

When Mom and I played the Ohio State Fair one year, Dwight decided to invite his family to our show, and he took me to his mother's house for a family dinner. Dwight and I both forgot our laminates, so we ended up having to pay to get back into the fair so I could perform at my own show!

I got my first apartment while dating Dwight. My new apartment—all nine hundred square feet of it—represented success to me. I felt like I was taking the first plunge into adulthood. The place was mine and I could do anything I wanted, come home as late as I wanted, grocery shop at two a.m., fall asleep with the television on. I could drink from the milk carton! I answered to no one but myself. I immediately bought a dog, a rat terrier, that I named Loretta Lynn. My new life with my little puppy began in that apartment. We would have a twenty-year love affair, were inseparable for nearly two decades. I didn't go anywhere without her. Even when I recorded, she sat there in the studio, waiting while I sang.

I got my furniture from a rent-to-own place in Nashville. My couch had a green background with calla lilies all over it. Everything was brass and glass. I thought I was so fancy! But I also had a few antiques from Mamaw Ciminella to remind me of where I had come from. I had already had several hit records and our career was rocking. But getting my first apartment represented real freedom for me personally.

My next move was to a log cabin outside of Franklin, Tennessee. It was out in the country. It had a huge front porch. Living there gave me a sense of solitude. I could lay on the porch and paint my nails with no one watching my every move. With this move, however, I took the concept of personal freedom a little far.

I was so frustrated with the record business, with the idea that you always had to show up on time, looking perfect and knowing the answers to all the questions. I still have a real problem separating business from personal. And back then it was especially hard for me to focus on what had to happen *before* we performed. I didn't pay much attention to the details prior to my stepping on the stage. Music was all I knew and cared about. I planned my whole day around jamming with the band. Mom planned her day around our schedule. She knew to the last second when we had to do our hair and makeup for preshow interviews, where we were having our meet & greets, and how many would be there. People labeled me a rebel. But maybe I just wasn't as excited about the other activities because I was an introvert. Onstage, the fans brought me out of my shell.

At that time I decided that I needed a personal assistant, and ended up hiring my best friend, Lisa Ramsey. Lisa had had no music business experience. She worked in the computer business. Neither one of us even knew what a personal assistant was supposed to do, but we loved that it gave us a chance to hang out together. It was a clear case of the blind leading the blind, but we had a blast. Lisa and I were like Thelma and Louise, and those days were some of the best times of my life.

Lisa helped me to come out of my shell socially. We went to a lot of events in Nashville. We attended all the cool parties. It was strange, but I began to enjoy this new experience. Even though I was only a moderate drinker and I didn't do drugs, I was the last one to leave the party. Lisa and I would often stay out way too late. Then we'd oversleep the next morning and miss our flight. We leased a lot of jets to get us to the show on time. It drove Mom crazy—but I never missed a show! I realize now that it was unprofessional—but I was living completely in the moment.

Living on a bus with Mom, having adjoining rooms, continued to take its toll. One night out on tour, after playing a college show, some fans invited me to a local fraternity party. I went, and had so much fun I lost track of time. By the time I got back to the backstage area, all the semitrucks and buses were parked in a line behind our bus, and I could see Mom sitting in the jump seat of the Dreamchaser. She was in her pajamas, with her arms folded and *that look* on her face. I was so embarrassed. Here I was, the lead singer on a major tour, yet I felt like I was a little kid getting scolded in front of my friends. Mom and I fought all night. We finally went to bed when the sun came up and slept most of the day. Now, of course, I have a better understanding of both sides of the situation. Mom and I were on different personal paths, and it affected our professional relationship. Both of us wanted to be in control.

As we continued to tour, I became immersed in other artists' music. Before we were the headliners, we opened for artists like George Strait, Alabama, Don Williams and George Jones. I became a huge fan of the traditionalists. The more country the better. I loved Merle Haggard and Glen Campbell records. George Strait had the biggest band I had ever seen, and I found myself wondering how he could afford that huge band on tour. Another favorite, Willie Nelson, also has a great number of people on his tour. The music was always wonderful, though! Years later, as a solo artist, I'd learn too well that having a big band does, in fact, mean great music, but huge overhead!

Mom and I were having the musical experience of a

lifetime—playing arenas and touring with all the big artists. But of all the people we worked with, Conway Twitty was my absolute favorite. I would stand and watch him every night as he stood behind the curtain and performed the talking part of "Hello Darlin'." Then when he walked out onstage in his polyester bell-bottoms and with that awesome hair, the women went absolutely berserk! He was such a gentleman, and to watch his female fans lose their minds over him was so entertaining. Another of the best periods of our early years was when Mom and I were out on the road with the Oak Ridge Boys. I consider that one of our career highlights. Those guys really treated us like royalty. When they spoke of us from the stage it was always with respect, even when they were kidding around! And kidding around was exactly what we did when we played shows with the Oaks. Once, we paraded across the stage holding a big "Applause" sign. Then the Oaks showed up during one of our performances dressed in drag! (We laughingly called it *Transvestites Night Out.*)

The more I performed, the more I thought about the way other artists presented themselves and their music, especially in the case of three of my favorites, Loretta Lynn, Tammy Wynette and Dolly Parton. Sexy, classy and fascinating—rare gems—all three of them! Each one has a rags-to-riches story, examples of the American Dream. Onstage, all three are captivating. They possess what only a few have ever had in our history—mystique and charisma. Loretta, Tammy and Dolly are my definition of the term "superstar." (People throw that term around too much.)

They are three of the most influential people in my life, and I think about them often because I know they are the ones who paved the way for me and other women of my generation. They are the ones upon whose shoulders we all stand.

There's a raw uncertainty to Loretta. She's so childlike in the best possible way. Loretta reminds me of one of my Judd aunts—sweet and tenderhearted. And funny! You never know what the heck she might say in interviews. She always says exactly what's on her mind.

Back when Mom and I had been in Las Vegas, long before we ever got our break, I would sit in the booths the Aladdin reserved for high rollers every night, sipping my usual Shirley Temple, watching everything Loretta said, did and sang. I loved watching Loretta's traditional backup band with their perfectly matching outfits that accented Loretta's Scarlett O'Hara–style lace and ruffled gowns. Her hair was my favorite part of her style. When she sang "Coal Miner's Daughter" people gave her a standing ovation every time. And I cried every time! To this day that song is one of my top five favorites.

Dolly Parton—well, there is no one else in the world like her. Her sound and her image were her own. She's the total package. She truly owns the performance patent on her songs. I remember wondering how anyone could ever try to cover songs like "Coat of Many Colors," "Life Is Like a Butterfly" or "Jolene."

When she walked onstage the night I first saw her perform, it was like seeing color television for the first time, or when you first saw *The Wizard of Oz* and the black-and-white world of a Kansas tornado turns into the colors of Oz. You can't understand it until you see her show. She has every element a concert attendee desires. From her long painted fingernails to her outrageous rhinestone outfits, I was totally fascinated by this woman.

Even now when I'm around Dolly, I find myself just staring at her. (And I'm not talking about her breasts, either!) She's eye candy from her wigs to her five-inch heels. She's not of this world. I *must* be in love with Dolly, because last year Roach and I rented a Winnebago and drove our three kids to Dollywood for a vacation. We rode rides all day, and at night we sat around a campfire and roasted hot dogs and marshmallows. We ate s'mores until our bellies ached!

Of the three Queens, Tammy was the closest to me, connected both personally and professionally. In the early days, Mom and I opened for her many times. (I've also worked with Loretta, but have never worked with Dolly. I'm available!)

I sat on Tammy's bus often and loved her like family. She gave me advice, and she hugged me every time I saw her. I was privileged to sing "Girl Thang" with Tammy on her 1994 *Without Walls* CD. I sang at her memorial service, and then rerecorded "Woman to Woman" on a recording George Richie did of Tammy's hits. She was one of the most beautiful and classy women I have ever known. She was country music royalty.

Mom and I were on tour with Tammy when my Mamaw Ciminella slipped on the narrow stairs to the basement at 1515 Morningside Drive. She fell the length of the stairway and, badly hurt, had to crawl to the telephone to call for help. Tammy was kind enough to change the time she went on, to allow us to get home as soon as possible. Unfortunately, by the time we arrived, Mamaw was in a coma. She lingered on, until her weight was down to around ninety pounds. It was heartbreaking to see this vibrant woman lay in that bed, so helpless. We had to return to the tour, and ironically, Mamaw finally died the night of our final show. I felt like I had lost everything. And I will always remember how gracious and kind Tammy was to us during such a stress-filled time.

All three women—Tammy, Dolly and Loretta—connect to the audience with their stories. Loretta's sweet spirit makes me cry. She taps into my Appalachian heritage, and I can't hear "Coal Miner's Daughter" without feeling a catch in my throat. Loretta takes me home to my people. Dolly seems to have left that mountain background behind, but I know it's still there inside her. She honors her roots through her music.

I always wanted to know what Dolly was really like. I could never get a handle on it. What is she like before she puts on that outfit? At one awards show, I even invited myself to her house. She said, "Well, come on!" But it still hasn't happened. And oddly enough, I ended up hiring one of Dolly's former assistants a few years back. It was all I could do not to ask her a bunch of questions. For the record, she never talked about Dolly. Darn it!

I respect her achievements so much. She's one of the most successful businesswomen in the world. Through all her enterprises, she supports *so* many people. It must be a blessing and a burden to have such a level of responsibility. Personally, I'd like to know what it must be like to be *that* rich and famous!

I can imagine that she's not able to be intimate with very many outside her inner circle. What I've learned is that it's difficult for most of us to be vulnerable. In order to be emotionally intimate with the people you care about, you have to be strong in your identity of *who you are*, not *what you do*. I used to have an identity onstage, but not off. That has changed.

By the late eighties, Mom and I were getting along better. We had survived the early years and were beginning to get more comfortable and accept the magnitude of our opportunities. We performed for President and Mrs. Reagan. We toured internationally. We traveled to Ireland in 1988 and

U2 came to our show at an old boxing arena! Bono tried to adopt Mom as his own mother.

I had actually met Bono a year before and I have pictures to prove it. I showed up at U2's *Joshua Tree* Tour at Middle Tennessee State University in Murfreesboro, Tennessee. (Five years later, Mom and I would play the last show of our Farewell Tour in that venue.) I had heard that on the *Joshua Tree* Tour, Bono invited someone to come up on the stage to play guitar. I showed up wearing white jeans and a white leather jacket with fringe. I wore bright red leather boots to match my hair. The production crew gave me a pass and let me stand on the side of the stage. Bono then introduced me and I walked out to sing with him.

The funny thing about that night is that it was as if all of my performance fears went out the window. All I cared about was that I was playing with *Bono*! (I was madly in love with him.) To this day, the *Joshua Tree* album is in the top five of my favorite albums. Since meeting U2, I traveled often to see their shows, ending up backstage and even at an after-show party where Bono and I started writing a song together. (We still haven't finished it.)

I gave Bono my satin tour jacket that I had gotten while touring with George Strait and Alabama. He loved country music. The *Joshua Tree* album marks a very poetic time in my life. Bono became my mentor. The U2 band with their fusion of blues, country and rock were so influential. "I Still Haven't Found What I'm Looking For" became my anthem. Personally and professionally, Bono is one of the most passionate, charismatic people I have ever known. People call Bono a rock god, but to me he is a spiritual and sentimental soul. He gave me one of the best pieces of advice I have ever received in my career. *Just show up and wait for God to walk through the room.*

I had really started to appreciate Mom's advice by then, too. I finally understood that she had knowledge she was trying to pass on to me. I might not have always liked her approach or her timing, but she did have meaningful values. Perhaps the most important thing Mom taught me during our career was to treat everyone kindly and with respect. She talked the talk, and she walked the walk. Mom wanted the limo driver to feel as loved and as special as she did. She treated the room service guy as well as she would treat the President of the United States. She never forgot a name. She never said no to an autograph request. If I ever walked past someone without acknowledging them, forgot to leave a great tip or say please or thank you, Mom would remind me of where we had come from.

In 1988, Pop started producing a group called Matthews, Wright and King: Raymond Matthews, Woody Wright, and Tony King. When I met the group, Tony was the only single guy. He had just broken up with a longtime girlfriend. Pop started bringing him around in an effort to cheer him up. It started out as strictly friendship. *Hey, want to go a movie?* It was completely platonic for months.

Tony King was one of the kindest, most gentle, humble, honest souls in the world. He came from a sweet Christian family. He was one of the straightest guys I ever knew. He didn't drink or "chew" (and he didn't go out with the girls that do!). My manager, Ken Stilts, wasn't sure Tony was the right one for me. I think he felt Tony wasn't aggressive enough or man enough for me.

By that time, Ken was coming out on the road with us more. He'd arrive in his own bus with a trailer hauling his Harley-Davidson motorcycles. He worked hard and he played hard. It was part of the package. Ken Stilts had a true spirit of celebration. He seemed larger than life, and he lived on the edge.

Ken's house seemed to get bigger and bigger as The Judds got more and more successful. We would do a tour, and he'd build another room. It soon began to look like a motel! He built a tennis court and put in a pool. Finally, he turned his basement into a fifties diner, complete with a full bar, a jukebox and a dance floor. He bought two limited edition Harleys, had them put in Plexiglas cases and suspended them from the ceiling. He had someone come in and paint a scene above the booths featuring Carl Perkins playing guitar with Mom and me singing backup. Ken and Col. Tom Parker were peeking through a curtain on the side of the stage, watching the show. Ken loved the idea of Col. Parker almost as much as he loved Elvis.

Ken Stilts loved Elvis so much that Mom gave him an Elvis costume that Pop owned. Once Mom and Pop started communicating again, they started seeing each other. Therefore, *Elvis Presley is responsible for Mom and Pop getting back together.* Isn't *that* a tabloid headline? Mom and I had a wax figure made of Elvis (like you'd see in a wax museum) and dressed him in the stage clothes Elvis had given Pop. It was all part of the fifties diner motif.

Maybe it was watching Ken's house grow by leaps and bounds, but I started wanting to own a home, too, and bought a house just outside of Franklin. The day I went to view it, I bought it. I knew it was my home—the place that I belonged. It was a big, meandering house: four bedrooms, four baths, four thousand square feet, but with a homey, cozy feeling. Built in 1889, it had original hardwood floors and four fireplaces on the main floor. Walking through the house was almost like being in a folk art/Americana museum. Everything in the house was handmade. I took great pride in hiring local craftsmen to do all the work. In many ways it was like our Berea experience, with local artisans and craftsmen playing such an important role. I bought Southwestern art and antique furniture, Indian rugs and artifacts I put in the game room with the Wurlitzer jukebox, a bar and a pool table.

There was a thousand-square-foot log cabin for guests and a twenty-five-hundred-square-foot barn for my animals. The Little Harpeth River was right behind my twenty-five acres of fenced pasture. There were flower and vegetable gardens. I planted flowers everywhere, and each spring I'd have thousands of butterflies! I quickly began acquiring what would amount to a petting zoo. I ended up with ten fallow deer including a beautiful white buck, buffalo, horses including four miniatures, potbelly pigs, raccoons, rabbits, dogs and cats. I started collecting old cars. It was a prosperous time in my life, when I was truly able to enjoy the fruits of my labor.

Mom and Pop got married on May 8, 1989. Mom chose an old-fashioned pink taffeta gown with puffy sleeves and a bustle. We flew family and friends in from all over. It was a classy affair and the reception was fancy. One thing I remember most about the wedding is that a van pulled up to deliver balloons and a couple of tabloid photographers jumped out with cameras and took off toward the mansion, where they held the reception. Another vivid memory is of people dancing to the music of the Dillards, the band from the *Andy Griffith Show*.

Right after the wedding Mom, Pop, Ashley and I flew to Lake Tahoe to play a show, so essentially I went along on the honeymoon. Mom and Pop bought a five-hundred-acre farm eight miles from my new house. They named it Peaceful Valley.

* * *

That "Peaceful Valley" feeling would only last around six months. I had noticed that Mom wasn't feeling well while we filmed a Bob Hope Christmas special in Hawaii that year. By the time we got back to Nashville, Mom was feeling unusually tired. She had to drag herself to the studio to sing her harmony parts on our new album, *Love Can Build a Bridge*. Around the end of January, just before we were set to leave on a new tour, I went with Mom to her doctor's appointment. It was there she learned that she had hepatitis. Mom tossed it off as just an inflammation of the liver. I had no idea that meant it was *very serious*.

I knew Mom was having difficulties, even though she continued on the tour. I kept thinking she had what people called the "yuppie flu." It goes by other names—immune dysfunction syndrome and chronic fatigue immune deficiency—but it means constant tiredness that a good night's sleep won't cure. When she got the final diagnosis, it was of "non-A, non-B" hepatitis. At the time, there wasn't a hepatitis C, so Mom started calling it a "designer disease."

On Monday, January 22, 1990, we were scheduled to cohost the American Music Awards in Los Angeles with Gloria Estefan, Anita Baker and Alice Cooper. Mom later said that she told Ken she felt we needed to make the appearance because we had to represent country music in a multigenre show. She also confessed that she hadn't known if she could make it through the show, although she was still covering up the severity of her condition with me. The day after the AMAs, Mom went to a specialist in Los Angeles. He told her that she had a "smoldering fire in her liver" and that it could erupt in flames at any time.

Since that time I have learned a great deal about hepatitis C. HCV is the most common chronic blood-transmitted infection in the United States, with an estimated four million sufferers. The most frightening statistic is that about 70 percent of the people infected don't know it! There are many ways to contract hepatitis C, including any kind of blood exposure. Mom had worked as an ICU nurse, and almost certainly got it from a needle prick. When Mom was diagnosed, there was only about a 15 percent chance of a cure.

Still, I was unsure of the seriousness of the situation. I even made jokes about bringing her Carter's Little Liver Pills. Over the next months, we canceled a few shows, but she still played others. Mom was being very strong and brave, concealing her lowest moments from me. She was even having panic attacks, yet never said a word about it to me. I kept thinking that Mom would beat whatever this condition was, and then things would get back to normal.

Then in July, unbeknownst to me, Mom phoned Ken and told him that she could go on no longer. Ken flew to Los Angeles, where we were doing the *Arsenio Hall Show*. The day after our appearance, we all went to San Francisco for a day off. I was still in the dark when Ken asked me to accompany him to Mom's room. I thought we were just having one of our routine skull sessions. He opened the door, and there she was in bed, looking very tired.

"Sweetheart, your mom is very sick, and she's not getting any better," Ken began.

The rest of the conversation is as foggy to me as it was on that very foggy day in San Francisco. Mom explained that she couldn't go on touring and that it was her "Sophie's Choice." She talked about me going on with a solo career, and how she knew that music was my life.

Her words filled the room, but were barely sinking in. She was talking about my career, and all I could think was *Are you dying*? And all I could say was "I feel like I'm dying."

Then I started crying and said, "I don't want to go on without you, Mom."

"I've always believed that I appreciated this career more than you, Wynonna," Mom recalls saying. "The reality is, you need it more than I do now. You need to sing like you need to breathe. I've crawled over broken glass to get us here, so don't you think that you're gonna throw it all away, young lady. You're gonna carry on without me. It's your destiny."

As it would happen so often in our family, there was no real warning. I was called to a meeting and delivered a bombshell about my mom. Yet it wasn't Mom who told me the devastating news. She wasn't able to do it, I think. It was as if saying the words meant she would die. So Ken stepped in and spoke for her.

We held a press conference on October 17, 1990, at the old RCA building to announce Mom's retirement. We chose that building because it was where we had started out. Neither one of us expected things to look so dilapidated. The offices were empty. There wasn't even carpet on the floor. The shabbiness reinforced the depressive mood of all of us at the gathering. It was one of the loneliest memories of my life. I felt like I was dying, too.

After the press conference, two things happened almost simultaneously. People started talking about a farewell tour and orchestrating my debut as a solo artist. It was like planning a wedding and a funeral at the same time. I didn't know if Mom was going to live or die. Why were people planning my debut when a new Judds tour was just beginning?

It seemed so wrong. Things between Mom and me were finally getting better. Then out of nowhere she became dangerously ill! First came denial, then anger. At the time, the person I was most mad at was Ken, probably because he had been the bearer of bad news. I was upset, worrying about Mom. Ken's way of coping with it was to begin planning a Judds Farewell Tour and the launching of Wynonna solo. We'd go to Ken's house in Florida between the Farewell Tour shows and Ken would talk to me about my solo career. It felt like I was cheating on Mom, like Ken and I were killing her off, burying her alive.

The Farewell Tour almost buried *me*. The nightmare went on and on. We kept getting offers to play more dates and Ken kept booking them. There were times when I was so worried about Mom—she kept taking on more and more. I guess she felt that she had to keep busy and I felt she needed to rest. I thought if she rested, she'd heal. And if she healed, our career together could be saved. Mom was determined to go on as long as she could. She loved the fans so much and being onstage became her therapy. I think there was a part of her that worried if she did go home that she would die. Her connection to her fans was her lifeline. Being onstage gave her energy. The music was soothing to her soul.

I felt like a multiple personality during that time. I seemed to be a different person at every turn. I often felt invisible. I tried to be a supportive player yet my role changed all the time. I tried to be a loving daughter, but I hated seeing people use her illness to sell magazines or get television ratings. One of the hardest things to see was how the fans reacted to Mom's illness. It was as if they were going through their own mother's illness and possible death. Everywhere we went, people cried. They would often try to hug Mom. I couldn't quite understand what they were feeling. Finally, I realized that she was not just my mom— there were many fans who felt like she was theirs, too.

Some interviewers were so invasive that it made me

sick to my stomach. Sometimes I got severe headaches. Why did people keep asking, "How do feel about the fact that you must quit your career, that you might die?" It's like when you see a story on the news where the mother has just lost her child and the interviewer asks, "How do you feel?" That's unbelievable.

And so, the drama continued, and I continued to feel more and more hopeless. Mom and I started going to a therapist together and individually. Any time one of us felt we needed professional help, we made an appointment. Then the counselor phoned anyone involved and called a meeting. That system is still in place in our family today.

It was difficult for me to say how I felt. I felt guilty about feeling angry with Mom for getting sick. I was mad at her for continuing to work, yet I didn't want to let her go. I wasn't ready and I continued, because of my debilitating sadness, to let her have her way about everything. This was her "going-away party." She was my queen but there was an undercurrent of resentment knowing that I had absolutely no control over what was about to happen. I felt like a part of me was dying, too. I tried to live each day as it came, being grateful for every opportunity to go out onstage and celebrate Judd music with the fans who had been with us from the beginning. But it was the most helpless feeling not knowing if the concert that night would be our last. I lived in constant dread knowing that at some point the Farewell Tour would come to an end. I just didn't know when.

I know that everyone wanted us to do the Farewell Tour for obvious personal and professional reasons. But watching Mom get sicker and sicker during that year was the most excruciatingly painful thing I've ever been through in my life. There were days when she was so sick that she had a hard time getting out of bed. I would go down to her hotel room and help her get ready for the show. I did her hair every night and helped her get dressed. I saw how weak she was, but you'd never know it once she set foot onstage. It was as if that love and energy coming from the crowd was her physical and spiritual therapy. She stepped into the light literally and figuratively every night.

People who came to see the show had no concept of what it really took for her to pull this off. It took every bit of her survival skills and sheer determination. I didn't know that Mom was going to make it out alive and I wasn't sure I would. I thought she'd collapse one night onstage in front of thousands, and I'd have a breakdown in front of everyone while holding her in my arms.

Sometimes Mom would call me in the middle of the night. I'd go to her in my pajamas and sit beside her in bed. Sometimes we'd cry. I somehow felt I was letting her down by not being strong all the time. One time, she called me to her room, and told me that she'd bought funeral plots for the whole family. From time to time she'd tell me things that were in her heart, and I was never prepared for what she might say. One night she came to my house:

"I went out today and bought presents for my future grandchildren," she added.

At the time she said it, I thought I'd faint. Now I can see that Mom was being the consummate organizer, planning for her death—and beyond!

Tony King and I were living together by this time. It was while the Farewell Tour marched on that he took me to an O'Charley's restaurant and proposed marriage. I accepted the proposal, but it was almost doomed from the beginning. I was in such a depressed state that planning anything, much less a marriage, was almost unthinkable. I lived day to day.

I know this sounds odd, but in the end, I think I felt like I had to choose between him and Mom. I chose Mom. I had become pretty codependent and probably addicted to her needing me so much and it separated me from Tony. I wanted to be the person she needed, yet I sometimes resented it. On the other hand, you don't *dare* admit you resent taking care of someone you love when they are sick because that makes you a bad person! Each time I reached a breaking point I felt like such a failure. I remember once saying, "I want off this tour." I immediately felt awful because I knew this was her last party. There were so many conflicting emotions surging through me.

Toward the end of the tour, I became more and more vulnerable. I turned away from Tony and to Ken's nephew Doug Stilts. He made me feel safe, and took great care of me during a very chaotic time. There were no strings attached to the relationship developing with Doug. Tony King didn't deserve the treatment he received from me at the time. He was too sweet of a person. Tony wasn't pressuring me, but I felt pressure. I just couldn't make a commitment. So I broke off the engagement.

The Farewell Tour happened a long time ago. Since that time, I've had a successful solo career and God has healed Mom. I'm thankful for Mom's health every day. Many people have asked me why I'm still struggling with my feelings about Mom's leaving the career. It's only been recently that I fully understand what impact that time in my life had on me. Mom leaving the road made me a psychological wreck. At the time when Mom was so ill, and so fragile, I was being intensely groomed to go solo.

My manager was doing what he thought was best for me by pushing me to forge ahead into my solo career. But I think that it was very damaging. I could think of little but Mom's health while I was in the studio working on my first solo album. I never truly went through a grieving process, so I continued to see the glass as half empty.

I ended up having nightmares almost every night. One in particular lasted for years. Mom was giving herself shots of interferon, a new drug being tested for hepatitis C. In the nightmare, Mom comes into my room on the bus and asks me to step back to her stateroom. Once in her room, she hands me a syringe and asks me to give her a shot. Then she lies down on the bed. As I put the needle into her hip, she looks up at me and smiles.

"Honey, when you give me this shot, I will go to sleep and never wake up again."

But I've already given the shot! I begin to weep. I sit there on the bed and hold her for a while. Finally I cover her up with a quilt, and go to my room to get ready for the show.

In the dream, hours seem to go by. Finally I'm walking to the front of the bus to go and perform. Mom walks out of the stateroom, fully dressed in her stage clothes, her hair done, lips perfectly lined. She's ready to go do her meet & greet! Then I would wake up.

I also had dreams about our house being on fire with Mom trapped inside. She was often strapped into a chair with flames getting closer and closer to her while I'm trying to get inside to save her. I must have had some pretty strong feelings. I now realize that there just wasn't time to process and heal the sadness. There was too much work to be done. I didn't want to let my manager Ken or my mom down, so I put my sadness aside. The show had to go on.

I was also struggling from survivor's guilt. This is a term used for how people feel who are in an accident where everyone dies but them. There's a feeling of "Why am I still here?" "Why did this happen to the other person and not to me?" It was so bizarre. It was agonizing for me to continue on with the process of accepting my fate. I found myself unable to focus on the future. I was still so stuck in the past, personally and professionally.

Mom often came by my house to visit. We weren't able to be out of each other's sight for long. When she pulled in the driveway, I'd immediately turn off the stereo and put away the demo tapes I was listening to for my upcoming album. I didn't want to hurt her. She was still in such pain about having to leave the road, that I had to be very sensitive to her feelings.

When she left, I found it almost impossible to bring out the tapes again. I would sit and cry for hours. On the days we booked sessions to record my first solo CD, I would drive to the studio and park my car in the parking lot. I'd sit there continuing to struggle with my emotions until I'd have a panic attack. It was as if Mom had died, and while being so caught up in the grief, I was getting ready for a party.

Overnight I was promoted to the leader position, the one in charge. It was a battlefield promotion. For so long I had followed Mom's lead. I wasn't used to making any of the major decisions on my own. I had to face the fact that, after a ten-year career, I still had little decision-making experience. It was terrifying.

If Mom was the head and I was the heart, then where was I going to gain the ability to run a corporation, to lead my band and crew? By that time I'd bought into the myth that I was "out of control." Everywhere I went, people continued to ask me if I thought I could make it without my mom. I remember being in a grocery store one time and a guy walked up to me and asked *the* question.

"Hey, Wynonna, how do you think you're gonna do without your mom?"

I stared at the man in disbelief. My heart started racing. I got a lump in my throat and began to cry. I ended up leaving my shopping cart and going home. Mom tried many times to talk to me about taking my life into my own hands.

"It's all up to you now," she'd say.

Our roles had started to become even more complicated than usual during the Farewell Tour. I felt as though it was my responsibility to save her, and she was beginning to feel as though she had to save me.

I would learn very quickly that even though my emotions were a mess, it was not appropriate for me to let anyone know that I wasn't capable of taking care of myself. Even starting over at twenty-seven years old, I still was bound by the need for Ken's and Mom's approval. I bought a Harley and got two tattoos, and when Mom and Ken found out, they barely spoke to me for over a week. I was humiliated. Instead of standing up for myself, and telling them that I was satisfied with my decision, I felt ashamed and embarrassed that I had done it.

Ken was becoming increasingly vocal with his criticisms of me. Now that Mom was leaving the partnership, it was just the two of us. He often told me that if it hadn't been for him I wouldn't have made it. Maybe it was his way of trying to keep me humble. I don't know. I can imagine his concern now that I was on my own. I was becoming more and more codependent on our father-daughter-type relationship and I soon found myself unable to make decisions without him. I took everything that he said as if it were the gospel. If the President of the United States and Ken Stilts had told me different opinions about something, I would have agreed with Ken. And yet, as I've looked back over that time in my life, I can imagine that Ken was growing more and more concerned that at some point I would make the decision to go on without him.

I truly loved Ken Stilts and I believe that he loved me, too. Everyone around Ken loved him. His family worshipped him. His office staff worshipped him. The band and crew respected him. We all believed he could walk on water.

I am loyal to a fault and nowhere was it more obvious than in my relationship with Ken. In the end it was a split between Ken and Mom that cost me so much. Ken began phasing Mom out of the career. It was very difficult for me to watch Mom as she began to feel less and less included or needed. Ken would remind me that business was business and this wasn't personal. Yet how can it not be personal when it's your mother?

Still trying to hang on, I'd call the office and ask them to fax Mom to keep her in the loop. Ken believed that it was important for me to move forward without her, to grow up and stand alone. It felt to me like it did watching Mom and Dad get a divorce. I felt once again like I was in the middle.

Even with Mom gone on a day-to-day level, I still wasn't involved in a lot of business decisions. The protocol was *Wynonna, you sing and leave the rest to Ken.* He made the decision to move to MCA Records although I certainly liked the idea of working with their label head, Tony Brown. Originally I wasn't involved in the decision to go by the name "Wynonna," dropping Judd. It was strictly a marketing call to take my new music out of the "J" sales bin, where the "Judds" CDs were, and putting it into the "W" bin so I'd have my own identity. (I finally had my own space—literally.) I'm afraid that many people thought that I made the decision because I thought I was famous enough to go by one name. What they didn't realize was that once again, the business heads had a meeting and I got the memo.

I never saw record contracts or written business proposals. I never asked to see financial statements or budget reviews. Artists don't usually go to school to learn anything about how to be in the music business! I knew the music, but not the business. I wasn't even sure what questions to ask, and it made my Papaw Ciminella crazy. He worried about me.

"Do you know how much you make per show?" he'd ask.

"No."

"Do you know what your expenses are?"

"No."

"Do you have any idea what you're worth?"

"No. But I think I know how much is in my checking account."

All I cared about was being the best singer I could be. I was not a business head. I trusted! I trusted Ken and the label. I was concentrating with all my might on surviving out on the road by myself, trying to become a leader and be a champion.

I wasn't encouraged to get to know the people involved at RCA or Curb and I didn't make the effort. I didn't push it. The same applied to my move to MCA. I didn't understand that it was appropriate for the artist to directly contact anyone in the industry. I did things the "old school" way. I always went through my manager. He spoke for me. Once again, I was the heart, while he was the head. A few years ago I was talking with Tony Brown and he said, "You know I never remember in the past having a real conversation with you. It's nice to have this new connection, this new relationship."

So many people have said almost those same words.

Tony Brown was one of the people in Nashville who never questioned whether I could make it without Mom, even though there were times I was questioning it myself. One day I was full of optimism; then the next I would head straight downhill. I couldn't even decide what I wanted for lunch!

People kept telling me that I was *already* a star, but what they forgot was that *Mom and I* were the stars together. We were a duo, which meant I was half. I continued to see the glass as half empty, and would do so for a long time.

I still felt nervous when Mom came to the studio. It was the darnedest thing—I just couldn't shake it. Regardless, I called and asked her to come by one day to listen to some of the playbacks. I remember putting her in the producer's chair right in front of the mixing board. I sat right behind her, feeling too vulnerable to look at her face while she listened. It felt so strange to not hear her voice on the tape, that I asked her to sing harmony on "When I Reach the Place I'm Going." It felt good to connect with her again—good for both of us, I believe. That door remains open, too!

Tony Brown and Don Potter got me through those first solo sessions. They were my bookends, the yin and yang of my solo experience. Like Don, Tony has a calm presence. I knew he would do everything he could to help me make this the best recording possible. Tony wanted to help me make country music history. Don was there to help me get stronger. Don made the experience about acceptance and healing. Don's being there was like having your guardian angel sitting next to you, saying:

"Everything's going to work out fine!"

Proving that you never know what the Lord has in store for you, the man who would ultimately prove to be the love of my life entered the picture during the Farewell Tour when Mom and I did our final show together in Murfreesboro. D. R. Roach, co-owner of Rock Solid Security. He so impressed our road manager, Mike McGrath, that he met with Ken and he hired him full-time as my bodyguard. Roach met me at the airport and off we went on the beginning of a thirteen-year adventure. It was April 1, 1992. How appropriate! We laugh about it every year on April Fools' Day. My first impression of Roach has lasted all these years. I thought he was one of the funniest and kindest people I had ever met. We laughed all the time then and we still do!

Looking back on it, Roach and I are so perfect for each other. We're both very adolescent when it comes to joking and fooling around. We made faces at each other, knocked into one another walking through crowds. In his effort to rein me in and keep me moving forward while walking to the stage, Roach had a hard time, because I would often stop suddenly to shake a hand or give someone a hug. He was constantly bumping into me. One day I turned around and socked him really hard in the arm. I will never forget the look on his face. Talk about bewilderment! Then we both started laughing. We were like a couple of thirteen-year-old kids but somehow it worked. Roach and Mike McGrath became the brothers I always wanted and never had. Mike was hilarious, too. He was so smart and respected within our group. He saved my life during that first solo tour.

Roach's sense of humor soon began to irritate Ken, who thought that his funny nature indicated that he didn't take his job seriously. Of course I saw it another way. Roach's humor helped me cope during a time when I was feeling extremely fragile. When Ken told me he was firing Roach, it would be the first time I would stand up to Ken. Roach was staying. Since Ken couldn't fire him, I think it became sport for Ken to try and give Roach a hard time.

Buying my 525-acre farm was the second time I stood up to Ken. I've always felt such a connection to land. Papaw Judd's sister, my great-aunt Pauline, was the woman who first introduced me to the spirituality found in nature and God's earth. I spent a lot of time at her Little Catt farm when I was a child. She lived in a big farmhouse with a screened-in porch. She and Uncle Landon didn't have running water but they did have electricity. I often spent parts of the summer there. It was always a joyful occasion. I couldn't wait to go stay with her.

Ashley and I spent a lot of time down at the creek catching crawdads. Some of my fondest memories are of sitting on the screened-in porch, watching Aunt Pauline rock in her rocking chair, shelling beans. Uncle Landon would cock his hat to the side, rock in his rocking chair and spit tobacco into a coffee can. Aunt Pauline always had a lot of animals. I think it was on that farm where I developed my love for all creatures great and small. She talked to the animals, but she didn't have much to say to humans!

Aunt Pauline was magic. She knew it was going to be a tough winter because of how the squirrels would gather extra food. They didn't have running water, so we would have to walk to the outhouse, which was out beside their garden. Ashley and I would play in the woods and get so dirty that we would often come inside with dirt rings around our necks.

My favorite part of the visit was that we didn't have to take a bath every day. Pure heaven! At night Ashley and I would lie in bed together and listen to the crickets. To this day I find myself drawn to the country because of Aunt Pauline.

I very much wanted land and a home where I could keep my animals, too. As it turned out, I found the 525 acres that backed up to Mom and Pop's farm. To own that property meant peace of mind, home, security. I think Ken was concerned to see me buy that much land and advised me against it. I held fast to my dream and purchased the land anyway. And if I may say so myself, holding tight to my feelings about Roach and the farm were excellent decisions!

* * *

Meanwhile, the Farewell Tour went on and on. We kept getting offers to play more dates and Ken kept booking them. Between February of 1991, when we started, and our final show in December of '91, we played 116 cities across North America, and grossed over twenty-one million dollars! It became the top-grossing act of 1991. I don't know how Mom did it.

The idea of turning our final performance together into a pay-per-view cable show was anathema to me but pay-per-view it was and the saga of the Judds in the end was as strange and wonderful as it was in the beginning. It's one of the most emotional nights of my life. For one thing, I was sick. I lost my voice completely, and was told that I might damage my vocal cords forever!

But I was also told that my solo career *depended on that performance*.

Onstage that night Mom talked of my upcoming solo career. She said, "I'm not going anywhere but you are. Fly, baby, fly." She was handing me the baton. We sang "Love Can Build a Bridge" together for the last time and then Mom laid her head on my shoulder and cried. We held hands and walked offstage together.

What happened after that final show of our Farewell Tour reveals Mom's wacky sense of humor. You would think that a wrap party after what at the time was the largest pay-per-view in the history of music would have been held at a nice hotel or a fancy restaurant. You would think that the wrap party would have been in an expensive suite. You would think that there would be champagne and caviar. Instead, we pulled the bus into a Krystal's. We were all still in our stage clothes. I still had sparkles in my hair. And instead of toasting champagne, it was:

"Would you like fries with that burger combo?"

Mom and I spent one last night together on the Dreamchaser, parked in the driveway at her farm. The next morning I helped Mom pack up all her belongings, and unload them off the bus for the last time. We took everything into the house, and she stood on the front porch and waved goodbye as the bus driver and I pulled away. I suddenly realized that it was over.

· 6 ·

THE WYLD UNKNOWN

I should have had a T-shirt made up that read: *NO, I don't know where my mom is!*

At age twenty-seven I found myself alone and starting over in my career. Anyone who was once part of a professional group knows what that feels like. I remember asking Marie Osmond if the fans ever stopped asking, "Where's Donny?" I think we know the answer to that.

Historically, fans have had a hard time when groups break up. It's like seeing a family separate. It's impossible for them to see each person individually. The other members are always missing. It's like the empty chair at the Thanksgiving dinner table. Much like children caught in the middle of a divorce, they pray for a miracle, that the parents might reconcile. Our fans supported me, but at the same time, they held on to the hope that a miracle would bring Mom back to the stage.

I had been part of something much greater than myself, and was now having a hard time with my own identity. I wanted to pay homage to the former identity, but not forget myself as a separate entity. I didn't want to ride on the coattails of The Judds, or have to stand in the shadow of the record-breaking success.

The Farewell Tour ended on December 4, 1991, and four months later, in March of 1992, I was out on the road doing my first solo performance. The label and Ken Stilts were planning a larger-than-life premiere, whereas the press and fans were speculating whether I could or could not survive on my own. I think that my personal feelings about whether I'd succeed were split down the middle.

Ken reminded me that I'd just finished a year saying goodbye to the fans as The Judds. At the same time Mom and I were saying goodbye, people were becoming aware that I was going to be coming out on my own. But four months between the Farewell Tour and my launch didn't feel like enough time. I didn't have time for closure and I didn't think fans of the Judds had time either. It was too confusing for all of us involved. MCA decided to release "She Is His Only Need" as the first single from my solo debut album, *Wynonna*. On the day that radio stations received the record, MCA's promotion staff called the programmer of every country station and played the song over a high-tech system hooked up to the phones. We had a private concert in Minneapolis, where I showcased the new music to retailers.

"She Is His Only Need" received more first-week adds than any other single by a female country artist in history. After the Minneapolis album debut, a lot of retailers doubled their orders. And so my first Curb/MCA CD shipped over 800,000 units out-of-the-box. Six days later sales hit the million mark, and debuted at #1 on *Billboard*'s Top Country Album charts. It also debuted at #4 in *Billboard*'s Top 200, which included pop and rock releases. *Rolling Stone* called it ". . . the most important release by a country artist so far this decade." They gave it a four out of four star rating. I was stunned!

The celebration would only be temporary for me. I was booked at the Chaparral Center in Midland, Texas, for the first concert, and wondered why I hadn't been booked in a major market like New York or Los Angeles. Given the label's buildup for the single and CD, it seemed odd. I can only believe that it was because Ken feared that I might not be able to pull off the performance. So much was riding on that night, and emotions ran high. I love playing in Texas, but it seemed to me that it made more sense to be in a major city where there was more press.

Appearances are often misleading in the entertainment world. Especially during the promotion of a new CD or act, when it appears that things are running smoothly and on time. On the afternoon of my first show of a nine-month, 110-city tour, there were fans waiting all day outside my windows cheering, chanting my name. I held the newspaper in my hands: *USA Today* said that I'd sold almost a million CDs with my solo debut. Yet I sat in a run-down hotel room that smelled like stale beer and cigarettes. There wasn't even room service. I laugh about it now, when I tell people, "Is that any way to treat a girl when she's having her debut?"

However, I guess if Ken *was* worried, it was with good cause. Mom was there in Midland with me, and I tried to put up a good front for her. But inside I was feeling like turning around and going home—just like I'd felt all those years earlier when Mom and I first opened for the Statlers in Omaha. I was experiencing all this too soon. Some people were coming to witness a rebirth, but I knew that others might be there to witness me fall on my face. It was a spectacle waiting to happen. Would I win or lose? I was very much aware that I, along with everyone else, would soon find out.

Standing there with the crowd chanting my name and cheering, I almost had a panic attack. Mom pulled me toward her, and said:

"Honey, the best advice I can give you right now is, *Never watch sausage being made*."

I looked at her with an expression that said, *What the heck?*

The lights went out and I walked up the stairs to the stage. I can only think it's like so many brides feel as they walk down the aisle. *Am I walking to my life—my rebirth? Or to my execution?* I wasn't sure. But then the music kicked in, and when I walked on the stage, the crowd showered me with total love and support. I was overcome with emotion. The thing I remember most is that I never left about a four-foot radius from the microphone throughout the performance. I constantly looked to Mom offstage. I could feel her sadness in my heart, but she smiled and applauded with the rest of the audience. The more I heard the applause, the more I accepted the moment as one that was meant to be.

Mom went home after the Midland show, and the first week on the bus without her was unbearable. I wondered if I should have bought a different bus. When you lose someone you love, is it better to get a new house or continue to live among the memories? But as painful as it was, the familiarity was necessary. Mom and I had adjoining rooms on the bus—you had to walk through mine to get to hers. My room had a pullout couch, and her room had a queen-sized bed. Yet I never moved into her stateroom; it wouldn't have seemed right. One night I found myself sitting on the bed in Mom's room. I opened the bedside table drawer and found that she'd left me the tiara and scepter that Pop had given her as a gift: the Queen of Everything. I wondered if she was passing me the torch, or had left it there to remind me who was Queen! As many times as I'd complained about being on a bus with Mom, I found myself wanting her back. As they say, *You don't appreciate what you've got 'til it's gone*. It took me a long time to accept that she really *was* gone.

John Lennon once wrote that life is what happens between the big plans you make. After the show every night during our years as The Judds, Mom and I would sit at the front of the bus together. Mom would make popcorn; we'd talk about that night's show. We would laugh about some crazy thing that had happened or something a fan had said or done. I didn't realize how many rituals like that we'd had. Then, seemingly overnight, she was gone. I would sit up in the front of the bus staring out the window as it rolled down the dark highway. Try as I might, I couldn't make peace with the change. I felt caught between the past and present, and I didn't handle being alone very well. What I didn't realize was that I was sinking into a severe depression. I began sleeping most of the day and eating a lot at night.

Food was becoming my greatest companion, my most loyal friend. It was the only thing that comforted me through those months alone. I ate anything I could find— so much that I had to get a trainer and began trying to work out on tour. It was such a struggle. I became more introverted and retreated to the bus more often than not. I didn't know what to say to people. I know they were curious, but people asked so many personal questions. I had a hard time balancing being honest about my sadness and trying to appear strong.

At the same time, my career soared. I played to sold-out

arenas and spent eight weeks at the top of the country charts with my first three singles on *Wynonna*: "She Is His Only Need," "I Saw the Light," and "No One Else on Earth." *Wynonna* went on to sell five million albums. The 1993 follow-up, *Tell Me Why*, produced the hits "Tell Me Why," "Rock Bottom," and "Girls With Guitars." My advisors all told me that between the healthy cash flow, diversified investments and properties, my finances couldn't have been better. Professionally, I was rocking!

And so, like the Kris Kristofferson song goes—I was a walking contradiction. I was successful, yet lonely. I would have traded all five million of my debut album to have Mom back out there with me.

Mom and Ken ended up parting ways and I started thinking about leaving his management, too. I had finally begun a period in my life where I began to question everything. As I got more proactive, I asked more questions and began to challenge Ken's authority. I think my trying to take such charge of my life threatened Ken. I'm sure he thought he'd created a monster. I wanted to be more included in the day-to-day business dealings.

Now that Ken was no longer managing a duo but a single artist, I felt that I should not have to continue paying the same management percentage. I think that was the final blow. I'm sure many artists and managers split over money issues. I was unlocking a mythology about myself, trying to decide who I was aside from Naomi's daughter and Ken's client. I was realizing more and more that I did want to be a better business head. I began to become more interested in how the career was handled. And as I became more proactive, I started referring to myself as Wynonna-Alone-a.

My attorney, John Unger, stepped in as my manager. I

welcomed this new relationship. I began feeling more involved in the career, and I felt more like John's equal. John felt I was not only talented, but bright as well, and he told me so. I wasn't used to someone telling me this! When John came to me and asked what single I'd like to release, I was stunned. I'd never been asked, not once. I thought, "Wow, this is the way it should be! He works for me!"

Of course, then I began overcompensating for my past lack of involvement. When John asked me to sit in on a meeting, I grew more and more excited about telling people my ideas and explaining how I wanted things done. I'm sure I irritated a lot of people at the record label. But the more John asked me to participate, the more activated I became. The more I got in the game, the more I became a ball hog, unwilling to pass off or let others take a shot. John tried to slow me down, but I was too far gone and swimming in the lake of *me*! It was only a matter of time before I drowned.

I will always appreciate John Unger for giving me the space and the opportunity to take back my career. Usually by the time an artist tries to do that, it's too late. It was a real turning point for me. I was now more involved and replacing feelings of helplessness with self-empowerment.

In 1993 I met my future first husband on a flight back to Nashville from the Academy of Country Music Awards Show in Los Angeles. He and a lady friend sat a few seats in front of me in first class. He told me he sold yachts for a living, started a conversation about a benefit Harley ride, and asked me if I was interested in participating. By the time we landed in Nashville, I'd given him my phone number.

As Mom would say, "He was slick as snot on a doorknob."

Not long after that, he called and asked me if I wanted

to go ride Harleys with him, and I accepted the invitation. Looking back on it, I guess you could call it our first date. (I was still dating Doug Stilts at the time, but had decided to end the relationship.) He next called and asked if he could bring a friend to one of my shows in Louisville, Kentucky. I got him two tickets, but he showed up alone. I think he was trying to impress me, showing up driving an expensive sports car. And I *was* impressed. He was very tan, buff, blond hair and had the whitest teeth I'd ever seen. Later he jokingly told me he'd chosen the whitest shade, called Hollywood white, because he thought it made him look more like his favorite actor, Robert Redford.

Not long after he came to see my show, my new Harley-riding friend called and asked me to go to lunch with him at the Cooker, a family-style restaurant frequented by a lot of music business people. At first, I wasn't really interested in a relationship with him, but I thought there would be no harm in going, since it was only lunch.

This man was cocky, aggressive and very attentive. He was the complete opposite of what I had experienced in the past. The relationships I had had were with artist types, laid-back, and gentle-natured. I was usually drawn to the down-to-earth types. This was new for me, and I found myself wondering if his self-assuredness meant that he was successful.

For about a week after the lunch, he called every day. When I finally called him back, he asked me if I wanted to go to Florida to meet him and spend the weekend on his yacht. Of course, I naively thought it *was* his yacht. (I later learned that he was supposed to be cleaning it for someone.) I not only went, but I didn't tell a soul where I was going. I hadn't traveled on my own since I was eighteen and became famous. I loved the idea of "running away" and didn't take into consideration the fact that I barely knew this man! I was also using the trip as an excuse to make the break from my present relationship. Doug had been asking me to get married, and I knew it wouldn't work. So the trip with this new man was my ticket out of that commitment. (By the time I got back to Nashville, things had fallen apart with Doug. We reconciled briefly, but I knew it was over.)

Something about this new man's manner on the Florida trip bothered me a lot, certain things that didn't feel right. For one thing, I felt like he was trying too hard to impress me by talking about money. Our conversations were more about what we did for a living than who we were as people. But I ignored those warning signals, as well as ones to come. The next time I saw my future husband, he showed up at my estate unannounced. I lived on a secured property, surrounded by fences and gates. But he climbed over the fence and knocked on my door at midnight. I was up, and instead of recognizing this incident as a red flag, I chalked it up to spontaneity. *He must really be interested in me,* I thought.

He started pursuing me with a series of random, extravagant acts, trying hard to create a shroud of mystery and excitement. He somehow found out where I was going, and had flowers and notes delivered before I got there. He was too attentive too soon. We weren't even officially dating at that point, but he was acting as if we were a couple in love. Even though I enjoyed this new game, I had a feeling in my gut that things were moving too fast. But I continued to accept his attention.

Our first official date was the 1994 Country Music Association Awards Show here in Nashville. I was slotted to sing my single "Is It Over Yet." I had a beautiful burgundy gown designed for me, and flew in a premier hair-and-makeup stylist from Los Angeles. I was very excited be-

Mom at nineteen and Dad at twenty-one at one of Dad's fraternity formals.
COURTESY OF THE AUTHOR

Me at nine months. My family says I was a very happy baby.
OLAN MILLS STUDIOS

One of our last family photos. Mom filed for divorce soon after. OLAN MILLS STUDIOS

I was four the first time I flew alone from California to Kentucky to visit Mamaw and Papaw.
COURTESY OF THE AUTHOR

Mamaw and Papaw Ciminella.
COURTESY OF THE AUTHOR

Ashley and I spent part of each
summer at Aunt Pauline and
Uncle Landon's farm in Louisa,
Kentucky. These are some of
my happiest memories.
COURTESY OF THE AUTHOR

Age four and already Mama's
little helper!
COURTESY OF THE AUTHOR

Going fishing (here at age six)
with Papaw was one of my
favorite things to do.
COURTESY OF THE AUTHOR

Mom became a professional model in 1972 when we lived in Hollywood. This is one of my favorite pictures of Ashley, Mom and me.
COURTESY OF THE AUTHOR

In second grade, at age seven. I have the tiniest Chiclet teeth!
COURTESY OF THE AUTHOR

My first grade class at Hollywood Elementary. I'm in the first row with Angelique and then Mariska to my right.
COURTESY OF THE AUTHOR

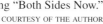

With my favorite teacher, Ms. Kolnosky, at eighth grade graduation. I sang "Both Sides Now."
COURTESY OF THE AUTHOR

I was all of fifteen when Mom and I started singing in public together and we shot our first professional portrait.
COURTESY OF THE AUTHOR

Visiting a friend's recording studio in 1978. It was the first time I had ever sung into a microphone.
COURTESY OF THE AUTHOR

I went to a bridal shop to have my senior yearbook photo taken. I wanted to make a dramatic presentation.
JAN FALK BUCK

I still feel like that eighteen-year-old sitting on the front porch swing singing my heart out.

SLICK LAWSON PHOTOGRAPHY

These are the outfits that we bought at the Alamo Western Store in downtown Nashville when we performed on the *Noon Show* in Nashville.

COURTESY OF THE AUTHOR

Our very first stage outfits (1984)—and the only dress I ever wore onstage!

COURTESY OF THE AUTHOR

1985, Omaha, in front of our dressing room door before going onstage at our very first concert.

Mom, Brent Maher, Don Potter and me celebrating my twentieth birthday at the studio while recording *Why Not Me*. What's up with that preppy sweater I'm wearing?

We traveled hours up to one of the highest peaks in Zurich to take this Christmas album cover. We almost died when the sleigh driver backed out over a ledge while trying to turn us around.

Accepting our Academy of Country Music Award for Best Vocal Duet, 1989.

© RON WOLFSON

Performing for President and Mrs. Reagan was one of the most exciting moments in our career. It has been an honor to sing for every president since Reagan was in office.

DAVID BALFOUR PHOTO

The legendary Carl Perkins had a tremendous impact on my life. I loved him so much. Mom and I sang at his annual Circles of Hope Telethon to benefit the Carl Perkins Center for the Prevention of Child Abuse.

LONNA KIRKJUNE

Backstage at the American Music Awards in 1990 with Dwight Yoakam.
COURTESY OF THE AUTHOR

Meeting Aretha Franklin at the Grammys was a defining moment for me. (She was walking around with a video camera filming other artists like a fan!)
COURTESY OF THE AUTHOR

Joni Mitchell's dressing room, 2000. I was getting ready to sing on the *All-Star Tribute to Joni Mitchell* television special. My (s)hero smiled at me the whole time I sang. I will never forget how happy I was that night.
COURTESY OF THE AUTHOR

Bonnie Raitt and kd lang are a major part of my musical life. I don't travel anywhere without their CDs.
COURTESY OF THE AUTHOR

The Country Music Association Awards, 1993. I was on my way to the stage to sing "Is It Over Yet" when I stepped off my bus and saw Loretta and Tammy. They both hugged me. I cried. I miss Tammy so much.

COURTESY OF THE AUTHOR

I attended the Aerosmith concert with friends last summer. Steven Tyler walked over to the side of the stage and stuck a microphone in my face during "Walk This Way" and I became a rock star for the night. Joe Perry is one of my favorite guitar players. Am I trying to be cool or what?

COURTESY OF THE AUTHOR

At the Rainforest benefit at Carnegie Hall. When Sting got down on his knees during our duet of "You've Lost That Loving Feeling" it took my breath away. He is absolutely DIVINE!

KEVIN MAZUR/WIREIMAGE.COM

December 8, 2002, my life changed forever. My dear brother/friend Bono invited me to spend a day with him in Kentucky during his Heart of America Tour. His crusade against the HIV and AIDS pandemic has earned him a nomination for the Nobel Peace Prize. Ashley and I are now Ambassadors for YouthAIDS. For more information, log on to www.youthaids.org.

PAUL NATKIN

Celebrating at Krystal's after our farewell concert. COURTESY OF THE AUTHOR

Shooting the video for "Give a Little Love." I remember standing out in the middle of that desert thinking to myself, "How did I end up being so lucky?" COURTESY OF THE AUTHOR

MCA hosted a party for me after my debut CD sold five million copies. Mom and Ashley and I continue to honor one another at our celebrations. COURTESY OF THE AUTHOR

With Ashley on Malibu Beach in 1985 after she went to Hollywood to follow her dreams. I remember not wanting to let go of her after Mom took this picture. I felt a great deal of sadness being away from her so much.

COURTESY OF THE AUTHOR

Mom and Pop. They've been together for twenty-five years now.

COURTESY OF THE AUTHOR

Elijah at age two with Elmo. Being on *Sesame Street* with my children was great—it definitely brought out the child in me.

COURTESY OF SESAME WORKSHOP

Singing at the Minnesota State Fair in September 1994. The bigger my pregnant belly and butt got, the bigger my hair got, too!

JEAN PIERI/PIONEER PRESS

Elijah and Grace graduating from first grade and kindergarten, respectively. I took all the furniture out of the living room and set out rows of chairs for the ceremony, and friends and family came to celebrate our first year of homeschooling. I cried as the children walked down the aisle to "Pomp and Circumstance." These moments are truly what life is all about. COURTESY OF THE AUTHOR

Rocking Grace to sleep on the tour bus (hadn't even taken off my stage makeup yet). I was never away from my children for more than a day. We were INSEPARABLE.
COURTESY OF THE AUTHOR

Polly Judd is one of the strongest women I have ever known. I don't know how she has survived all that she has had to endure. She is truly a miracle.
TIM WEBB

At Mom's fifty-ninth birthday party with Mom, Pop, Dario, Ashley, me, Roach and the kids.
COURTESY OF THE AUTHOR

When I went solo in 1992, I bought my first Harley. It represented freedom and helped me face my fear of cruising alone in this world. I love to pull up next to someone at a stoplight and just when they recognize me—take off!

RANDEE ST. NICHOLAS

Someone brought this fawn to me after finding her alone in a field during hunting season. I pray constantly for a compassionate heart and gentle hands to care for these lost, wounded and mistreated animals. I have learned some of life's most joyful and painful lessons from these innocent creatures great and small. JINNI THOMAS

Clementine was one of the greatest friends I have ever had. She was with me for fifteen years, and I was holding her in my arms when she died.

COURTESY OF THE AUTHOR

Grace, age eight, and Elijah, age ten. These two marvelous beings continue to be my teachers.
DANA FINEMAN

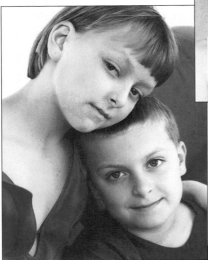

I look at this picture of Charlie Jordan and wonder what kind of life my birth father had. I missed out on so much not getting to know him. Doesn't Elijah look like him?
COURTESY OF THE AUTHOR

Roach and I in Ashley's kitchen in 2000, spending our first Thanksgiving together.
COURTESY OF THE AUTHOR

Being Mrs. Roach has done wonders for my personality! I truly didn't think I would ever get married again. I'm living proof that miracles do happen. I'm telling you: Don't ever give up on love.
TRACY NIEDERMEYER

We may not have it all together but together we have it all!
TRACY NIEDERMEYER

Ashley has always been there for me no matter what. I trust her with my life.
TRACY NIEDERMEYER

We put the fun in dysfunctional! Our family has a lot of spirit. We laugh all the time. KRISTIN BARLOWE

A friend told me years ago that being unique is lonely. Coming home to myself has been a lonely journey at times. I have spent a great deal of my life out in a wilderness of feeling lost and sad. At forty-one, I can finally feel myself beginning to come out of that wilderness into a place of love and acceptance—for my SELF and for my life.

KRISTIN BARLOWE

cause the CMA had agreed—for the first time—to hire an orchestra for my performance. I felt it was wonderful to be one of the first female artists to have such a production. Vince Gill introduced me, and I gave the most dramatic, passionate performance. It was very emotional for me to sing "Is It Over Yet," because I was ending a relationship, and embarking on a new one.

My family was far more impressed with my performance than with my date. Mom and Nana were both at the CMA show, and when I introduced my date to Nana, she said almost nothing. I didn't pick up on it, because I was so caught up in the festivities. Later, after the divorce, I learned that Nana hadn't trusted him from the beginning. Not surprisingly, Mom expressed her feelings right away. Mom's first reaction was to question his intentions. Like the feelings I'd brushed aside in Florida, Mom felt that he was moving too fast. Sensing my vulnerability, I believe this new man saw an opportunity to move in and that's exactly what he did. I was at an unprotected place in my life. I was newly separated from my mom and had recently left my manager of twelve years. I guess you could say that I was ripe for the picking.

Soon after I went back out on tour, he flew into L.A. to surprise me at a show, and ended up staying on the bus with me for over a month. I enjoyed the attention. The bus had felt lonely for some time, and I welcomed his company. Very quickly, I began to feel I needed him around.

"Doesn't he work?" Roach asked.

"He's independently wealthy," I explained.

"What is a grown man doing showing up and hanging around for that long without paying his way?" Mom asked.

I didn't see the things others saw, I guess. I chose to see only the good, and before I knew it, we had grown close and had become intimate. Looking back on it, I think the intimacy did happen far too quickly. I should have waited until I knew him better. I didn't have any boundaries, and was in such need of love and attention. I didn't listen to my gut instincts, but decided with my head that I needed someone to take care of me.

That feeling didn't last long. Within a few months I decided to break up with him. I phoned and asked him to meet me at a nearby church parking lot. All the way to the meeting place, I lectured myself.

You've got to get out of this deal! Things are moving way too fast!

When I pulled up beside his car, he got out and got into my car with me. Before I could say anything, he reached in his pocket and pulled out a ring box.

"Wynonna, I want to marry you."

He opened the box and I stared down at the diamond engagement ring.

"I can't accept this," I finally said.

He took back the ring but continued with his declarations of love! So even though I had broken up with him, he continued a cat-and-mouse-type game. This was the most persistent guy I'd ever met. *He must really love me!* I thought. I finally gave up running and the two of us began a courtship. I was pregnant within four months.

I found out about the pregnancy through a voice mail message from the nurse at my doctor's office, and the first emotion was absolute and sheer joy. I was so elated! Then I thought, *Oh, my God! Mom's going to be so mad at me!* I was twenty-nine years old and still worried about what my mom's reaction would be.

Mom, of course, was shocked when I told her. What should have been a joyful moment between mother and daughter ended up instead being a tense conversation about the timing of the pregnancy, my career and the fact that I wasn't married. I can imagine that Mom felt as though history was repeating itself. She didn't want me to have to face the same judgment she herself had experienced twenty-nine years earlier. But I couldn't have been happier about being pregnant. I sensed right away that it was a boy, and knew immediately that I would name him Elijah, after my great-great-grandfather Elijah Judd.

As word got out among my immediate circle, I sensed an immediate feeling of panic among the Wynonna, Inc., employees. Some people were happy for me, but at the same time concerned about themselves and their families. What would happen to my career and, in turn, theirs? I felt caught between two different dynamics. One of my dreams had finally come true. I was going to be a mother! But would I be able to take care of everyone on payroll? I knew people wanted me to be happy, but it felt like they wanted it on their terms. For me it all felt natural. I'd wanted a baby for as long as I could remember. Some career women have a hard time fitting a baby into their agenda. For me it was the opposite. I relished it, loved the idea of singing and mothering. I began daydreaming about my child. I felt closer to God. At that point, although I was nervous about public reaction, I was too thrilled to let anyone steal my joy! I found myself becoming intensely protective of what felt right for me and for the baby.

My manager, John Unger, advised me to hold a press conference and try to control the media before it controlled me. It felt like the right thing to do. On the day I held the press conference about my pregnancy, I met someone who would become one of the most important and influential people in my life and career: Kerry Hansen.

I wish I could say this was a friends-at-first-sight relationship, but I didn't care for her the first time that we met.

This is a story of wrong first impressions, assumptions and misinterpretations that so often can affect both business and friendly relationships. Thank goodness this one has a happy ending.

I was contracted to attend a meet & greet prior to a concert in Maine, the first stop on my thirty-five-date Dial-sponsored tour of 1994. A great many company executives and contest winners were coming. Because of the press conference about my pregnancy, I was late getting to the venue. I walked in to find a beautiful young woman working the crowd. I stood and watched as Kerry moved from person to person, smiling and schmoozing. It seemed phony to me. I thought she was the ultimate Ms. B.S.

As it turned out, Kerry worked for the Chicago company that had set up the tour for Dial. PS Productions had a client list of Fortune 500 companies that they brought together with touring artists for sponsorships. Her job was to go out on the road and set up elaborate backstage parties where everyone could get to know each other.

She'd been putting the final touches on this event when my tour manager approached her and said, "By the way, Wynonna is going to be late, very late."

Kerry says she almost fell down. "What do you mean? This is the first date in the tour! All the Dial heavy hitters are coming in from Phoenix!"

"Wynonna is having a press conference today in Nashville to announce that she's pregnant, out of wedlock," he confided.

Kerry later told me that she sat down and tried to assess the situation. She decided she could do one of two things. She could say, "Well, damn. This is a problem. The clients are going to be really upset." Or, she thought, she could turn it into a positive and say to the Dial people: "Guess what? I have the greatest news! Wynonna is in Nashville holding a press conference to announce that she is pregnant with her first child. She'll be a little late getting here, but she is thrilled at the prospect of being a mother!"

She decided to spend the night reassuring her corporate clients that everything was going to be just fine. We ended up working together during the tour, but never really clicked. It wasn't until 1995 when John Unger convinced Kerry to work with him on the management team that I would begin to fully appreciate how remarkable and talented this woman really was. Twelve years later this woman would not only be one of my best friends, but would become my personal manager as well.

She and I still laugh when we talk about that night we first met. We were both so young, so ambitious, and so determined to cover our butts. Unfortunately, I wasn't covering my butt on the home front.

Soon the father of my child moved in with me, and encouraged me to allow him to take complete control. And take control is what he did. And the truth is, it felt good to let someone else drive. He accompanied me everywhere I went. He started doing things for me that I'd always done for myself. He answered the phone, read the faxes and opened the mail. Before I knew it, he was involved in every detail of my personal and professional life. In my past relationships, I had always kept the personal and professional separated. But I soon found myself asking for his opinion about everything, soon couldn't make a decision without him. I began taking on the role of a stereotypical traditional housewife. I was used to partnerships and I liked having someone around to help me make decisions. But I think my increased estrogen levels must have caused me to lose brain cells!

Yes, honey. No, honey. Whatever you think.

But more than anything—more than another hit single,

another platinum album, another sold-out tour—I wanted a family, so I began doing anything and everything I could to preserve and protect that dream. Instead of going to visit my friends and family, I stayed at home. Instead of going to meetings about my career on Music Row, I went to bookstores and purchased books on pregnancy and child care. Instead of traveling to award shows, I built fires and got massages.

I sent out the message loud and clear: *I'm barefoot and pregnant and remodeling my kitchen!*

Together, my baby's father and I began a nine-month love affair with comfort food. I became a carb chaser. I was ravenous all day and all night. I couldn't get enough to eat! The baby's father seemed to enjoy watching me eat. Every time he came home, he brought me doughnuts, pies, comfort foods, casseroles. It was the first time in my life that I ate whatever I wanted and didn't feel guilty.

"I'm eating for two and loving every bite," I'd say.

I continued to tour, and in spite of my weight gain, I was singing better than ever. I loved being pregnant and onstage! It was the best of both worlds. I was creating life and music all at the same time. By the time the yearlong tour ended, I was eight and a half months pregnant. I had gained about seventy pounds and was still trying hard to rock onstage.

One night a man in the audience heckled me about how much weight I'd gained with the pregnancy. I remember he shouted out:

"You are *really* pregnant!"

I leaned over to the microphone and asked: "Really? What's your name, honey?"

"Frank!" he shouted out.

"Is that your wife sitting next to you, Frankie?" I asked.

"No, she's at home," Frankie answered.

Well, right then some of the audience started giving him a hard time. Some of them even turned *their* heckles into baby-related comments.

"Yeah!" one woman shouted out. "Right now she's probably home washing *your* poo-poo undies, you big baby!"

The audience went *wild*!

Each night after the show, I'd ride down the highway, lying in bed and listening to Elijah's heartbeat on the Doppler I'd borrowed from my doctor. The sound gave me inspiration when I'd get so tired that I wasn't sure I could continue on. I was determined to finish out the hundred concert dates I had committed to before I was pregnant. I was in a good place, and at peace with myself. Some felt differently.

I became a regular headline in the tabloids. It seemed that everywhere I went, all journalists wanted to talk about was how I felt about being judged for being pregnant and not married. I began to dread doing interviews for fear that I'd spend the whole time defending my choice to celebrate this birth. It seemed like some people felt that I had destroyed the legacy of the Judd dynasty. I tried to understand that some people were disappointed that the Judds' story hadn't continued as they had envisioned. I knew that where I'd come from, the way I was raised, I'd been taught that a woman is supposed to get married and *then* have children. A friend told me that a local preacher scolded me during one of his sermons. It took every ounce of strength that I had to shield myself from the bad press and harsh judgments. I even got hate mail backstage at some concerts!

But I was determined to hold my head high and march through the judgment. People speculated whether I could finish the tour. I planned to prove to them that I could. I was exhausted, but satisfied with what I was accomplishing. Primarily, I was determined to be truthful with both my family and my fans, and the truth about my own beginnings was starting to unfold.

TELL ME WHY

Mom and Dad had been fighting for thirty years. As far back as I can remember, I've always felt as though I was stuck in the middle between the two of them. Both Mom and Dad used me as their sounding board. For years I had taken on the role of mediator. I don't know which burden felt worse: the fear that I would be forced to choose between the two of them or feeling as though it was my responsibility to repair the damage. After all, it was because of me that they had had to get married, and why they got divorced, or so I believed. I had done my best to defend one to the other. But I had finally decided that it was not my responsibility or place to challenge what Mom said about Dad on national television. I think to this day that it's one of the main reasons that he ultimately chose not to have a relationship with me.

I had spent a lifetime wanting Dad to love me, and yet it seemed like something remained in the way of that happening. During holidays, Dad complained if I didn't come to visit him. But he was a single man with a singles lifestyle. Only recently have I come to understand why I didn't visit him more. When I was a little girl, Dad was usually working and my memories of my visits are of waiting for him to come home. So, as a result, I often put off going to see him as an adult. Today it makes me sad to realize all the opportunities we missed being together.

Once I had made it in the music business, I thought I could win Dad's affection by sharing my newfound wealth. He loved the Rolling Stones, so I took him on my bus to a concert. Dad and I ended up hanging out backstage and playing pool with Keith Richards. Anytime I had the chance to invite Dad to a special event, I did. Our love for music was what connected us. It had once been our bond, and I was paying him back for the times he took me to hear live music when I was a young girl. I wanted to celebrate that part of our relationship.

In 1994 I performed at the Super Bowl's halftime show. Dad came to the game and asked if he could ride to Nashville on the bus with me. When John Unger learned of Dad's plans, he said he would ride on the bus, too, which did strike me as a little odd. Dad didn't say much. Looking back on it, John controlled most of the conversation. John would ask a question and Dad would give a short answer. I assumed everyone was tired, so I said good night and went back to my room to go to bed.

We arrived at my home early in the morning, and I stayed on the bus to sleep in. Dad went on into the house. The next time I saw him, everything in my world, in our relationship, was changed forever.

I woke up in the morning and checked my cell phone first thing.

"Wynonna, would you please call me as soon as you get this message? Your mother has requested a meeting with you and Ashley."

It was our family counselor. My heart almost stopped. This is it! Mom's terminal and she has only a few months to live! So I quickly got dressed and drove straight to the counselor's. I felt sick to my stomach, so numb I couldn't even cry. Both Ashley's and Mom's cars were there.

When I walked in, Mom immediately began to cry. Ashley was sitting at her feet, leaning on her knee. I wondered why Pop wasn't there. If Mom's health had taken a turn for the worse, why wasn't he there? I guessed he must have stayed out in the car, and it seemed odd. I looked at everyone, but no one said anything for what seemed to be an eternity. Sadness permeated the room. The counselor looked at Mom, who continued to cry. By that time I was convinced that what I was about to hear was devastating.

But nobody said a word. Since the counselor's usual way to begin a session is to let the person who called the meeting begin, she continued to look at Mom, and then back at me. After a few more minutes, I couldn't stand the silence. I leaned forward and looked directly into Mom's eyes.

In a soft voice I asked, "What is going on?"

Still no one spoke. Mom kept crying. Finally Ashley spoke:

"Michael Ciminella is not your biological father. Your father is named Charlie Jordan."

I was so stunned that I couldn't speak. I stopped breathing. My heart was pounding. This wasn't happening! My ears started ringing and I felt sick to my stomach. I felt a lump growing in my throat. Adrenaline kicked in and I felt incredibly hot. I think my spirit must have left my body, because all of a sudden I couldn't feel my hands or feet. I saw Mamaw Ciminella's face, then flashes of darkness, then Papaw smiling at me. I wanted to run, to rewind time and erase what I knew now. I sat there in that room, and stared at my mother.

Finally, all I could think to say was "It's all right, Mom."

I wasn't angry. I wasn't sad. I wasn't anything. And I belonged to no one. I felt like I was in a space between earth and hell. I looked at Ashley and saw the pain on her face. I continue to see that moment in my dreams, still feel the sting even as I write this page. This kind of sorrow never truly goes away. It was devastating for all three of us.

All my life I've been told that I'm too sensitive and too emotional. But after hearing the news, I became neither. I couldn't even cry. All of a sudden, Mom seemed so little and fragile sitting there. Looking back on it, that day must have been so hard for Ashley. It wasn't her place to be the one to have to tell me. I've never gotten over that.

I knew that day that I must not attack Mom. Children learn very quickly what pleases their parents. In the book *The Highly Sensitive Child*, a woman talks about how she learned to soothe herself instead of crying when she was a baby. If she cried or became emotional, her mother got agitated and immediately lit a cigarette. The woman says she learned at a very early age that it was *her* job to soothe herself so her mother wouldn't become upset. And she was rewarded. Her mother often told people, "She's such a good girl. She never cries." This selfless act became her pattern, and in the end, it shut her down emotionally for years. It wasn't until she had her own child, and found herself becoming agitated when her own child cried, that she realized that she was repeating the cycle.

I can't speak for anyone else in the room that day. Each family member has a different reality of what took place. My own, about what happened in that room, was that it felt like the energy during the appointment was more about telling me the news than how the news affected me.

I couldn't think of anything to say, so I got up and left.

Driving home, one of my first thoughts was about Dad. For the first time in my life, it all made sense. I had always felt that Dad preferred Ashley to me. I'd always felt like I didn't fit in. I'd always wondered why Ashley and I looked different. Why did I struggle with my weight—why? Now I understood why, and in a way, it set me free.

I drove home thinking what in the world I would say to Dad when I walked in. It was going to be a long afternoon. When I got back to my house, Dad was sitting in the glassed-in great room. He didn't say a word.

"I've just been with Mom and Ashley," I said. "Ashley told me."

"Well, now maybe we can develop a relationship based on truth," he said.

Develop a relationship. What a strange thing to say, I thought. I sensed fear in Dad. There was no embrace. No *I love you anyway*. There seemed to be a filter over the house, over the day, over Dad and me.

I know now that I'm not crazy! I thought. *Thank God I know!* All those years I'd felt that Dad was unable to really love me, that something was wrong with me, that I was not lovable. I always thought to myself, if I could just do one thing to make him really love me things would be all right. I wondered over and over, *What's wrong with me? Why can't I be who he wants me to be?* Now I knew why! Even as down as I was, I felt thankful for that knowledge.

"Why am I only finding this out now?" I asked.

"I didn't think it was my place to tell you. I feel that it was your mother's job."

It's still about Dad and Mom, I thought. *What an odd thing to say*. It's about him being mad at her. I felt I was caught in the middle once again.

"How long has Ashley known?" I asked.

"Since she was eleven," he said.

I hadn't thought anything else could surprise me, but that certainly did. *Since she was eleven?*

"Did Mamaw and Papaw know?" I asked.

"Of course."

Later that night a memory flashed in my mind. One day when I was about ten years old Mamaw Ciminella took me into her bedroom, sat down on her bed, took both of my wrists and pulled me close to her. "I want you to know that ever since I found out that you were conceived, I've loved you. I will love you no matter what, and I will love you forever." When I recalled that moment, I wept for the first time since learning about the thirty-year lie. Mamaw was planting the seed so that when the day came that I found out, I would have that sacred moment to hold on to. You never forget moments like that, moments when you are a child and someone validates their love for you.

"Nana and Papaw Judd?"

"Yes."

"Who else knew?"

"Everyone else pretty much knows by now."

Well, I thought, *the joke's on me!*

Dad got up and started upstairs to the guest room, where he was staying. I followed him.

"Do I know the man who fathered me?" I asked. "Does he live in Ashland? Did I ever meet him?"

"No," Dad said. "You don't know him."

It seems strange looking back, but it was quite a while before I started seriously wanting to connect with my biological father. The news of *who I wasn't* took precedence over *who I was*. I thought more about Papaw Ciminella than anyone else. Mamaw had died years ago. What could I say to my sweet papaw? What would he say to me? How could I face him? I couldn't stand to see him cry. He and I had such a bond. But in the end, Papaw gave me a great gift, just as Mamaw had done. When I next saw him, he hugged me and held on tightly. He wouldn't let go for a long time. When he did, he looked into my eyes and reassured me of his love.

I started finding out who the people were who'd known. Ken Stilts knew. Woody Bowles knew. Our wardrobe assistant knew. Mom had told them all. That was the thing that I had a difficult time accepting. Mom had told everyone but me! Woody Bowles said he had come close to telling me one time, but stopped himself. In the end, I found out that Dad came to my Super Bowl performance planning to tell me. He told Mom that if she didn't, he would. That's why John Unger had come on the bus with us, to prevent him from giving me the news.

How much longer would it have gone on?

I felt a double burden. There I was, unmarried and pregnant. And my dad was not my biological father. The only thing that saved my sanity during this confusing time was the fact that I was pregnant with Elijah. I had my baby, no matter what had happened all those years ago. I think that is why I became so attached to Elijah that I almost wouldn't let anyone else hold him from the day he was born! Elijah was my truth. And I made a promise to God that I'd never keep secrets from my son.

On July 4, 1994, Mom and I were scheduled to be a part of a weekend-long celebration in Ashland, Kentucky. Mom was set to host a food drive, and I was scheduled to perform. There would be a lot of press there. Before we left for Ashland, I learned that my dad had given an interview to the hometown newspaper in which he said he was not my biological father. I knew it would be front-page news.

I was shocked but not surprised. Dad had long been angry about the things Mom said about him to the press. Mom had been unfair in the past and Dad was determined to get even. I would end up being the biggest loser in the deal. I called the paper and asked if they'd consider holding the story until after the July Fourth event, but they refused.

I felt like I was going home as the town joke, the bastard child. I called a meeting with our counselor before Mom and I left for Ashland to try and set some boundaries with Mom about what we would and would not say about Dad's article. I had nightmares of the two of them trying to fight it out with each other on Ashland's Main Street during the parade.

As usual, the counselor told Mom I'd requested a meeting, and asked if anyone wanted to start. She didn't have to ask twice.

"I'm really concerned about what's going to happen on July Fourth, Mom," I said. "You're asking me to go with you to Ashland, and *if* I go I need you to promise me that you won't spend your time and energy defending yourself in the press against anything Dad has said in that newspaper article. What Dad did was wrong, but this weekend is about celebration, not airing our dirty laundry."

"I give you my word!" Mom said emphatically.

"Even if during an interview somebody asks your feelings about the newspaper article?"

"I give you my word."

We shook hands.

I drove to Ashland in my car, arriving a little before six a.m. It was still dark. I drove straight to the nearest newsstand to buy a paper, and there it was. Front-page headline. I panicked. I got back in the car and started reading. This was no *I've always loved Wynonna anyway* piece. This was a shot sent out toward Mom.

I wanted to get back in the car, turn around and drive straight home to Nashville. But I knew I couldn't let my family or our fans down. So I drove to Nana Judd's and got ready for church. When we arrived, people turned their heads and stared. Nana and I took our seats in the front pew and the service began. Mom was the guest speaker that morning. She gave an inspirational talk as if nothing had happened. I was amazed at her ability to keep herself together in the face of fire.

After the food drive, and an autograph-signing session, camera crews came on the bus and did some interviews with Mom and me. As the last interview was wrapping up, Mom suggested that I go back to the stateroom to change clothes.

As I started to shut my bedroom door, I heard Mom say, "I'd like to say something about Michael Ciminella."

She said she thought that Dad was being very cruel to me, and that she didn't like it a bit. She said that the two of us really loved Ashland, and we were trying to do something for the town.

To this day I regret that I didn't go back and stop the interview. There's a part of me that wishes I could turn back the clock and walk right back to the cameras and say, *Stop this right now!* But there's another part of me that knows that if I had, the film footage of me doing it would have been even more tabloid fodder.

When Mom finished up her speech and as the film crew packed to leave, I did go back up to the front.

"I cannot believe this is happening, Mom," I said. "It's got to stop! I won't be any part of it."

Mom started to try to explain herself and I stopped her.

"I don't know how I can ever trust any of you ever again," I said. Then I walked off the bus. I got in my car and took off for Nashville. The thing I remember most about leaving so suddenly is seeing Roach standing there by the bus with a bewildered look on his face as I waved goodbye to him. He must have thought, *Oh, my God! What now?*

I stayed in a siege mentality for years. Now I can have compassion for both Mom and myself. This was Naomi Judd's hometown, and she was determined to not let Dad have the last word. Mom and Dad had been getting back at each other for years.

Dad called me later and said, "Wy, the tabloids are offering me a bunch of cash for an exclusive. Let's do it together and split the money." He said he was just kidding, but I didn't think it was particularly funny. I just wanted the fighting to stop. It drove a wedge between us for a long time.

My husband-to-be helped to keep that wedge in place. During a trip to Los Angeles, he brought me a tabloid that featured an interview and a picture of Charlie Jordan. I couldn't believe it. The first picture I saw of my biological father was in a tabloid. I freaked out, but I didn't hold it against Charlie. I know how the tabloids get their stories. They often stalk their victims until they finally give in just to get rid of them. In the piece, Charlie said that he was proud of me. I held on to those words for years. But what a strange place to read about how your real father, whom you've never met, feels about you.

"This article is your mom's doing," my partner said.

I was in such a vulnerable place that, like a fool, I believed him. Somehow he convinced me that it was all part of a conspiracy against the two of us. I decided to concentrate on the impending birth of my child.

Hindsight is 20/20, so now I can say that I very much regret putting off meeting my biological father. I sensed that Charlie Jordan was a good man, a simple man. He'd known all those years that his daughter had become famous. And he must have believed that with fame comes fortune. But he asked for nothing—not a meeting, not a favor and not money. He stayed quiet. I sometimes wondered if he felt that since he'd not been a part of my life, he didn't deserve to meet me. Maybe he thought that I had known about him and had chosen not to contact him.

I tried to remain in touch with my dad. I kept inviting him on the road, and tried to maintain a good relationship despite his talking with the press about Charlie Jordan. I offered to give him a Mercedes-Benz that Ken Stilts had given me. Dad said he had no use for the car, and would I mind very much if he sold it to help pay for a house? I then offered to help him buy a house. He found a beautiful old house that needed work, so I gave him the bulk of the money, and he began the renovation process. Dad agreed to will the house back to me as repayment. So things seemed right in my world. I was in such great shape financially that I'd been able to help my dad with a house, my career was going strong, and I was having a baby!

Christmas of 1994 was especially festive at my house! Our baby was due at any time, and I went all out on decorating the house. I bet I had about a hundred thousand lights. We lit a huge star and the word *Believe* on the barn. Lights were on every fence! One of my favorite displays was an incredible almost life-sized nativity scene that I bought in Italy.

On the night of December 22, I came home from having supper with Mom and Pop with terrible lower-back pain. I took a long, hot bath, but even that didn't help me sleep. I got up and started wandering around the farm, looking at all the out-of-doors decorations. I noticed that one of the sheep had fallen over in the nativity scene, and went over to set it back up. All of a sudden, right there on the hay in the manger, my water broke! I couldn't stop laughing! The concept of my water breaking in a nativity scene was just too hysterical!

Before I did anything else, I went back inside and tried

to phone Mom. It was on DO NOT DISTURB, so I called the police and asked them to go wake her and Pop up so they could meet us at the hospital. We lived forty-five minutes away, so I was already nervous and running around the house trying to get myself together. I called upstairs, and woke up the baby's father. He jumped out of bed, buck naked, and started running through the house like a madman. By the time he got his act together, the pain was unbearable. And by the time we got into the car, I was cussing like a sailor.

We went into the hospital the back way and they wheeled me to a labor room. I was in labor for five hours before they determined that Elijah's cord was wrapped around his neck three times. They rushed me in to have an emergency C-section. Mom was in the labor room with me—she kept modestly covering me up so nobody would see me half-naked. Honey, by that time I couldn't have cared less!

"Mom! I don't care if anyone sees my vagina! I'm trying to have a baby!"

Then she went into the delivery room with me—my nurse-mommy. Everyone should be so lucky! While a team of nurses and two doctors worked, Mom sat at my head, patting me and saying, "You're still my baby." She looked so cute in her scrubs, in full makeup, lips perfectly lined, sitting right there ready to assist if they needed her.

Elijah was born in the early morning hours of December 23, 1994.

After Elijah was born, my partner got much more aggressive and demanded, though we were not married, that Elijah take his last name. When I tried to use both our last names together, he went berserk and I ended up calling in a mediator. This all happened within a few hours after I gave birth, and it broke my spirit. This wasn't exactly the way I had dreamed being a new parent would be. What a beginning.

I had decided to take a year off after Elijah's birth. Against the advice of my financial advisors, I opted to keep my band and staff on salary for the time I didn't work. It wouldn't have seemed right to put everyone out of a job just to allow me some time off. I had made those commitments prior to getting pregnant and felt strongly about honoring them. I believed it was a win-win situation for all of us.

Many people, including Mom, felt I was shooting myself in the foot career-wise. But I was determined not to let the guilt associated with career versus family overwhelm me. Instead I focused on being a new mother. I hadn't had that kind of time off since I was eighteen. I was ecstatic. I hired Mary Eller, the head labor and delivery room nurse at Baptist Hospital, to help with the baby, and she turned out to be a lifesaver.

I knew that I'd slowed down at a crucial time in my career. I knew that any time you slow down, for whatever reason, there are plenty of performers ready to step onto center stage. I well remember the day in 1995, when I first saw a Shania Twain video on Country Music Television. I was rocking Elijah, while breast-feeding and feeling postpartum. I was still carrying most of the seventy pounds I'd gained. I felt terrible! I was in no mood to see Shania's belly button. Then I chuckled to myself, and realized that I was just feeling insecure because my belly button had a few layers of fat around it. I tried to laugh at myself. *If I had a flat stomach*, I thought, *I'd probably flaunt it, too.* But then I realized that I had never felt that free and comfortable with my body in the first place—even when my stomach *was* flat!

I made the decision not to marry Elijah's father. The dynamics of our relationship began to change. We grew more and more apart, but stayed together to care for Elijah. We already had separate bedrooms, so I set up the nursery in my room. My partner stayed gone a lot. He didn't have a steady job, so I grew curious about what he was doing with all his spare time. However, I was so content with Elijah that before long I grew used to the routine.

By the time I got pregnant with my daughter, I'd decided to ask my live-in partner to leave. He and I had not been intimate in months, so imagine my surprise when, after one brief encounter, I discovered I was pregnant again. With a second child on the way, I felt that the right thing to do for my family was to get married. I decided that with two children, I must fight to keep everyone together. So I began to plan a wedding. Even though my relationship with the children's father was falling apart, I kept faith that I could make things better. If I just prayed hard enough about it, things would change.

At one of our meetings with our counselor, Mom said I was making a mistake and said she wasn't going to come to the wedding. She didn't want to have anything to do with the wedding, or the reception, which was to be held at our family restaurant, Trilogy, in Nashville. Pop stood up to Mom, telling her that regardless of whether Mom agreed with my decision, he'd be attending. That meant the world to me. It was one of the few times I'd ever seen him go against her, knowing full well that he was crossing Mom, and I know it must have been difficult for him to have to make a choice between the two of us. In the end, Mom did decide to attend, despite being convinced that I was making a very bad decision.

A few weeks before the wedding, my future husband went jogging with my manager, John Unger, and told him that we'd decided we didn't need a prenuptial agreement. John called me immediately. Later, as calmly as he could, John told him if my partner didn't sign it, there would be no marriage. He was worried sick about what could happen if I didn't protect all that I'd worked hard for.

John had been worried ever since he learned I was pregnant for the second time. As a manager, for him one pregnancy in the middle of a career was a challenge. But two pregnancies posed a real threat to career momentum. John called Kerry into his office and said, "I don't know what I'm going to do. Wynonna is pregnant again. Her career has been on hold for a year and a half since she had Elijah. If she chooses to take more time off with this child, I'm afraid that the label will begin to lose faith in her. They won't wait much longer."

Kerry stepped up to the plate. "You're looking at this the wrong way, John," she said. "You have children of your own. She's about to have another child! This is a gift from God! Be happy for her, and figure out a way to deal with what her life brings to the table. She's a woman having a child. Don't make her think there's something wrong with that. Don't judge her, because if you do, you'll lose her."

I think that the beginning of the end of our management agreement came when I walked into J. Alexander's restaurant one night to find John having dinner with Mom and Pop. Why hadn't I been told about this meeting? It suddenly hit me that the three of them were having a meeting about my personal life behind my back. It was an opportunity for my future husband to create more drama, to play on my emotions. I was so upset.

"They're trying to come between us."

"I'm the father of your children."

"It's none of their business what you and I do."

I felt defeated and fell even deeper into the us-against-them mentality.

Besides being my career manager, John had begun to take on the role of personal manager as well. He was concerned that large amounts of money couldn't be accounted for. I was beginning to make some bad choices, and on the verge of giving my future husband power of attorney. But even knowing that John's concerns had merit, his involvement with my personal life felt invasive. People tried to give me advice but I was too busy fighting for what I'd wanted my entire life—family.

The wedding and reception cost a fortune and turned out to be a nightmare. My bridegroom invited so many people, most of whom I didn't know, that I ran out of space for some of our family. I asked Dad to read something during the ceremony, and he declined. He said that he hadn't brought his glasses. Ashley was my maid of honor, and because her makeup and hair took longer, our ceremony ran a half hour late. D. R. Roach and Rock Solid were hired for the entire event. Roach personally walked me into the church.

I saw Mom crying as Pop walked me down the aisle. And I learned from one of my backup singers that she kept her head down during the entire ceremony. Her tears were clearly not those of happiness but of despair. In my heart, I knew that I was not being supported in my decision. John Unger didn't come at all.

But even though it was not a joyful occasion, I knew it was the right thing to do. My children deserved to come into the world with a mother and a father who were husband and wife. I told myself that once we were married, things would get better. I have always believed in miracles.

Tabloid-hired helicopters followed our family from the moment I stepped out of my house to the church, and they continued to circle the church throughout the ceremony. At one point I thought they were going to land on the roof.

The sound got so loud, it drowned out our vows. Thank God I can laugh about it today.

Later that night, in the bridal suite at the Opryland Hotel, Ashley showed up at our door with members of the Nashville Bluegrass Band. They came in and serenaded us with "Good Night Irene."

"You can't have a honeymoon without me," she said.

Soon after we were married, my husband said he needed me to sign over power of attorney so he could sell a few of our cars. I was about to do it. But one night I got a call from my business manager.

"First, we need for you to understand what power of attorney means, Wynonna. It will mean that your husband will have the right to sign any legal document in place of you, including business concerns. And second, if you do this, we'll resign. We can no longer represent you. We advise against you allowing your new husband to make these kinds of decisions for you."

I had no idea that power of attorney would give my husband complete control over my business. Mom and I were still doing business together and I couldn't imagine the three of us being involved together!

When I phoned and confronted him, he laughed it off.

"All I wanted to do was sell a car," he said.

Things began to fall apart right away. Within the first year of our marriage, I lost six employees. The relationship between my manager and my husband deteriorated further. There were continuous disagreements. My husband felt as though my manager was too involved in my personal business, and my manager felt as though my husband was too involved in my career business.

I continued to believe that I could have both a family and a career. While pregnant with Grace, I played an out-of-door show in 110-degree weather and did everything I could to keep our family going. It was complete insanity. In fact, I almost died working right up to the time my daughter was born on June 21, 1996.

On that morning, I had found myself getting really busy, cleaning and doing chores. I decided to water my whole garden, and it was while I held the hose on a bed of flowers that I felt something shifting in my body. I don't know how, but I knew immediately that something was very wrong. I followed my intuition and had my husband drive me to the hospital to see my doctor. By the time I got there, my blood pressure was sky-high. I was immediately admitted as a high-risk patient. Thank God, I had followed my heart and gone straight to that hospital!

My husband caused such a ruckus that you'd have thought that he was the one having a baby! He went all over the hospital calling for extra security. Everyone was so nervous! The staff was frantically trying to meet his every request. I didn't even know it was going on, but he was developing quite a reputation for being high mainte-nance! It was a long time before I heard the whole story.

Within an hour they started labor, and I tried to push for a couple of hours. Finally the doctor informed me that we'd have to do another C-section. I was so disappointed when they wheeled me into emergency surgery. Then, within minutes, something went drastically wrong and my blood pressure went drastically low.

"She's bottoming out!" somebody yelled. "Get a crash cart." That's what they call for when someone is in grave danger. My mom sat beside me, watching everyone work frantically to get my vitals under control. I started shaking violently.

"Uh-oh!" one of the doctors said. As the two doctors were cutting me open, a small tear appeared in my uterus. Fluid started leaking out into my body. I know now that if

I'd been minutes later getting to the hospital that day, my baby and I would have died.

Mom stayed right there, quietly stroking my hair and telling me things were going to be fine. She was the consummate nurse and an even better mom.

I still have a hard time comprehending that both the baby and I nearly died. But through God's Grace and the good hospital staff, here we are! I named my new baby Grace Pauline, after my great-aunt Pauline, the one with whom I'd spent so much time on her Little Catt farm in Kentucky, and Grace for God's Grace.

Although I didn't know it at the time, the seeds were being sown for the end of my marriage. Show after show, people were going to my manager with complaints. This wasn't just my own band and crew, either. I was told that I lost some tour dates and sponsorships because my husband had tried to take charge. John would come to me and ask me to tell my husband to stay out of the business. When I performed at the Super Bowl again, Roach came to me with complaints from the show's producers about demands made by my husband. It seemed that everywhere we went he took every opportunity to try and sell a boat and do his business. He wanted to be liked. He wanted to be successful. And he wanted to be famous.

I really wanted to give my husband the opportunity to be a man, to feel wanted and needed. So even though those early days when I had felt so dependent on him were long gone, I often asked him to take care of certain things. But he did business differently than I did. People were not used to his aggressive personality like I was. I continued to lose employees, from bus drivers to farm managers.

Roach was one of the few people who could deal with my husband. Shortly after the marriage, my husband called Roach.

"I want you to start coming out here once a week to mow our farm," he ordered.

"I don't work for you. I work for Wynonna," Roach said firmly.

He set that boundary early. Others were not so proactive. I've long thought that Roach felt *he* couldn't quit because he knew that I needed someone around who could be objective and fair, someone who couldn't be bullied. I believe that Roach was strong enough in his own identity that he continued to be loyal and he didn't budge in his commitment to Wynonna, Inc., and to me. Roach never quit.

But John Unger finally did. I hated it that he told me he was quitting on the telephone instead of in person. Pop stepped in as my new manager. But it wouldn't be long before Pop questioned whether he, too, could survive my marriage.

According to people on the road with me, problems with my husband accelerated when I wasn't around. He was eager to have respect, and seemed to have a deep need to be needed, to become the middleman. I've never known anybody who wanted to *be somebody* more than my husband. He had created a position for himself at Wynonna, Inc. His actions had often separated me from my family, and now they separated me from my staff.

Finally, after losing so many employees so quickly and learning of lost dates and sponsorships, I began wondering what was going on. When I first got married, I thought it was because people were having a hard time accepting my new husband. But people were saying that they were leaving because they felt I'd changed and was no longer accessible. I began to see a pattern. Things weren't being communicated to me. My husband was making decisions *for me* and not *with me*.

He wanted to attend every record label meeting,

every management meeting. He wanted to translate everything any employee wanted to communicate to me. If I forgot to wear my wedding ring, he had fits. He was furious when I filmed a video and my dress showed cleavage.

I didn't hold my husband accountable for a long time. I wanted to trust him so badly that I gave him the benefit of the doubt. Isn't that the way it should be? We all long for a partner that we can trust. Speaking of trust, I started to doubt the ones around me, even those who had been around me for a long while. I stopped speaking to my best friend, Jennifer Ferreri, for a while after she gave me her opinion about my relationship. I was more concerned about being right about my husband than being loved by my best friend. It was a decision I would come to regret. But my best friend is still around, and my husband is not.

A close friend of mine, who'd been with me for ten years, who was also my wardrobe assistant, left me without notice. I hugged her goodbye one night and never saw her again. Her name was Vanessa Ware. She died last November, and I never got to say goodbye to her. When she was on her deathbed, I wrote her to tell her I loved her. But she never responded. She was a colorful character, and I still have fond memories of our years together.

Having my husband on the road *clearly* wasn't working out. He and our nanny, Ya-Ya (which means "second mother" in Swahili), did not see eye to eye on much. She was and is an alpha female, one of the strongest women I know. He was always jacked up, edgy and ready to challenge anything and everything she said and did. It got crazy!

I think I mistook his edginess for passion. Plus, I have always been a little crazy myself. There was a lot going on at home and on the bus. I found myself having to do a lot of damage control. I started having to spend time talking to people to reassure them about how I felt. I didn't want anyone, not even my husband, speaking for me.

I realized that never before had I set this kind of boundary for myself. But if I wasn't able to do it for myself, I was sure as heck able to do it for my children. More than anything, I wanted them to live in peace. I began to work hard for it. It worried me that he seemed to bond more with his son than with his daughter and took Elijah with him so much it created a separation between the two children.

I made a difficult decision. I felt it was best that my husband not come on the road. So we made a pact that he would stay home and help take care of the farm.

Five weeks after Grace was born, I was back out on the road singing "No One Else on Earth" at the top of my lungs and feeling the sting from my C-section stitches. After the show each night, I'd get on the bus and start making snacks for the kids even before changing out of my stage clothes. Life was good. There on the bus, it was just the driver, Ya-Ya, the kids, Roach and me. We were a family. A road family. Though I still longed for a family at home.

The studio was the one place where my husband didn't try to dominate. I felt once again in charge. Part of that was the fact that Tony Brown was so supportive of my choices. Even though Tony was a label executive, he was also my friend. I had put Tony through a lot during the making of my first record, and I ended up putting him through even more during the making of *Revelations*.

Even though my husband didn't try to control things in the studio, he was controlling how I felt by the time I arrived! By this time we were fighting even more, and in public. We were fighting so much that I was often late and constantly in tears. I canceled sessions, which cost me thousands of dollars. Finally, the problems between my husband and me had caused so many delays that Tony had to leave the *Revelations* project to start on a project with Vince Gill. Many critics questioned my including a song I'd recorded for another project, "Free Bird," on the record. Now you know why. Time had run out.

I'm one of those people who believe that marriage is truly a God-given gift. Two people are joined together and their two bodies and souls become one. So a divorce causes a tearing of the flesh; it leaves a big, open, gaping wound. The suffering can last a long time, and unless healed, everyone involved, including children, can suffer endlessly. I hung on in this chaotic situation as long as I could, knowing that the marriage hadn't worked and believing that I should end it. My husband and I barely related to each other anymore. All we did was fight, and it was harming my career and almost all of my other relationships. A conversation with Pop helped me make my final decision.

"I love you and will always be your pop," he said. "I'm not giving up on you but I can no longer be a part of your life professionally, and watch you struggle the way you are. I can't help you anymore. You have to help yourself. I can't be your manager anymore."

I honestly didn't believe or understand how badly things had gone. You can live a long time in denial. Insanity is what happens when you continue to do the same thing over and over again and expect a different result. Nothing seemed to be changing in a positive way. If anything, negative things were beginning to happen more and more.

I think at the moment when Pop said those words to me I realized something had to be done. Something major had to change. I had come to a crossroads once again and was standing there alone. This wasn't about some manager getting a better offer from someone. This was my pop, some-

166 · WYNONNA JUDD

one who had known me and believed in me since I was fifteen years old. He had stuck by me through thick and thin. He'd never given up on helping me in the entire time I'd known him. Things must be unbearable for him to quit!

Even though I'd been struggling inside about my marriage for quite a while, I didn't want to give up. I wasn't a quitter! I didn't feel like it was the Judd way. But I felt like I had settled for less. I had become the very thing I had told thousands of women to not ever become—the Martyr.

I feel that the standard I had set for myself was this: I would rather have been in a bad relationship than no relationship at all. I had two children and they needed a father. I needed a husband. I had hung in there, believing that a miracle could and would happen. I really believed that if I loved him and took good care of him that I could help him want to change. I had taken on a lot of the responsibility for everything that had happened since our relationship had begun. It was very strange. I could handle failure in my career, but not in my personal life. I didn't want to be another tabloid headline!

It was while I sat there in Pop's office that I really *knew* that I was never truly in love with my first husband. I felt hopeless. If I was never in love with him, why had I stayed? Then it hit me. No wonder I tried so hard, after all I had been through with my mom and dad.

I had a long conversation with Pop about my personal feelings regarding my husband. I heard some details that made me realize that I had to get divorced or I'd lose everything. The statistics proved it. The biggest thing I had lost was myself. People were losing faith in me, too.

"I've got to take my life back," I finally told Pop. "I've got to try and get out of this marriage. I'm scared and I don't know what to do."

"I'll help you," he said. And that very night he made a

phone call to a top Nashville attorney. After dark the next evening, we drove to Music Row and parked in an alley. We entered in through the back door so no one would see us, to Rose Palermo's office. When Pop introduced me to Rose, I shook her hand. I had placed one of those gag windup buzzers in the palm of my hand, and when I squeezed, it shocked her. We both laughed.

"Thank God for a sense of humor," I said.

"You and I are going to get along very well," she replied.

And that was the beginning of a wonderful relationship between Rose and me, and a very messy, scary divorce. Rose, Pop and I took our seats, and from across her desk, Rose told me that I had to say the words.

"What do you mean?" I asked.

"You have to say the words, *I want a divorce*."

"I want a divorce," I said and signed the papers. My heart felt like it was pounding so loud that Pop and Rose could hear it. This wasn't the way it was supposed to be, I thought.

After our appointment, Pop drove me back to our office so I could get my car. So many emotions ran through my head on the drive back. I knew that I absolutely had to get out of this marriage. I had an obligation to not allow things to continue on as they were. It would be too unhealthy. Still, I felt guilty. Would Elijah and Grace grow up hating me?

I spent most of the next day in my room, composing a letter to my soon-to-be ex-husband. When I finished, I called for him upstairs to come down, that I had something to give him. I sat him down and handed the letter to him. I sat with him while he read it. When he was finished, he looked at me with sad eyes and walked over to me. I thought he was going to grab me and give me a hug or a kiss, to try to change my mind.

In a broken voice, he asked, "How can you do this to our family?"

I didn't respond. Instead, I got up and left the room. He followed. We walked through the kitchen into the dining room. There, I turned around and calmly said, "Don't try to change my mind. I've made my final decision. The papers have already been signed."

I will never forget the look of panic on his face.

For a moment I had a feeling of guilt that he must have sensed, because he then said, "What are you going to tell the children? That their mommy broke up their home?"

All of a sudden I realized what he was doing. This was not a loving husband trying to win back his wife. This was a desperate man trying to use his children to manipulate their mother.

Wrong day. Wrong girl.

I stood there looking at him. I didn't speak. I think the look on my face said it all. He started walking toward me, and I thought, *Oh, no, he's going to try and kiss me*, like he'd done so many times before when he saw that I was mad.

I certainly didn't expect what he did next. He got right up in my face, and in a calm, cold voice said:

"I'm going to do everything that I can to ruin your fucking life."

· 8 ·

I SAW THE LIGHT

I was soon living in fear, feeling like I was being stalked. My soon-to-be ex-husband moved into the log guesthouse, and it would be a long time before he would be willing to actually move from the property. By the time he did I was starting to have mixed feelings about my beloved home—it started to feel unsafe. That feeling heightened after he finally left.

Once, when I was standing in front of the bathroom mirror, brushing my teeth, I suddenly felt uneasy, as if someone was watching me. I glanced out the window, and there he stood in the yard, staring up at me. He began following me and showing up at functions I attended.

It was an odd feeling of déjà vu. I thought back to when he first courted me by coming onto the property unannounced. I thought back to the times he sent flowers to me, somehow tracking my every move. In the beginning, I had thought it was exciting, a real show of affection, but now I felt afraid. I was advised to take out a restraining order and change the locks on the doors to the main house.

I felt I couldn't turn to my family for support. They were all relieved that I had gotten the divorce, so when I got depressed about things, I felt I couldn't go to them. I couldn't turn to my office staff either, since they were working hard to keep my career on the right path. And so, in the end, I went in for therapy. It was often the only sympathy I got and I didn't mind paying for it. In addition to the divorce, the reality of Charlie Jordan, my biological father, weighed on my emotions. I wanted to know him, and yet I feared it. So I did nothing.

The impending divorce affected everything around me. I was turning to food more and more for comfort and companionship. I was constantly on edge.

My divorce was final in 1999, but not before some well-publicized battles. Both the *Tennessean* and the *Star* reported that I had had to pay my ex-husband to leave the property where I lived. When the information appeared in public, I filed suit against him because the terms of the divorce were to have been kept secret. He showed up at the courthouse alone and asked my attorney, Rose Palermo, if she would help him out. But of course she couldn't—he had to have his own lawyer! It was such a bizarre scene. There were the three of us, sitting, waiting for the judge to hear our case.

When we finally went before the court, the judge ordered him taken into custody. I sat there next to Rose while two policemen handcuffed him. He turned to me and asked if I would help him. He continued to stare at me as they led him from the courtroom. The whole scene became surreal. I couldn't believe it was happening. I felt an overwhelming sadness, for him, for me and for the children. Months later, sitting at breakfast, Elijah asked about it. "Mommy, why did you put Daddy in jail?"

"Where did you hear that, honey?" I asked.

"Daddy told me."

I almost choked.

One morning I woke up, and before I even got out of bed, the words *I need to sell this house* came into my mind. I had lost my life savings during the marriage and the divorce. I didn't want Grace and Elijah to have to carry the burden for my choices. So I decided to sell the property and put the money in savings for them. It broke my heart. But while it was devastating on so many levels, in some ways I felt relief. By then the house had many bad memories. And it no longer seemed like the place where I wanted to raise my children and create a new life and new music. Plus, though I would be selling this property, I would still have the 525-acre farm next to Mom and Pop's land. That would be where I would one day build, I promised myself.

I then took a look around the house and realized just how much stuff I had collected over the years. Since 1980 I had kept everything that I had ever bought—whether it came from a designer boutique or a truck stop. It was an amazing collection: antiques, stage clothes, boots, memorabilia. *Two hundred pairs of stage shoes!*

I had so much that was important to me, things that I normally wouldn't want to get rid of. But the more I realized that I was starting over in my life, the more I felt the need to lighten the load. I was moving on, literally and figuratively. I thought that wherever it was that I was going, I needed a fresh new start. And the more I really thought about it, the more I realized that it was a death and a rebirth all at the same time. Once again, I was at the crossroads. I had been there before in my professional life, and now I was there in my personal journey.

I decided to have a garage sale and get rid of all the excess. I put an ad in the local newspaper, and my staff and I began preparing for the few hundred people we hoped would show up. By the time we'd finished organizing the sale, we had ticketed over four thousand items! I rented a tent for the items I cared most about, just in case of a sudden rainstorm.

I woke up at five a.m. on the morning of the sale. When I went outside, I was shocked to see that hundreds of people were already at the gate, and there was a line of cars that stretched for as far as I could see! We were not prepared for this! Hundreds more cars continued to arrive every hour and they kept right on coming. We had to open the gates and let them park in the fields next to the horses and buffalo. I panicked and called Roach, who sent ten security guards to help manage the crowds.

I stayed inside with a walkie-talkie so that I could communicate with people if they wanted more information about an item, or when a fan wanted to bargain about a price. In some ways, the whole thing was a revival for me. The more things I sold, the freer I felt.

It was quite a crowd. A Wynonna impersonator showed up and bought ten pairs of my shoes. A lesbian couple bought my bed. (I autographed it.) Two women got into a fight over one of my Harley outfits. I ended up inviting people into the house, where they could look at more racks of clothing and shoes. We were sold out of everything in two days. People came from as far away as Canada! I don't even know how they heard about it! It had turned into a Fan Fair–type event with over five thousand people attending, so big that *USA Today* even did a story about it. It went on long after the actual sale, too. Later, people told me they'd sold some of the things they bought on eBay. I autographed items for months at my shows.

Once I shed all the excess baggage, the children and I moved to a nearby rental house that my farm manager, Bill, learned about. It sat on top of a hill out in the wilderness, with few neighbors. I named our new place Faith Hill, because it was faith that was keeping me from giving up.

It took a while to get used to the change. I developed insomnia and found myself wandering around the house at night. I was used to living in the country, but the rental house was so far back in the woods—and nighttime seemed so much darker and more isolated than where we had lived before. I would look out the windows at the inky blackness each night, and be reminded of just how dark life can get.

It seems to me that there are three groups of people. There are the ones going into the wilderness, the ones *in* the wilderness, and the ones coming out of the wilderness. I was definitely "going in." I clocked in hours with the therapist, fighting the depression and anxiety attacks. I felt exhausted and overwhelmed most of the time. I would go for four or five days in a row with only three or four hours of sleep (and I require at least eight hours for my brain to fully operate). I felt like I was once again at the top of the bottom. I felt a great deal of guilt over having had a failed marriage. I had such swings of emotion! Each day I would thank God for Elijah and Grace, the two greatest miracles that have ever happened in my life. Then, I would curse the devil—"Get thee behind me, Satan, and don't push!"

The children and I got very close during this time. Elijah was five and Grace was three when the divorce was final. At night the three of us would pile into bed together and sing songs and tell stories. I remember some of those nights when it was so cold and dark outside, so quiet. Grace would lay on my right and Elijah on my left. We held each other until we fell asleep. I couldn't get enough of their sweetness! Some nights we would jump up and down on the beds and then the next morning we would go out and play in the woods. I became a child again myself.

My biggest mistake as a newly single mother was that I operated a lot out of guilt. I was often tired and depressed, and I had a hard time saying no. Out of exasperation I gave in to their every request. In some way, I was trying to make up for the fact that I believed I caused all that was happening to us. Because my own hours were inconsistent on the road, I had a hard time keeping the children on a schedule. Children need consistency, stability. I guess it took me almost a year to start to learn to time manage. When you don't say no to your children, giving in to all their whims, they don't feel safe. Without boundaries, children live in fear of never knowing where they can and cannot go. Even if they push them, boundaries are absolutely a necessary part of parenting. You either say no now or suffer the consequences later.

Being a child of divorce, I *did* understand how important it was during such an uncertain time to give Elijah and Grace a solid foundation. Regardless of *what,* I wanted them to both understand who they ultimately belonged to. I wanted them to know that although they had earthly parents, their truest identities were in being children of God. With that in mind, I enrolled them in a faith-based preschool.

Like so many single working mothers, I tried to be Wonder Woman! I would be in the recording studio until late, then come home and try to get a few hours' sleep before waking the children at six thirty. Then—chaos! I would make breakfast, pack their snack bags and try to dress them in clothes that matched with their socks and shoes. (Yeah, *right*!) Then I would drive them to school singing Bible songs the whole way, trying to get them there in time to park and walk them into the school with all the other mothers and their children. I wanted to fit in so badly! I tried so hard to be what I thought was good and right.

I wanted people to know who I was as Grace and Elijah's mother, not the tabloid headline in the grocery store checkout line. In just the years since I had gone solo, those headlines had included my unwed pregnancies, weight gain, the thirty-year lie about my biological father—and now my contentious divorce. It was going to be difficult!

As it turned out, the thing that separated me most from the other mothers bringing their children to preschool was my wardrobe. I usually wore pajamas underneath my coat. I remember Elijah pleading with me one morning in the parking lot.

"Mommy, please don't come inside with us."

"What's the matter, babe?" I asked.

"It embarrasses me when you wear those slippers," he answered.

In the rush of trying to be on time, I had forgotten to put on my shoes! But hey, I remembered the snacks! God bless all single parents. Hang in there and don't give up!

One morning when I got to the school, one of Grace's teachers took me aside.

"I understand that you let your daughter listen to Britney Spears," he said.

"Well, I know Britney personally," I said. "I don't always agree with what she says, but I support who she is—a child of God."

"All right," he said. But I could see the disapproval in his eyes.

"I love the fact that this is a Christian school," I explained. "I sing about the Lord, and I am a spiritual person. I will continue to praise and worship through what I do and who I am. But I live in the secular world. My daughter will be exposed to many kinds of music."

"Well, we're concerned about influences," the teacher said.

I tried to be polite about it. "My job continues to be to guide Grace and Elijah, and to do so with real words about real people in the real world. I don't want them to be so naive and uninformed that they can't cope when they get out in the world." Then I added, with a smile, "Besides, in six months Grace will move on to someone else's music, like you and I did."

I'm not sure that my message got through.

Then, right before Elijah's kindergarten "graduation," he came home and told me he didn't want to go to school the next day. When I asked him why, he said, "The teacher says we're going to practice the graduation procession until our feet bleed."

I was livid! *It isn't healthy to get this riled up,* I thought. But I did. Man!

I spoke with the principal about it, and he said it was just the teacher's way of getting the students to work harder. I was outraged! I began to question this teacher and her ideas about discipline. More and more, I began to feel that we didn't fit in. And it made me think about the dynamics of the school. I had been looking for a structured situation, but I also wanted my children to feel joy and freedom while learning about the Lord. I wasn't looking for a correctional school. I realized that this school was too strict, and could end up breaking their spirits.

I then spoke with a woman who lived in my area, Karen Costello, who is a pioneer of the homeschooling movement and very involved in encouraging other parents to teach their children at home. I told her right away that I felt inadequate to homeschool. I had no college degree. I hadn't even been that great of a student myself. She quickly assured me that you don't have to have a Ph.D. to homeschool your children, just four hours a day to devote to it. "But be ready for some people to question what you're doing," Karen laughed. "They'll think you've joined some granola-eating hippie cult!"

She gave me a homeschooling manual that detailed the

teaching process, taking you through every step of setting up a program that fit your family best. The book also said that a parent's spiritual IQ was every bit as important to a child's development as was intellectual "book smarts." I was encouraged. I prayed about it.

What is important to remember if you are considering homeschooling is that lots of materials are available to guide you through. Nobody expects you to say, "Okay, kids. Now I'm your teacher." You get a curriculum that lays out what to do and when. It lays out what a child should know at certain ages. The materials give you the confidence you need.

I decided homeschooling sounded like the perfect solution. I could participate, but because of my schedule, I knew I needed to hire a teacher. I could give the four hours a day when I was in town, but if I had to be on a tour where the kids couldn't go along, I didn't want their schooling to suffer. The first person I hired for the homeschooling was a young woman who was working on her teaching degree. She had been teaching at a preschool, and so was perfect for the first years. Then, as they got older, I hired a "manny" to work with them. Both of the children responded to him right away, and they continue to thrive. Now I'm an established member of the rising tide of homeschoolers, and I am glad I chose this path.

It was the best thing that could have happened. I was looking for a place to belong. I needed some consistency in the kids' lives, and in my life! I needed something to throw myself into with all my power. I had given myself so completely to the marriage that I had to find a foothold and start coming back.

Even given my tight tour schedule, I found that in most cases, I could move the school along with me. When Grace was very little, I would give her baths in the bus' sink, and sing some of the school-related songs. If I went on a lengthy tour, the kids and books came along. I remember taking Grace to the recording studio with several pages of homework in language arts. I believe it helped both Elijah and Grace to be self-starters. And numerous field trips, some led by Mom or Ashley, taught them things that being in a classroom did not always do, like respect and manners, and compassion for people of all walks of life.

Some people question the concept of a four-hour homeschool day. Fact is, in public schools a great deal of time is spent just getting the children to and from classes. Teachers spend even more time with large classes trying to deal with so many distractions. Actual pencil to paper time ends up being about four to five hours a day as well.

The children and I enjoyed the freedom to travel and I was grateful that the road allowed us to learn so much about people from all walks of life. It was very important to me to show Grace and Elijah how other people live. They learned early a tolerance for all mankind. They don't just read about it in a book, they have witnessed it. They saw all of us together on the road—people from other races, religions and sexes—working together as a family and I believe the children don't see a separation, like some do. To them, differences between people are based on trust and spirit, not color or class or sexual orientation.

Another benefit I found to homeschooling was that Elijah and Grace continued through the years to remain close. The two of them didn't experience classroom separation by age or sex. In a public school, Elijah might have started snubbing his younger sister on the playground to be cool in front of his classmates. They're certainly not perfect, but because of homeschooling, I see a real difference in them. They're calmer and less consumed with peer pressure.

Though they have normal struggles when it comes to being siblings, I see them working together.

We start out each day with the Pledge of Allegiance, followed by Bible study. They learn about the Bible in a very simple and joyful way. There are no sermons. There are stories. They really are encouraged to think on their own. I ask a lot of questions. Grace and Elijah talk about the Bible like they talk about any subject in school. Teaching Elijah and Grace has allowed me to want to have more of a personal relationship with God again. It has allowed me to be renewed. By teaching them, I am reteaching myself. I discovered the Bible once again, and have found myself drawn to the Word. My children remind me constantly that I am loved. Too many times, people use religion in order to be *right*. But what Jesus taught is *love*. Children understand that.

It was vital to me also that my children be taught a great amount of creativity—painting, writing, and dramatics—in addition to subjects like math and science. And even those subjects can be approached creatively. Grace is such a free spirit that she would have felt crushed in a school that didn't support creativity. And Elijah has a high spirit, so much energy. He does better in class after I give him short breaks to allow him to release energy by listening to music, playing drums or going outside to jump on the trampoline.

When I was growing up, I often felt like a robot in school. Moving as much as we did, we learned that in too many places the state spent more money on roads than on schools! Ashley and I both went to many different schools. I found myself struggling to concentrate. I daydreamed a great deal, and felt so different from my classmates.

Many schools do promote individualism, but in some,

children learn to be mediocre, to do just enough to get by, to fit into the rest of the world like everyone else. Paying attention to a child's distinctive needs is so important, and there just isn't enough time for teachers to give individual attention.

Homeschooling has worked out beautifully for my children. They've developed and grown at their own pace. Grace is about a year ahead in several subjects. She's a math whiz. Elijah loves the logic and creative thinking involved in chess. They both love the fact that they get an immediate response to their work. I remember handing in papers and waiting days to receive my grade; my children get feedback while the assignment is still fresh in their minds. Homeschooling promotes their unique, authentic personalities. In some cases, I think it's the difference between surviving and thriving.

I also believe that it has been important that I teach the children the way that Mom taught Ashley and me. We were taught not to just exist, but to excel. "If you can't do it right, then don't do it at all," Mom would say. Also, Ashley and I were never compared to boys. Mom didn't teach us based on gender—she taught us based on spirit. It was about imagination and passion. There was no penis envy at our house! I still remember when I played Annie in *Annie Get Your Gun* in the eighth grade, singing at the top of my lungs, "Anything you can do, I can do better." We were taught to believe that! It was the Judd way to "do it better."

I continue to try and do it better by teaching Grace and Elijah that they are the hope of the world. They both know how to take care of themselves, that their precious bodies belong to no one but themselves. I try to answer each and every question that they have—whether it's about an art project or about sexuality—as openly and honestly as I can (sometimes trying hard not to laugh)! And every day, I tell them in some way or another that *the world is a better place because you're in it*!

I don't want to appear to be casting stones at the public education system, because there are many wonderful schools and wonderful teachers. In public schools, I learned how to deal with the real world. I learned how to survive in a tough environment. Homeschooling may not work for every family, but it was a godsend to ours. After four years we're still rocking and the children continue to be excited about receiving information. I've learned how important it is to recognize when they are motivated to learn more about a certain subject and to act quickly on that inspiration! And I've come to believe that one of the most important goals of education should be expanding horizons and promoting initiative. That's what our homeschool is all about. My kids are already deeply involved in their education.

During the years since the Farewell Tour, Mom had been taking very good care of herself. Her doctors said she was very fortunate to have had a strain of hepatitis that could be effectively treated. In fact, her health was so much better by the time the children were coming with me on the road that she started coming along, too. I knew she had missed performing, missed the lights, missed the fans and being on the road. So one day, when we were sitting together on a beach in Florida, I said, "How would you feel about doing a show with me to celebrate your healing?"

Before you could say *Judds reunion*, we were in rehearsals and Kmart had signed on as our Power to Change Tour sponsor. Ironically, Mom felt great, but I got very sick. I woke up delirious in the middle of the night with a

104.5-degree fever. I still don't know how I did it, but I somehow drove myself to the emergency room and was admitted to the hospital immediately. I told the nurse I couldn't spend the night because I had to rehearse the next day! The doctors reminded *me* that if I hadn't come in when I did, I might have died. It turned out to be a case of streptococcus bacteria similar to the strain that killed Jim Henson. Once we got past that initial scare, we were back going ahead full steam.

The record label got involved, and it was decided that Mom and I would record four new Judd songs to add to my upcoming Mercury Records CD, *New Day Dawning*. The show would feature those four songs, some old Judd material and my own songs that I would perform solo since we wanted people to know that we were definitely continuing to pursue our separate careers. We planned to keep the tour short-term.

NOT!

Like the Farewell Tour before it, the Power to Change Tour kept on going and going and going!

We officially kicked off the tour with a New Year's Eve Millennium Concert in Phoenix. Mom and I called a press conference to announce the exciting news. When one reporter asked us why we were doing the tour, Mom said:

"Because I'm not dead and Wy's not pregnant."

I gave her that *Do I know you?* look. Some things had not changed.

I had truly believed that on this tour I would not feel obligated to live up to anyone's expectations but my own. I thought that enough time had gone by that when Mom and I performed together again, things would be different. After all, it was eight solo years and nine million CDs after that final show in our Farewell Tour. And this time we were traveling in separate buses. But from the beginning, I was torn between setting boundaries and putting my ego aside to allow Mom to celebrate being back. It was a *real* test for me. Mom immediately walked in and I felt her desire to be in charge. I learned to physically take a step back to give myself space when I needed it!

I would often complain to Roach, telling him my frustrations. I would cry and say, "I don't think I can do this." (And there were days when I didn't think I could!)

"Sure you can," he would say. Roach believed in us, and he was one of the most optimistic people on the entire tour. He kept me from blowing my cool so many times. He was the calm before, during *and* after the storm.

Mom is a bulldog when it comes to doing things the way she considers best. On the one hand, I love her for it. There is no one who is a better team leader or better at getting things done. But Mom and I had different ideas and different ways of communicating them. When Mom wanted to tell me something, she would send her personal assistant to my bus with a message. One time she was very concerned about my being late because the show had a curfew and we would be charged a thousand dollars for every minute the show ran too long. Mom reminded me several times throughout the day, as if she was telling me something I didn't know.

"Mom, I *hear* ya!" I said, with each reminder. It was starting to feel like I was eighteen years old again.

Then, just to make sure I got the point, when it was nearing showtime, she got on the production manager's walkie-talkie and said to the entire crew:

"Wynonna, remember—we can't run over tonight. If we do we'll be charged a thousand dollars for every minute we run over. We have a curfew tonight. Be on time!"

I couldn't believe it! I sat on my bus, fuming. From the beginning of our tour, I had decided that we couldn't go back to our old ways of fighting and yelling at each other. Mom and I had been through so much together. Now I wanted things to be more constructive. Not only was everyone watching, but people on this tour were depending on us.

So after Mom's announcement, I stepped off my bus with Roach and walked to the backstage area. I pulled Mom and her assistant over to our quick-change area and proceeded to set a boundary.

"Mom," I said, trying to be polite but firm, "that didn't work for me. I need for you to not discuss our issues in front of the tour personnel. When you do, you embarrass me. And secondly, if you have something to tell me personally, I would prefer if you would do it instead of having your assistant give me messages."

The whole time I was talking to her, Mom just stared at me, showing absolutely no emotion. Mom's assistant gave me a go-to-hell look. I was trying to be proactive, but I still felt like an idiot. I guess better late than never. I left the two of them standing there. Later, as we were walking to the stage, Mom hurled a water bottle as hard as she could at one of our equipment trucks. Then, without missing a beat, she took her microphone and the two of us stepped out onstage holding hands and began singing "Love Can Build a Bridge" in front of fifteen thousand people.

Later on in the tour, Mom went to Roach to complain about me. "Wynonna's getting a little arrogant," she said. "I think she's forgetting about me during the show."

That's when I realized that we both felt like we had to dance around each other onstage. A big tour can do that to you—make you paranoid. You start letting nitpicky things bother you. I think both Mom and I were getting tired. The shows were two hours long and we were doing large meet & greets every night. It was like having a wedding and a reception every single day. I was trying to honor the Judd music, as well as celebrate my new CD, and it was a tough place to live. I didn't want to lose myself in the tour and I didn't want to abandon Mom and what she had hoped for. It was a continuing struggle.

But despite any conflicts, the Reunion Tour changed my life because toward the end of it Mom introduced me to Mona Lisa Shulz. Mona Lisa is an M.D., a Ph.D., a neuropsychiatrist, neuroscientist and a medical intuitive. Her books include *Awakening Intuition* and *The New Feminine Brain*. You may have seen her on PBS, *Oprah* or the Discovery channel. Mona Lisa is the doctor who changed my life. She prescribed the first medications I had ever taken for depression or ADD. I had put off taking anything, thinking I was too strong and that I didn't need help. I could do it on my own. It's been some years now, but I have my depression and ADD under control (I can still be sassy and creative, though). It has accentuated the positive and eliminated the negative.

Mona Lisa helped what I call "rewire my brain." Once I got on medication, instead of trying to process hundreds of thoughts running around in my brain, I can now concentrate on a few. I can now do an interview and not cut the other person off before they complete a sentence. I was able to write this book. I would not have been able to do that before taking the medication. I process quickly. But I'm able to slow down and enjoy myself. Mona Lisa was the first person to ever truly understand me and help me see that I wasn't lazy or uninterested in other people or incapable of achieving success in business. I just didn't have the ability to sit still long enough to focus and to pay attention. She told me that I was gifted, unique—and sane. We should all be so lucky to have someone tell us those things!

Mona Lisa continues to teach me how to prepare and organize my activities so that I can get to where I am going, show up on time (still waiting on this one) and not have anxiety attacks by keeping myself calm and taking the time I need to prepare. It has changed my life personally and professionally.

I don't know what advice Mom thought Mona Lisa would give me, but after seeing the chaos and pain I was living through, she said, "I don't know how you've continued to thrive!"

For me to hear that validation from a top professional was life-affirming.

9

NO ONE ELSE ON EARTH

As the years went by, D.R. Roach and I developed the ideal working relationship. I had complete trust in him, felt safe with him and genuinely liked him as a person. But at the end of each tour, when we came in off the road, we went our separate ways. It would be a long time before I knew much about his personal life. All I knew was that, like so many security guys, he worked hard and played hard. He was a partying bachelor who loved a good time.

Roach was always the "go-to" guy on the tour. People knew if something needed doing, he was the guy who would see that it happened. He was also highly protective of my children and me, on both a professional and personal level: whereas a lot of tour managers, when their boss is criticized, will respond with something like, *"Yeah, well, you know how artists are,"* Roach was not like that. He always came to my defense. His answer would be along the lines of *"Well, she's really trying"* or *"She's working really hard right now."* You need those people in your life—people who care about you and protect you, people who know your heart. Roach understood how hard I was trying and always gave me the benefit of the doubt.

In time I learned about Roach's personal life, and started worrying when he was in bad relationships. Roach was such a great person and I thought that he deserved a great girlfriend! But he made some bad choices. Sometimes when he got on the bus I could see he was depressed. I would listen to his story, and try to give him advice. (Talk about the blind leading the blind!) He even asked me to talk to his girlfriend at one point. I did, and it was obvious that the two of them were in trouble. Roach was miserable, but he worked overtime trying to make her happy. He thought a lot of their problems were his fault. It's unusual for a guy to stay so concerned about what he could do to fix a relationship, and he stayed torn up about it most of the time. I would ask him, "What the heck do you think you're doing?"

But he would still go on and on about what he was going to do so that his girlfriend wouldn't be mad at him. Some might have thought he was a wimp, but I knew it wasn't that—it was because his sense of loyalty and dedication was so fierce. He didn't give up, and it cost him dearly.

On August 1, 2000, I went to Los Angeles to visit a dying friend, the Academy of Country Music's legendary Gene Weed. He only had a few days to live. As my road manager/bodyguard, Roach often accompanied me on personal trips as well as professional, and on this day he drove me to Gene's house. It was a spiritual day, the room filled with light and angels. I watched Roach with Gene that afternoon and was touched.

I had always known Roach as a professional guy in a suit, doing his job. And although we were close on the road, working side by side in many different situations, I had never been with him in such a spiritually intimate setting. I was used to seeing Roach walk into a roomful of people and take charge. No one is better at making people laugh or feel special at a meet & greet! Roach has a boyish charm; he can tell you to go to hell and you'll thank him for the directions. I've watched him for thirteen years now. It's a show before the show, and Roach is the star!

Roach and I had been on the road all those years and not once had I ever thought of our working relationship as anything but platonic. Our relationship was asexual. The way I felt about our bond was that it was the truest of all relationships. We showed up and gave 100 percent of our hearts and souls to the cause. What we did together was above and beyond us.

That day, as I stood there watching Roach be so real, so authentic with Gene, I realized that after all that time I was meeting the spiritual D. R. Roach for the first time. I fell instantly and completely in love. I had long *loved* Roach, but this was different. I was falling *in love*. I guess I felt an immediate need to share this feeling, because I called my dear friend Vickie Hampton, who sings with me, after we left Gene's house.

"Where are you?" she asked.

"California," I said. "Roach and I came out to say good-bye to Gene. He's crossing over any day now."

"I'm sorry," Vickie said.

I explained that Gene was peaceful, and that I knew he was in God's hands. We talked a few minutes about what a good man Gene was, and how much he had done for both country music and for the people within the industry. Visiting with Gene had been both sad and hopeful. I was sad for myself and for the others who loved him; we wouldn't have him much longer. But the visit had also left me with a renewed knowledge of just how awesome life is and why we need to live every moment to the fullest.

"Where's Roachie?" Vickie finally asked.

"He's sitting right here next to me," I said. "Right where he's always been."

"That's right," Roach called out.

"We're calling to tell you we love you, Vickie," I said, then looking at Roach, added, "We're professing our love to each other, too."

Roach just smiled at me.

I had made reservations for dinner at one of my favorite places in Malibu, where we planned to celebrate Kerry's birthday. Roach drove and we stopped along the way to take some group pictures. We were like teenagers on spring break.

The sun was setting over the Pacific when we arrived at Geoffrey's, and a glow settled over us. It was magical. I remember that Roach was wearing a cable-knit sweater, the richest shade of blue that I had ever seen. I looked at him with his tan in that manly blue sweater, and thought, *This man looks so good.* It was like I was staring at a man I had just met. I continued to stare at him while we sat in the bar, waiting for our table. We were all sitting so close together that I could smell Roach's cologne. Something was happening.

When they seated us, it was at a table that overlooked the ocean. It couldn't have been more romantic! I couldn't stop thinking about these new feelings throughout dinner. The funny thing was, Kerry had no clue. She was busy celebrating her birthday, and I was celebrating Roach. I ordered crème brûlée for dessert, which is odd in itself, because I'm not usually a crème brûlée–type person. It was sweet and warm. I took another bite, tapped Roach on the shoulder, and when he turned his face toward me, I leaned over and kissed him. The look on his face!

"Do it again," he said, barely missing a beat.

And so I kissed him again. Thinking back on that moment, I realize what a chance I was taking after eight years of friendship. Later, Roach told me that he had gone back and forth over the years. There were times when he felt platonic about me, and other times when he thought he would like to have a romantic relationship. But he never would have initiated it.

Kerry thought we were joking around until that second kiss lasted, and lasted. When she finally figured out that this was real, she squealed!

"This is too weird!" she gasped, like seeing a sister and brother kissing. The three of us left the restaurant and drove along the Pacific coast on our way back to the hotel. We parked the car to take a walk on the beach, and ended up going swimming in the ocean for hours. After that, we drove through a Carl's Jr. (home of the world-famous bacon cheeseburger) and arrived at the hotel around four a.m. Roach and I fell asleep together in my room just as the sun was rising. A few hours later, the phone rang.

"Hi! It's me," Mom chirped. "Guess what! I'm in the very next room, and I'm coming over."

Unbelievable! We were in Los Angeles! Mom had said *nothing* about coming to California!

"Well, could you wait a few minutes?" I said. "Kerry and Roach are here and we're eating."

Then I frantically phoned Kerry, who ran over in her bathrobe to make it seem normal. When Mom and Pop knocked on the door, the three of us were sitting around like we had just finished breakfast. We tried to be casual, but I had the feeling Mom was checking us out. She came over and hugged me. Then she looked right at me and said:

"What's going on? You all look different."

You can't get much past Naomi Judd. Of course, Mom now says she knew all along that Roach and I would fall in love. She adores him, so in her terms, it couldn't have worked out any better.

We waited almost four months before we let people in the organization know what was going on because we wanted to enjoy our secret romance. Roach made an extra effort to be very professional in front of others.

"Yes, Ms. Judd. No, Ms. Judd," he would say.

We would walk to the stage together as we always do, with me in the front and Roach following close behind. I would get backstage, and when the house lights went out, he would pinch me on the butt just before I walked on-stage. We were madly, passionately in love.

When we finally did let everyone in on our secret, Roach went the extra mile to be humble, kind and gener-ous. He tried very hard to assure people that his job re-mained the same, and that they could still treat him as they had—like one of the guys. He wasn't an extension of me. He didn't want people thinking that he had changed. It didn't matter, though. It got sideways for a while, and there was some resentment.

Guys said, "I guess before long you'll be tryin' to run the show."

The people at his company, Rock Solid, were merciless, because they think it's a cardinal sin to date your client. Even guys who had been very close to Roach for a long time gave him a hard time. His best friend of twenty years said, "Come *on*, you're not messing around with the boss!" I know it was sometimes hard on Roach. That's not an easy position to be in, when people you've known for years start treating you differently. But he marched through it.

It was important to both of us to maintain our profes-sional integrity, to keep our personal and professional lives separate. We wanted people to know that when we came to work we were the same people as before. At home, it was different. When we first began the new relationship, Roach said:

"When it comes to work, you are still the boss. You have the say-so. When it comes to love, we're partners, and I do have a say-so."

All right, Mr. Roach—come on with your bad self! I loved his attitude!

There is a reason that when Charles Dickens began *A Tale of Two Cities* with "It was the best of times, it was the worst of times," the line became one of the most quoted in literary history. It contains a universal truth found in so many life situations. It certainly has seemed to me that in my life the very good and the very bad have often come in rapid succession.

I was sitting at home in my office on Thursday, August 10, 2000, when Kerry called me on the telephone sounding upset.

"I don't know how to tell you this, Wy," she said, taking a deep breath.

"What's the matter?" I asked.

"Your biological father died. Charlie Jordan is dead. I just received a telephone call from *Star* magazine and they wanted to know if you had any comment."

The first thing that flashed into my mind was that it must be a lie. The people who write for this *use-the-page-for-the-bottom-of-the-cat-litter-box* are always spreading rumors. A feeling of relief washed over me. Of course it was a lie!

"Kerry, this is crap! I don't believe them."

"I'm so sorry, Wy," she said softly. "We've checked out the facts. Charlie did die this morning."

I couldn't even cry. I hadn't cried when Ashley told me that Michael Ciminella was not my biological father. And I couldn't cry now, hearing that the man who *was*, Charlie Jordan, had died. I found myself very short of breath.

"The funeral is in two days," Kerry said. "I'll call and give you the details as I receive more information."

I hung up without even saying goodbye. I didn't think I could speak.

I sat there in my office for a long time, staring out the window, trying to think what to do next. When I thought about the funeral, I felt hopeless. I tried to think it through.

I can't just show up at my father's funeral and introduce myself to a family I've never met. I can't show up at my first family reunion like that. What could I say—that I put off going to see my father because I was too afraid that I might be rejected? That I was afraid he had never ever contacted me because he didn't want anything to do with me?

Then I realized that the first time I ever saw a picture of my biological father was in the *Star*. Now it was the *Star* that had called to tell me that he had died. What a tragic way to begin and end a relationship, one that never was to be.

I had put off contacting Charlie when I first learned the truth, back in 1994, until I felt strong enough to do it. This year, I had finally thought about trying to contact him possibly in September when I came off the road. But I had put off meeting him too long.

I decided not to attend his funeral service because I knew the tabloids would turn it into a circus. I didn't want his family to think coming to the funeral was about me in any way. His funeral should be about *him*.

Not long after Charlie's death, I prayed for something healing to happen. I needed to know what to do next about this sad situation, and didn't know how I could ever move forward. I received the answer to that prayer one morning at the Nashville airport.

In all the years that we've worked together, Roach has never forgotten his briefcase. But on this morning, he left it at his condo and had to run back to get it. I stayed at the curbside checkout counter to wait.

It was about seven thirty a.m. I was sleepy. (I'm not a good morning traveler.) But I love people-watching, so I sat outside the terminal, smiling at people as they went in and out the automatic doors. I must have looked like the official Nashville International Airport greeter. A few minutes after I sat down, a young woman came walking toward me smiling as if we knew each other. I reached into my purse to pull out an eight-by-ten picture and an autograph pen.

Mom taught me to be prepared to sign an autograph at any time, so I'm usually prepared for anything. My philosophy has always been, once I leave the front door of my house, I'm open for business! I was not, however, prepared for this. She didn't ask for an autograph—and what she did say completely blew me away.

"I'm Charlie Jordan's brother's daughter," she said. "We're cousins."

I couldn't speak. I thought, *Okay, God—I know I talk onstage about how you're always on time, never early and never late. But this might be too early.*

Finally I stammered, "Oh, my God!"

She laughed. I hugged her. It felt a little awkward, but it also felt right somehow.

"Well, hello, cousin," I said.

"Hello, cousin," she said with a bright smile. "I was supposed to come here later today and pick something up. Then I decided to go ahead and come early and get it done! By the way, my name is Melanie. I know who you are!"

"I'm glad you're here—I'm glad we're here!" I said. "I'm glad you came early. This was meant to be—the answer to a prayer. I've been wondering how to move forward with all that has happened. You are the answer."

Melanie reassured me. "We've all been wondering when you were going to contact us. We want to welcome you into our family and want you to know that Charlie was proud of you."

Then, for the first time, I cried. Tears streamed down my cheeks. For a moment I wondered if it made Melanie feel uncomfortable. But I realized that finally, after all these years, I was starting to feel what I was supposed to feel. This felt right. This moment felt authentic. There were no more secrets, no more lies. What was happening was real—it was true.

Not long after the miracle at the airport, I ended up meeting my uncle William—Melanie's father, Charlie's brother. I saw pictures of my father as a baby. I saw him as a young boy, a teenager, and the way he looked right before he died. I found out that I have a brother! His name is Michael. He has two children, so I'm an aunt. It was almost too much to take in at once. Waves of sadness, fear and joy came one right after the other.

William gave me the lantern Charlie used when he worked on the railroad. My father was a railroad man. William said my father was never quite the same after he broke both wrists and had to retire. He lived alone. He was a quiet, shy man. He was simple. I liked that. After his death, his family found that he had kept a desk drawer filled with clippings of my career. It was then that I knew that my biological father was proud of me. He cared about what I was doing. I'll never get over the fact that I won't ever have the opportunity to look in his eyes and thank him.

10

HEAVEN HELP MY HEART

Ironically, after suffering this great loss, I entered into some of the most creative and productive years of my career. I coproduced my new CD. I began writing and performing in television and film and, all the while, played a solid tour schedule. My professional life was full. With Roach in my life, my personal life was wonderful. But while I was taking care of business, I was neglecting my health. It was only a matter of time. . . .

In 2003 I was the first country artist ever asked to serve as Grand Marshal of the Indianapolis 500. I was so honored! I had a red, white and blue fringed denim and leather jacket custom made and was so confident and full of myself as I rode down the street in the parade. My makeup was perfect, my hair sparkling. I felt great. I turned and waved first to one side of the street and then to the other. People ran up to my float to get photos. It was so all-American. So perfect for someone who *loves* a parade!

Suddenly, a guy who stood on the sidewalk swilling beer called out to me, almost as if it was in slow motion:

"Hey, Wynonna!"

I turned to him, smiled and waved.

"You need to lose some weight!" he shouted.

"Haw, haw, haw," his buddy added.

I was humiliated. I quickly turned to the crowds on the other side of the street. Weight had *always* been a concern of mine. I had had a manager make pointed comments. My weight had been reported in the tabloids time and again. But it had never been thrown directly and personally in my face in such an unkind manner. Nothing like that had ever happened to me in my twenty-year career. Despite my professional success, personally I felt like a complete failure.

Something was obviously wrong. Just *how* wrong was soon brought home loud and clear, moving from insult to injury.

I was in the middle of recording my sixth solo CD, *What the World Needs Now Is Love,* when Disney asked me to record Elvis' song "Burnin' Love" for their upcoming animated feature *Lilo & Stitch*, and I was ecstatic! Little did I know that one of my biggest thrills would be accompanied by one of my biggest scares.

Roach, the children and I were right in the middle of watching a screening of the movie at Disney World, when my cell phone rang. I stepped out in the hall to take the phone call.

"Are you somewhere that you can talk?" my doctor asked as soon as I answered the phone.

"Yes," I replied.

"Your cholesterol and triglyceride levels are dangerously high," the doctor said.

"What?" I asked.

"You should be in the hospital right now. You're considered to be high risk."

"That's impossible," I said. "I've got a press conference tomorrow with people from all over the world—Japan, Singapore, Thailand. I'm doing seventy-five countries in eight hours!"

"I'm concerned about a heart attack, Wynonna," the doctor said firmly.

"Well, I can't have a heart attack," I said. "I've got to fly to Los Angeles for the *Lilo and Stitch* premiere in a few days."

"I'm concerned about *you*, not press conferences and premieres."

Despite the warning, I continued with the promotional tour. I felt like a walking time bomb, waiting to go off at any minute. *This cannot be happening to me now,* I said to myself. *I'm only thirty-eight years old. I'm too young.*

I knew I was carrying too much weight. I knew that my lifestyle was stressful. But stress comes with any job. When much is given, much is required. I had no complaints. I had chosen this career and the pressures that went with it. But I felt, too, that there were many women and men out there in the world with much bigger problems than mine. There are many people struggling with careers and families who don't have the choices I have. I saw my mother struggle for years.

You can handle it, I kept telling myself. *This is just a bump in the road. Suck it up and deal with it!* Over and over, I told myself that I could fix things—that I was a Judd, my mother's daughter. I continued on with this same conversation that I've had with myself a million times before. Then it occurred to me: *Wynonna, you cannot disregard the numbers.* Those numbers kept ringing in my head. It's obvious to me now that I had been in denial about my health for quite some time. The numbers were reality. No matter how much I told myself that I could handle, no matter how much I told myself that I could do, the numbers didn't lie.

So what was I going to do about it? It came to me in a flash, in a moment of truth. Stop the madness! It's your decision—life or death. I decided to choose life. I reached out to some people who cared about me and asked for some time in dealing with this. Different people offered different strategies about my health. I didn't like any of them. One thing that kept coming up is places you can go where professionals and support groups surround you and help you work through your addiction.

I noticed, though, that the more I talked about doing something, the more irritable I became. I kept saying that I didn't have thirty days to go away like that. I couldn't leave my family or my work for that long. I said it wasn't an option.

By the time I arrived in Los Angeles for the premiere of *Lilo & Stitch*, I was a wreck. I walked the red carpet, smiling and waving. It was like that commercial where the actress is walking the red carpet, looking beautiful. Then they flash her cholesterol numbers up on the screen and she collapses. I agonized about what to do. I wanted to be well, but I wanted drive-through service, a quick fix.

I panicked, and decided I wanted gastric-bypass surgery. I will never criticize those who opt for surgery, because I understand that for some it is a last resort. To them I say, *Do what is right for you. Take care of yourself.*

For me it was a rash decision. Willing to do anything, I went so far as to book the surgery.

Sitting there in my hotel room in Los Angeles and using a false name, I got on the phone and started asking questions about the operation. The nurse I spoke with started telling me what a long, involved process it was. She explained that I would have to undergo therapy to emotionally prepare me for the changes in my body. She said I would have to learn to eat all over again. She wanted to know about my insurance. I told her I would pay cash. I didn't want anyone finding out. I felt ashamed, like I was doing something illegal. But I was so afraid of dying.

After learning that I could pay cash, the nurse told me I could have the surgery done right away. They could schedule it in two weeks. If you had cash you could be slipped in under the radar.

I decided to stay in Los Angeles and have the procedure as soon as possible. In the middle of it all, I called my counselor in Nashville, the one who had been there with Mom and me for years. She was against making a decision like that so quickly.

"Wynonna!" she said. "You are making a decision out of fear. Let's take a deep breath and talk about this! There are other options."

But they aren't fast enough for me, I thought.

After our talk I went back and forth with the decision, crying, uncertain. I was afraid that I was going to have a heart attack. I was afraid of the surgery. And it finally came to me that my counselor was right—everything I was doing right then was based on fear. I wasn't making rational decisions. My doctor had wanted me to go in the hospital and try to get the numbers back down. I knew what he would say about undergoing surgery before even trying to handle the problem in another way.

Roach was freaked by the prospect of the surgery, but he knows me well. He knew that in the end, a decision like that would be mine and no one else's. By day I convinced myself that I was making the right choice. But my nights were filled with bad dreams, nightmares about dying. Before too long it occurred to me that my subconscious was trying to warn me that I might be making the wrong decision. The closer I got to the date of the surgery, the more frantic I felt. I kept myself distracted by making a lot of phone calls and engaging with my family and friends. I often get involved in other people's lives when I don't want to deal with the problems in mine. But before long I found myself really sad, more so than I had ever been in my life.

A few days before I was scheduled to have the surgery I woke up and couldn't stop weeping. No matter how I tried to get on with my day, or to tell myself that everything was all right, I couldn't focus on anything but the surgery. How had I become so desperate?

Finally I said the words out loud: *I can't do this. I am making a terrible mistake!*

There had to be a more organic way to heal my life. Somehow I knew that if I had the surgery I was clever enough to find a way to eat more. I knew in the deepest part of my heart that the bypass surgery was not the answer. For me it would have been like putting a Band-Aid over a gaping wound.

But if surgery wasn't right, what was? I needed more answers.

Looking back on it now, it reminds me of one of my favorite stories:

A man is sitting on the rooftop of his house, which has floated into the river during a flood. Convinced that God is going to save him, he waits. A guy comes by in a rowboat and offers to help him.

"Hop into my boat," the man yells. "You'll be saved."

"No, thank you. God is going to save me," the fellow on the rooftop says. So the fellow in the boat heads on down the river.

Hours later another man in an even bigger boat comes by.

"Sir, I'll pull close enough to the house so you can jump into my boat. You'll be saved!"

"No, thank you. God is going to save me," the fellow on

COMING HOME TO MYSELF · 203

the rooftop answers. So the man takes his boat and cruises on down the river.

Finally a helicopter flies low over the man and calls to him over a loudspeaker.

"I'll lower the ladder down to you. You'll be saved!"

"No, thank you. God is going to save me," the fellow on the rooftop shouts back.

Not long after that, the house under him collapses and the guy drowns. When he gets to heaven, he meets God. Sobbing, he asks:

"God, why didn't you save me? I waited and waited! I thought you would save me!"

And the Lord said, "My dear child, I sent two boats and a helicopter."

It was after my health scare that I both made the call to my manager, telling her that I had hit a wall, and that I first met with Oprah. Roach and I were planning to get married on November 22, 2003. Oprah's staff had been in contact with us about the possibility of filming the Judd/Roach celebration. When Kerry called Julie Colbert, my agent at William Morris, to talk about Oprah and the wedding, she mentioned that I had hit a wall, and was going to take some time off. And then, during a girl-to-girl talk between my agent and one of Oprah's producers, they talked about my intense struggle in trying to balance career and self. It's a universal theme. Not long after that, Oprah called me personally and asked me to come to Chicago for a visit in October.

When I initially went to see Oprah, it was for personal reasons, not about being on her television show. I was not promoting a CD or a project. I was searching for some answers in my personal life. It was about me visiting her woman to woman. She is one of my (s)heros, both personally and professionally, and I felt like this woman coming into my life on a personal level was a miracle.

I went because I have such faith and trust in Oprah. I was in hopes of receiving inspiration from a woman who had walked the walk. I was looking forward to hearing her words of wisdom. It occurred to me that since she had been to hell and back in her own journey to health, she could give me insight about where I was going in mine. She was on the other side of her struggle with weight and food.

When we arrived on October 29, 2003, we were escorted into Oprah's personal office at Harpo Studios, and as people filed in behind us, I started to understand that this was not going to be as personal as I had naively envisioned. My heart started beating really fast when I saw Bob Greene and several people from Oprah's production staff. *So this is a typical day for Oprah,* I thought.

When Oprah walked in, it hit me. *This is the Queen of daytime television!* She's a powerful woman running a billion-dollar business. I tend to think of her as a woman who cares about people and who just happens to have a television show. She's from Nashville and I have known her since the eighties. So even though we were not close friends, I have always felt a personal connection.

Oprah talked with Roach and me for a minute or so and then asked if it was okay to film the meeting.

"Can we put a mike on you?" one of the production guys asked me.

It had all happened so quickly that I know I must have looked like this was the first time I had ever been to the city. Ugh! Then, of course, I realized I should just go with the flow. Bob Greene spoke about his work with Oprah. He said that addressing overeating is long-term, and can't be entered into lightly. It's important to have the commitment and see it through. The first thing one must do, Bob said, was to change the metabolism. That meant working out and not eating for several hours before bedtime. He also said that only five percent of the people who try to lose weight and keep it off actually do it. Only five percent!

Oh, I'm so glad I came, I thought. *Tell me more great news, Bob!*

That first meeting was tough. I was so nervous. I felt self-conscious. And at the time I didn't feel like one of the five percent who would ever make it. I felt like one of the ninety-five percent who wouldn't.

After the meeting in Oprah's office, we adjourned to the conference room. It was there that they asked me about going on the show and sharing my story with others. They all felt that I was someone that many people could relate to. I hesitated. I thought, I'm just a soap opera waiting to go into production. Am I willing to sit in front of a mass audience and talk about my failures? I had worked so hard for twenty years to overcome my weaknesses, to be a champion. It was not the Judd way to complain on national television. I was taught to be strong, to be grateful for everything. But at night I would lay in bed and hear the words *keep it real.* I thought about what I was teaching my children. What example was I setting for them?

I leaned toward declining Oprah's invitation because I realized what a huge commitment it was. I thought it might be a better idea to face my burden privately. It was a personal matter. In the end, it was my heart that made the decision. My career and my personal life *are* connected. My music comes from the heart, and my fans have always meant a lot to me. Starting out when I was eighteen, I felt I was raised with these people, and maybe I could help someone by helping myself. That would be a bonus.

Yes, I thought. *I have made my decision.* I called Kerry.

"I'm going to do Oprah's show," I said.

"What made you decide?" she asked.

"This is a *try-to-be-perfect* world," I said. "But perfect is not real. Life is hard for most people, and I want to admit that I'm struggling to keep it together, too."

The very *instant* I hung up, I started to have more doubts! It was too much! I think now I have a little understanding of how gay people must feel when they make the decision to come out. I felt a little like I was getting ready for surgery. I was apprehensive about the process—unfamiliar surroundings, anesthesia, the surgery itself. And I was anxious about the outcome—would I be better for having done it? The world is so jaded. Would people think of me as a victim, or a victor?

It was a paradoxical time. I felt that taking my journey in public could be a tremendously positive step, or it could be a complete disaster. As a performer, I like to have information about the shows up front—everything from sound and lighting to hair and makeup. I don't want any surprises, no chance of a last-minute mess. It doesn't always happen that way, but it's what performers strive for. But I would have little control over this appearance. This wasn't my show.

As it turned out, there was a big surprise. Less than two weeks prior to my wedding, I ended up splattered all over the headlines. And this time it was not just the tabloids. It started innocently, when Roach and I took a dear friend to dinner to celebrate her birthday at a Nashville restaurant. The three of us laughed and talked. We ordered some wine. After dinner, Roach got tired and decided to go on home. I had been tired when I arrived at the dinner, having been at a business meeting at my office. But by the time we finished eating, my energy was back. I stayed at the restaurant with my friend, talking and drinking. Then we decided to go to a blues club and listen to some music.

I was too distracted that night to pay attention to what I was eating or drinking. I had had the first meeting with Oprah about my health, but I wasn't thinking "healthy" that night. I felt on top of the world, and was too excited to go home. I'm the type of person who goes to a party planning to stay about thirty minutes, then ends up being the last one to leave. The hardest part for me is showing up, making the first move. But once I do, you can't get me to stop. I was taught how to act and what my responsibilities were from the day Mom and I started. But I realize that in my personal life, I often still react as an adolescent, a child who wants to play. What I must now learn is when it's appropriate to act like an adolescent, and when I have to be an adult.

If you have bought this book, you probably already know that I was pulled over that night, November 13, 2003, and charged with a DUI, nine days before my wedding. I went over and over the incident in my mind while I rode in the back of a patrol car to police headquarters. I thought I was capable of driving! I thought I was in control! How could this be happening to me? Why *now*? Later, when I was sitting at the police station, something happened to me.

That night—and I believe it was partly because I was getting ready to get married and beginning to take baby steps on my journey—I decided I had to grow up. I had been off the mark. If I was ever going to get it together, I realized that I had to be held accountable. So many of us try to sidestep incidents like this. I called Kerry and told her I wanted no spin, no excuses. I had gone out, had too much to drink and arrogantly had gotten behind the wheel.

Whatever the punishment, I knew I had to face it. And face it I did. It was one of the most humiliating experiences of my life, but it opened my eyes. When I think about that night, I still feel guilt and shame. I think about families who have lost people in drunk-driving accidents. I was sentenced to two hundred hours of community service, and I did those hours and more. I served Meals on Wheels, worked at Clover Bottoms developmental center, read to school children. It was a healthy dose of reality. Seeing that awful mug shot of mine on the news was also a dose of reality. I knew that it would be used on my televised *Oprah* appearance, and started trying to prepare myself for it.

At the same time, I was also preparing for a wedding.

Roach and I both knew that we were taking on a great deal, moving in together, bringing Zac, Roach's son, to live with my children, Elijah and Grace. I had read about a wedding where the couple getting married included their children in the ceremony. Since we were integrating the two households, I thought it would be fitting to have the three children take part. I thought it would be wonderful for Grace, Zac and Elijah to be joined together as well as joined with Roach and me.

I ordered three rings mounted. On top of each ring were three small circles. One circle represented the individual child, one circle represented all three children, and one circle represented all of us—the family. During the ceremony the three would read individual vows. I didn't know what they were going to say. I had told them to write whatever they felt.

The morning of our wedding, November 22, 2003, I stood looking at myself naked in the mirror. The feelings that I had about my marriage certainly did not match the feelings I had about my body! Just as I began to self-loathe, I said out loud, "Stop it!" I knew that this should be one of the happiest days of my life, and if only for a little while, I had to stop beating myself up.

I put on my wedding gown, designed by Jane Booke. It was beautifully handcrafted, beaded, cream-colored Italian lace. We had picked a small country church that sits at the edge of our farmland. The historical country church was a perfect setting for the seventy-five guests we invited. Everything should have run smoothly. We had hired our good friend Randi Lesnick from Hospitality Consultants. She's the best of the best. But even the best can't always control outside events.

The first mishap involved the Rolls-Royce that was taking me to the church (hopefully on time). It caught fire and rolled down the hill and crashed into a tree just as I was getting ready to come out of the house. That was exciting, but the biggest surprise happened at the church before we even got there.

The inside of the church had been draped in cream-colored silk (in honor of that crème brûlée kiss, of course). In the room where Roach and I planned to sit right after the ceremony, Randi, our wedding designer, covered the couches and chairs in creamy silk. It was to be our special room, where we would have a few minutes alone before we took pictures.

Just as Randi was finishing putting the silk cover on the last couch, a stray dog that had been hanging around outside the church for the past few days ran inside. He ran up the aisle, and into the fellowship hall, jumped onto the freshly covered couch and peed all over it! Randi got hysterical! She had to completely redo the couch just minutes before our arrival. But, having survived the car and the dog, we did get under way!

My backup singers walked down the center aisle of the

church singing a cappella to begin the ceremony. Then, as each person in our wedding party walked down the aisle, Don Potter led a trio. Kerry stood up with both Roach and me, as our "Best Person." Ashley was my Matron of Honor. Roach's best friends, Scott Calderhead and Burt Butler, were Groomsmen. Pastor Dave Foster and my uncle Mark performed the ceremony. And as I mentioned, Roach and I had decided to include the children because we both felt that Zac, Elijah and Grace were making a commitment to each other, too.

The children read their vows to each other:

Zac said to Elijah: "I promise to do my best to love you as my brother. As brothers we will not always get along, but I will be there when you need me. I promise to lead you as a big brother should, and listen to you as we grow older."

Elijah said to Zac: "This day is really special to me because you are finally my brother. It meant a lot to me when you stood up for me at your house. That made me feel cool, to have a big brother who would do that for me. I love it when we want to play separate things and you usually do what I want. That shows me that it is important to you that I am happy. You and I will have lots of fun living together. If I could change one thing, it would be your age. I would make you eight years younger so that we could always be together, even at college."

Zac said to Grace: "I promise to do my best to love you as my sister. I promise to be there when you need someone to talk to, whether you're happy or sad. I will protect you; I will comfort you when you hurt. I love you so much, and I love being your brother."

Grace said to Zac: "I always knew I would have a big brother, but I never dreamed that I would have two. I could not have picked a better new brother than you. It means so much to me that whenever I want to talk, you listen even if you are in the middle of something. I cannot wait to grow up and have you as my biggest brother. You always make time to be with me. I feel safe when you are beside me. I am so excited you will be by my side for the rest of my life."

Roach and I read vows we'd written. For my part, I promised that:

"I will always be as affectionate with you as I am with my animals, and *try* to never give you directions."

Our guests burst out laughing.

Roach said: "Wynonna Ellen Judd, I promise I will stand beside you and protect you to face the challenges, big and small, that we will go through. Just as you have believed in me when many did not, I truly believe in you. Since that day we kissed, my life has forever changed. I never realized what love could be, an intimacy I had never known before. I promise to support the person that you are, to keep my heart and mind open to you. I promise to respect and love you, keeping you only to myself as long as we both shall live. I will serve a Living God and seek the wisdom from Him to guide this gifted family."

We decided to postpone a honeymoon and concentrate on family. The Judd/Roach Party of Five—Your Table Is Waiting!

And so, in the month since I had first met with Oprah, a great deal had happened! When we had our next meeting, parts of our conversations were taped for the February appearance that was being planned by Oprah's producers. They asked me how I felt about talking about the DUI and showing my mug shot on the actual show. I said that while I didn't look forward to it, the show had to be real, and that included talking about the DUI in public.

At this second meeting I admitted to Oprah that I

weighed more than I had ever weighed in my life. I said I knew I was in trouble, that somewhere along the line I forgot to put myself on the list.

Oprah knew that food was a symptom of a much greater problem. I had to understand that problem before I could really get healthy. One of the questions she asked me was this: do you know why you are using food this way? It was the same question Bob Greene had asked her when they started down their journey together. I said I thought it had started when I was about eight years old and my parents got their divorce. I began to use food as comfort. Even if I wasn't obese then, the fact that I started eating when I was lonely marks the beginning of addiction. The definition of an addict is *a person with a passionate interest*. And my interest in food had turned passionate.

I also said that my weight kept me insecure, that I felt uneasy going to functions because I never knew what to say. But after I left our meetings, a thought nagged me. What if it was the other way around? What if my insecurities were keeping me overweight?

I knew who I was when I was onstage. I was Xena with a guitar. But back in the hotel room, or on the bus, I wasn't sure what my purpose was. I know that there are many women *and* men who feel that way, too. I knew because my fans often confided in me. Each time one of them said they didn't feel loved, even if they were in a loving relationship, I knew what they meant. I was right there in that boat with them. If they said they were too easily hurt, wounded, I knew about that as well. There's a lot of shame that one carries in being too sensitive.

Oprah wasn't surprised that I suffered some setbacks. In fact, she told me that she had had many herself.

"I've been there," she said. "It happened to me, too."

"You can't just lose weight," Oprah said. "You have to

figure out why you eat. I did the same thing. I would lose weight, then gain it back. I did this so many times. I'm fifty years old, and I've finally figured it out. You're forty, so you have a head start. You'll do it."

Oprah went on to talk with me about some of the mind traps you fall into when you try to lose weight. Friends who are not on a diet will sabotage you by saying things like "Oh, have just *one* bite!" If they continue to stay heavy and you are trying to lose, they may sometimes feel threatened by your desire to be thin. If you are a public figure that becomes magnified because some of your fans may see it as an abandonment and accuse you of turning your back on them. You aren't one of them anymore.

She told me that she had listened to me make a commitment with Bob Greene that I would do all the things we agreed on. "I knew you'd try," she said. But, she also said, she knew from experience that it was easier said than done.

"It's a process, Wy. You can say 'I'm gonna do this and I'm gonna do that' but then real life steps in. Something happens and you fall back into your old habits. You'll have to redefine your relationships, rethink old patterns. But because it's a process, you have to go through all of it, including the successes and the failures."

I came home determined to give it my best. But because of the demands of my career, I knew how difficult staying on a healthy schedule was going to be, and from the beginning of our talks, Oprah had stressed consistency. So as I began my journey to health, I started rearranging my household schedule and trying to get more organized. I talked with my trainer, Dominick DeVito, and tried to start moving more. Dominick is a fifth-degree black belt, a self-defense expert, and a certified personal trainer and nutritionist. He had been with me since 2000.

Another important member of my team would be Cathy

Lewis, a graduate of the Culinary Institute of America with twenty-eight years of experience. She had owned the Nick of Thyme Gourmet to Go and Café in Nashville. She had catered many of my recording sessions and family dinners, and even a *Life* magazine photo shoot of The Judds. Someone made Cathy an offer and she sold Nick of Thyme, which gave her the freedom to do more private catering and to offer lessons. Ashley took cooking lessons with her for about two months. Then Cathy decided to move to Florida. I hadn't seen her in a long time.

I had been trying my darnedest to stay committed to my program. Each day I tried to do my workouts, tried to eat healthier and take better care of myself. But then I got caught up in all the things you go through in your first year of marriage—setting up a new household, getting used to new schedules and dynamics—and I started putting my workouts off. One day I was feeling bloated and blue (that almost sounds like a song title) and I decided to try to call Cathy on her cell phone. I hoped she still had the same number.

"What are you doing?" I asked, almost surprised she had answered.

"Just sitting here on the beach thinking about what I'm going to do for the rest of my life," she said, laughing.

"Cathy, I'm looking for someone to help me on my journey. I've got to take better care of myself, and I need help. Want a job?"

"Sure," she answered. It was that simple. Sometimes things are just meant to be.

Having Cathy here to help me plan meals was such a blessing! In the beginning I felt guilty about it, because I knew that everyone who faced food and weight issues couldn't have a chef. I realized that I was giving myself a gift, the gift of learning how to take better care of not just me, but my whole family. Everyone began to get educated about nutrition, portion size and daily food requirements.

Oprah sent Bob Greene to my home in Tennessee to meet with Dominick, Cathy and me. "We won't make any radical changes right now," he said. While he was there, I admitted that my wedding day had truly opened my eyes. I truly needed change in my life, and I tried to continue to honor that commitment.

Dominick made our workouts fun, and he tried hard to keep me inspired by mixing up our morning routines. I even began looking forward to the appointments each day, as we concentrated on cardiovascular and strength training. I was rocking and rolling and starting to see changes in my body. I was less bloated, stronger and far more energetic.

The most difficult part was stopping my habit of nighttime eating! I was like Elvis, a night person with an appetite. I love feeling full when I go to sleep, so right before bedtime was when I was most likely to slip. I was also vulnerable when I was out on the road. If I found myself alone, I wanted food to comfort me.

But for the most part, great change was happening in our household. Immediately after Cathy Lewis came back into my life, two wonderful life-changing things happened. We started our Judd/Roach family tradition of eating supper together every night at six thirty p.m. I cried during Papa Roach's prayer on the night of our first supper."

The second thing that happened was that the children began learning about nutrition, about what foods to eat and what foods not to eat, how much and when. They now understand just how dangerous the "supersize" is to their bodies. They already know what a "portion" means. They were learning early what I was learning late.

I thought that I now had the time to focus on getting physically healthy. But one more time, life had something else in store.

· II ·

RESCUE ME

I was working hard on my health issues, when Kerry, my manager, and two of my financial business advisors called and asked me to come to their offices for a meeting. It was December 4, 2003. I thought it was to talk about the financial details of my upcoming tour. Boy, was I wrong!

When I arrived, instead of being escorted to the large conference room where we usually gather, I was taken to a smaller meeting room. We always started out our meetings in a casual manner. The mood was usually upbeat. People would get their coffee and talk for a few minutes before getting down to business. So when I opened the door, I was surprised to see everyone seated and engaged in what appeared to be a serious conversation. I was obviously interrupting something. Everyone stopped talking and stood up. We exchanged hellos and hugs and took our seats. The mood was somber. I could sense that something was up.

Kerry looked at me, I looked at my business managers, and they looked at Kerry as if to say, "You're it." Kerry took a deep breath and said, "Okay, I'll start." She then turned to me, and the look on her face seemed to say, "I'm smiling at you because I love you. I hate to be the one to have to tell you this."

In meetings, Kerry is impressive to watch. She's dynamic and powerful in her approach. She has an aggressive nature, but she'll tell you straight up if she doesn't know the answer. She'll rock your world with her ideas. There aren't many managers who do business like she does. Kerry and I are close friends, but we work to keep our business and personal relationships separate. Within the first few minutes of sitting together, I realized that she was there as both my manager and my friend.

"I care deeply for you, Wy," she said. "For the last eight years I've seen you try hard to keep everything in your personal and professional life going. It's been hard for me to stand by and watch the stress take such a toll on your health. I'll do anything I can to help you. I just want to see you healthy and happy."

I could tell this was extremely difficult for Kerry. She is always the first person in the room to say that "the glass is half full." But I had a gut feeling that she was about to tell me that it was half empty. Her heart seemed heavy. It was as if she believed that she had one last chance to tell me something that would save my life. Her words were precise, as if she had practiced them.

Oh, I know what she's getting ready to say, I thought. *She's going to say,*

"I love you but I'm quitting."

Then I had another thought. *Maybe it really is about my health. Maybe she is going to say,*

"The doctor called and doesn't want you to tour until you get your cholesterol down and lose some weight."

It had been six months since I received the bad news about my health. I could imagine that people were concerned about my well-being. It would make sense that Kerry felt responsible for telling me.

"I really appreciate your concern, Kerry," I said, thinking that at that point she would finish with the personal and move on to the professional. Instead, Kerry looked at my senior financial counselor. I was not prepared for what she said.

"Wynonna, you are going bankrupt. If you continue to spend at the rate you are currently spending, you will have to sell the farm."

What did she just say? Did she just say "bankrupt"? I thought I was going to throw up. I stared at her, waiting for her to say something like "But we have a plan" or "We're here to help you." Nobody said a word. I couldn't look at anyone. I just sat there with my hands folded in my lap. Finally she spoke again.

"Do you remember a conversation we had several years ago? I said you should be putting away enough money in savings so that within ten years you could live off the interest."

"Yes, I remember," I said.

"As your business manager, it pains me to see that you've worked so hard for twenty years and have so little to show for it."

Then she picked up a picture of our business team.

"This was taken on the day you sold your house. You were putting the money away for Elijah and Grace."

Yes, there I was, smiling and celebrating my decision to establish the Judd Family Trust. I put my head down. I remembered that day and it had not been that long ago. But instead of the money remaining in an account, earning interest, I ended up having to sign papers and take it out of savings to pay off debt. I felt complete shame. What a failure.

Finally my day-to-day financial advisor spoke up. On the one hand, I didn't think I could take any more. Still, I respected these three people so much that I knew what they had to say was vital. I owed them that much.

"It's getting harder and harder for me to do your daily balance sheet, and I'm not sure I can continue to do so. I watch you make so many choices that contradict each other. One day you put money aside for your family, and then you sabotage yourself by making random large purchases or charitable donations. In good conscience, I can't continue to watch you make these choices, knowing that the end is inevitable."

He then showed me a map he had made of my 525-acre farm—the farm I had felt so proud to have saved when I sold my home and the property surrounding it. He had divided the property into one-hundred-acre lots. I looked at the five vertical lines drawn through the map.

"I'm not interested in selling any of my land," I said quickly.

"But you'll have to, Wy," he said. "If you don't drastically reduce your spending—and I mean by fifty percent—each year you'll be forced to sell a portion of the farm." Then he took a pair of scissors and cut the first hundred acres off.

"In a year you'll sell this much. And by 2005 you'll sell this much."

He cut off another hundred acres, and continued doing it until all the land was cut off. Suddenly, there was no farm! The visual made his point very clear. If I didn't change my life, we would not live up on the farm with Ashley and Mom and Pop. I had bought that farmland in 1990 and had been working my way up there. Now the pieces lay on the table, and it was up to me to pick them up and put them back together. My senior advisor spoke up again.

"Here is a card with a name and a phone number if you should choose to reach out and ask for help. These people come highly recommended. They are aware of this meeting and that you might be calling." She then handed me the card. I stared down at it. The first thought I had was:

What did you tell them?

That's how I felt, like someone had told on me. People were starting to find out already. And my advisors hadn't offered a financial plan. They had basically told me I needed therapy to learn how to handle my finances.

I wanted to run out the door as fast as I could. Instead, I calmly took the card and said:

"Thank you. I appreciate that you care about me."

With those words, tears started to come, so I quickly turned and went out the door. I blinked back the tears, then walked slowly down the hallway, smiling and saying hello to everyone as if I didn't have a care in the world.

It was a little like the time I told Mom *It's okay* after finding out about Charlie Jordan. I guess even in my moment of grief, I wanted to believe that it really was going to be okay. If other people had given me that kind of information, I would have been mad at them. But these people had been with me for a long time, and I knew they did it from love.

As I was going down the last set of stairs, I looked up to see one of my platinum records hanging on the wall. There I was smiling back at me in all my splendor. Professionally I had sold millions of CDs but right then it felt hollow.

When I stepped outside, it had started to rain. *How perfect.* I didn't even care if I got wet. As I walked, I looked down the street and saw a guy get out of his car and go into a strip club. I wondered if his addiction was as bad as mine. Will he feel as guilty when he walks out of there as I did walking out of here? I sat in my car for the longest time, listening to the raindrop patterns on the windshield. I was so sad. Too sad to think. Too sad to cry. I felt like I had nowhere to go. It was cold and I could see my breath. It all seemed like too much to deal with.

"Call Roach," I said to myself, then immediately reconsidered. *I can't call Roach! I'm scared to death to tell him!* What am I gonna say? *Oh, don't worry, honey. I'll just take out another loan. Or maybe: we'll book even more shows this year. It'll be okay.* What I felt like doing was calling a press conference and making an announcement.

"Hey, everybody—I'm the biggest loser in the world."

I reached into my pocket and pulled out the business card that my senior advisor had given me. It was the name and number of a therapist at a facility called Onsite. What could I say to this stranger? *Hello, this is Wynonna. I'm bankrupt, so I hope you aren't too expensive!* I don't feel that it was my physical self that made the decision to pick up the car phone. It's as if my spirit took over. I could picture Grace, Elijah and Zac's faces. I feel it must have been God giving me snapshots of the children to keep me focused when I was about to give up. It's like when, during the last moments of childbirth, a mother doesn't think she can push one more time. Then someone gives her something to focus on. Without those images, I might have remained in denial or tried to figure out a way to "fix" everything myself. But something told me I needed to try to do something different. Like they say: insanity is doing the same thing over and over and expecting a different result. I also knew that I couldn't continue to live with the shame I had felt during that intervention.

I dialed the number and was relieved to get voice mail so I could just simply leave my phone number. After I hung up, I just sat there in the parking lot. Within minutes my phone rang.

"I cannot believe this is happening," I said aloud, then picked up the phone.

"How are you feeling?" a male voice asked.

"F.I.N.E.," I said. "F'd up, Insecure, Neurotic and Emotional."

He didn't laugh. I wasn't used to this! Wasn't that funny? *Oh, I'm just too hilarious for him! He didn't get it, bless his heart!*

He gently guided me through the process.

This is what it must be like to go to your first A.A. meeting, I thought. *I'm officially in the club!*

Ironically, I already had heard of Onsite, a healing center in Cumberland Furnace, Tennessee. Several years earlier, Mom had suggested that we go there together as a family. She had told me that she had heard that the workshops changed people's lives, that it was a highly respected healing center.

Coincidence is God's way of staying invisible.

Roach and I attended our first Onsite workshop the following month, in January of 2004. They have several kinds of programs, including some communal workshops. But since I was known, I didn't think I was ready to talk about my finances in front of strangers just yet, so we entered private counseling with several life coaches.

I felt incredibly vulnerable in the days leading up to the workshop, which would deal with finances. The idea of digging down into the roots of my problems seemed overwhelming. I knew that I was embarking on complicated territory. I felt a little like I suspect people feel when they join the army. I was signing up for boot camp and wondered if I was strong enough to finish the course.

Roach and I were signed up for a week, but it felt like I was going to be gone a lot longer, so I packed a lot of clean socks and underwear and brought my incense and serenity candles along with me. I brought along a CD player and soothing music to play in the evenings. I packed loose-fitting clothes, the kind I would wear to curl up on the couch on a rainy day to watch old movies. I wanted to have everything—just in case. I get that from my mom. *Just in case we get stranded on an island.*

I knew I was definitely not going to a party. I knew that there would be no communicating with the outside world, no television, cell phones, faxes or e-mails. I wondered if I would feel solitude or isolation.

The only other time I had been that removed from society was back in 2000 when I went to a yoga retreat called the Ashram, outside Malibu, California. People go there to hike the mountains and cleanse with healthy foods, to find physical, mental and spiritual healing. Ashley took me there for my thirty-fifth birthday. I was nervous because it was way up in the mountains, far away from town. As we were checking in, one of the girls told me that a super-model had only lasted three days before ordering a limo to come rescue her. Sure enough, after three days, I called Roach and said I was in camp hell and didn't think I would last and that I had wanted to call a car and escape, just like the supermodel had done.

It was funny, because Roach and I started out our journey to a stronger marriage by disagreeing about how to pack the car! It was my first introduction into how differently my husband and I did a routine task. It didn't matter in that moment that Roach had worked with me for thirteen years. We were finding that marriage changes a lot.

But I felt excited about taking our commitment to the next level. I was looking forward to the challenge. We were starting out with the financial workshop, but I had been told that Onsite also offered help on everything from money to marriage, from setting boundaries to communicating in a much healthier way and finding new ways of parenting. It seemed like a perfect way for us to begin our marriage in a positive way.

Before we left, we prayed. We have a family rule at our home. Because Roach and I travel so much, we always hug and kiss each child, join in what we call the circle of life, then have prayer. As we pulled out of the drive, I thought about a conversation that I had had with Grace a few days earlier.

"Where are you going, Mommy?" she asked.

"We're going to a workshop, a kind of camp for adults," I answered.

"Why?"

"We're going to learn how to be a better mama and papa to you all, and a better husband and wife to each other."

Grace got very excited. "Will you get to play games there? Will there be a swimming pool with a slide? Will you get to ride horses?"

"No, this is a different kind of camp. It's like school."

Grace frowned. "Well, that doesn't sound like a very fun camp at all!"

I had a feeling that she might be right. *What was I getting myself into!?*

Onsite is one of the most respected places in the country. People from all over the world, from all walks of life, have come to Onsite workshops, and they'll tell you that the experience changed their lives. I have traveled to a lot of mind/body/spirit centers over the years, but I had never signed up for a workshop to understand my relationship (or lack of it!) with money! It would be the first experience for Roach and me to discover what our issues were, and to find a new way to handle our finances personally and pro-

fessionally. We wanted to begin our marriage with new
ideas on how we could work together and do business. I
was ready to do the work. I knew it was going to be difficult and sometimes overwhelming.

I was overcome with thoughts about my emotions being
stripped bare for my husband to see. He would be there
when they in effect read me my rights. Roach had no idea
how many bad choices I had made throughout the years involving finances. I was horrified at the thought of sitting
next to him when he found out. I worried he would feel
trapped and want out. I was so afraid that it would change
our relationship—that Roach and I would end up feeling
like cell mates instead of soul mates at the end of the workshop. But once again I had to ask myself, Which is worse,
the pain of changing or the pain of not changing?

The first thing we did on the morning that we arrived for
our financial workshop was say how we were feeling, to
address our emotions before we began to work. I said I felt
guilt, and Roach said he felt anxious. Not long after we
moved on with the session, Roach and I began to give each
other a hard time. The life coach walked over and stood between Roach and me. He stretched out his arms and said:

"Stop, stop!"

The life coach sensed that we were nowhere close to being ready to deal with money issues. We had intense relationship issues as well. Before we could deal with money,
Roach and I would have to deal with our wounded, broken
hearts from past relationships. We were taking jabs at each
other, going for each other's jugular, being sarcastic.
Roach would make a comment, and I would crack a
(somewhat hostile) joke. We were acting out on an adolescent level, and it was getting in the way of the work we
were there to do.

Our life coach told us that we had much healing work to

do before we tried to tackle our financial issues, and the work had to be from the heart. You can't be in these workshops and expect results unless you're ready to show up and be honest. You can't stand there and say, "Uh, I don't know." You say things you wish you'd said ten years ago, twenty years ago. I thought I would lose my mind several times that first day.

I hadn't realized just how hurtful these digs that Roach and I were making were. The coach had to stop us several times and tell us that what we were doing wasn't helpful. I got so aggravated a couple of times that I cussed. I truly didn't know if I was going to be able to do the work. Our life coach said that it was entirely normal to feel like running out of the room, grabbing the suitcases and jumping into your car and taking off. It becomes a fight-or-flight decision. Do you stay and work through your issues, or do you make a run for it?

It was then that I understood we were going to have to go to square one. Roach and I were going to have to admit that our past relationships had wounded us so much that it was affecting our marriage. We had both brought a great deal of pain with us to our relationship.

We learned that communicating within a relationship involves compassion first, finding out where someone is and—whether you agree or disagree—understanding why they feel the way they do. Next comes empathy, which is the beginning of healing.

In some forms of therapy, the counselors act as mediators, translators, explaining to each person what the other is saying. But at Onsite, they also teach you to do it for yourself. They give you and your partner the tools to stay connected during conflict. One of the tools is called "mirroring."

Roach and I used an example of something that happened one Easter morning before we were married. Roach and Zac still lived in Roach's condo, and they had come the night before to attend church with Grace, Elijah and me the following day. At the last minute we discovered a problem with Zac's clothes and we were late for church. I had gotten Elijah and Grace ready and felt really frustrated that this had happened with Zac in the last ten minutes before we were to have left. I was upset and took my disappointment out on Roach, putting everything on him, casting blame:

"You know how much church means to me, how much I look forward to going, especially on Easter. You didn't have Zac's clothes laid out for him. Why didn't you take care of that last night before you went to bed? If he had tried on the pants last night, he would have realized then that they don't fit instead of at the last minute. And he didn't bring a backup pair."

Our old way of dealing with this might involve Roach coming back at me with:

"What do you mean? I told Zac to get a pair of pants for church! How would I know that they didn't fit? Zac's responsible for his own clothes. I'm doing the best I can. Zac and I don't have this going back and forth from the condo to here worked out yet. We live forty-five minutes away and can't go back for another pair."

Roach might say:

"What's the matter with you, firing off at me in front of the children? I thought we were trying to parent together."

We would both be in a survival mode. We would be so busy defending ourselves that we would miss out on an opportunity to resolve the argument by having compassion for what the other was feeling or experiencing.

But using the mirroring technique, he could answer: "So you're saying that church means a great deal to you, and you especially look forward to going on Easter Sunday. I should have had Zac's clothes laid out last night so that he could take responsibility for being ready on time. Is that what you're saying?" He would then pause.

"Yes," I would answer.

"Is there more?" he would ask.

As that conversation unfolded, both of us were starting to cool down a little. But I might feel I had something else to say:

"Yes, when we're late, you drive too fast and it scares me. I don't want to be late to church anymore. I get too stressed-out, and it isn't worth it. It's our family time. It should be fun and relaxed."

Roach would again mirror what I had said, showing me that he really was listening and my complaints were important to him. And he would ask me if I had anything more I wanted to say.

"Yes," I might say. "I know it's hard on all of us to have to get where we're trying to go. I feel like a failure as a parent when our children don't have what they need."

The thing is, when you mirror you must give the gift of letting the person begin and end, however long it takes. Being a good listener is part of being a good partner. Roach would mirror my statement as he heard it, once again.

"You know what, it makes sense to me that you would feel that way. I didn't have Zac's clothes laid out, and it caused us to be late. When I run late, I drive too fast. You get stressed-out and you don't want to be late for church anymore. You feel that our family time should be relaxed and fun. You feel like a failure when our children don't have what they need. I can understand that you'd feel that way. You want to be a good mom."

Now it's Roach's turn and he can add new information to the situation.

"You know what, I did forget to get Zac's clothes ready last night, and when I got out his good pants this morning, they were too short. I was trying to fix them so that they fit because we didn't have another pair, and I didn't want him to be embarrassed because of improper planning on my part."

I then mirror him. This part would be a real test for me. My old way would have been to be sarcastic, and say, "So you haven't even checked his good pants since *last* Easter." But in the new way, I repeated what I heard him say to me. Then I asked if there was more.

"Yes. When we started running late because of Zac's pants, I was embarrassed. So I tried to run around and fix the problem because I didn't want Zac to have to go to church with pants that don't fit."

Then I mirrored him, and asked if there was more.

"No," he said.

Then I would summarize.

"I can imagine that this is new to you and Zac. You're still learning. You're a single father, raising a young son alone. You're both still in the mode of trying to get it all together. I've been living at this house for enough time that I have Elijah and Grace's routines worked out. And in my heart I would see that you were doing the best you could between hiding all the Easter eggs and playing with everybody, trying to be fun Papa Roach."

By this time Roach and I would have had time to calm down. We both would feel heard and understood.

The other emotion I would feel is sadness that Zac might have been put in an embarrassing spotlight over a pair of too short pants. I would realize that I didn't want to be judgmental. Roach has already said he knows he must start to get more organized when it comes to Zac's belongings.

In the end, I said, "Honey, I can understand how hard

that was for you, and how it might have happened. You're Zac's father and you're trying to raise him the best you can."

What this process has done is to allow us to stay engaged while working through a problem. Often, couples completely disconnect when they have a misunderstanding and get into a fight over it. And Roach and I have learned that if something is said that causes hurt or shame, the injured party should say: "Is it your intent to hurt or shame me?" In almost all cases, the answer is, No, of course, that wasn't the intention. So then you apologize if you hurt their feelings.

We did this work again and again, until sometimes I was almost nauseated by it. At times I would think, I would rather just have the fight! Sometimes one or both of us would revert back to sarcasm and at other times to condescension. When that happened the life coach would step in, saying, "That didn't help."

He would remind us that we were both wounded and trying to learn to do things differently. Both of us had to win. You couldn't have one walking away feeling like a loser.

"Win-win or no deal!" Roach would say.

At first, Roach was much better at this work than I was. He comes from a more stable home life and he has faith that things can be and will be worked out. I came from divorced parents. Even with Pop, the love of Mom's life, it was touch and go for years. I did not come from a place where I felt that relationships could and would work out. I came from a place where I thought it all might go to hell at any minute.

Mirroring works in most situations, not just marriages. Think about how you deal with people in the workplace. How many times have people had their feelings hurt because they didn't understand what a boss or coworker was trying to say? How many projects fell apart or were delayed because of miscommunication?

Most of us are not really taught to communicate, not with our partners, our children, our associates. For example, one night our children had to do hours. (They are given "hours" for consequences. They do chores that Roach and I select.)

Elijah knocked out some of his hours. But Zac, our teenager, had put off doing his. He knew his time limit, and would get to it. But Roach said something to the nanny about the fact that he was pleased that Elijah had already done his work. When asked about Zac, he said, "No, he put his off." Both boys were in the room when he said it. What that did was put Elijah in the role of the good son, and Zac into the bad one, in that moment.

As soon as it was said, I realized that we were leaving Zac feeling bad about himself. I took Roach aside and suggested that he soften the situation. Roach immediately went to Zac, and said, "When I brought up the fact that Elijah had worked on his hours, it was not my intention to hurt your feelings." Zac's face lit up as if to say, "Thank you, Dad." Roach went on to explain:

"Mom just pointed out to me that I was comparing you and Elijah, and that's not fair. You're both individuals."

We learned that the best way to work through things was to excuse ourselves from the room where all the children were located. That way, when we came back, no matter what we'd decided, we stood together. That makes the kids feel safe.

The more we worked at communication skills, the easier it got. They say a habit takes thirty days to break. A lack of communication skills may take even longer, because you are changing patterns that have probably been set from childhood.

One day, during a couples workshop, Roach was asked to wear earmuffs, dark glasses and big, heavy gloves. I was instructed to have a conversation with him, and as I talked, Roach kept leaning in, frowning a lot. When I got finished, Roach looked at me and said, "I didn't hear a word you said."

"That's what happens when you try to communicate with each other when you don't have communication skills," the life coach said. "Before Roach did the work, and received the new information, he was unable to see you, hear you or feel you. It's the way too many of us communicate."

Moving into the financial realm, the next thing we did was to write out life scripts, which not only involved attitudes about personal relationships, but attitudes about work and money. We took Post-it notes and wrote down "truths" we had grown up believing because our parents or other authority figures had told us. These truths make an imprint, and affect how you behave as an adult: "Don't put off until tomorrow what you can do today" or "Money doesn't grow on trees." What's important is not that they are necessarily true or profound, but that you end up living by them.

"The early bird catches the worm."

"Judd women always land on their feet!"

"It's a man's world."

Life scripts affect all we do—our relationships with people, food—money.

Then the life coaches asked me to try to think of some of my earliest memories about money matters. Some of my earliest memories involved the Ciminella family, and how Mamaw would take me for lunches at the country club, how she would save up money to buy me new clothes. How wonderful it felt to be in Mamaw and Papaw's home, where money and food made me feel safe. Then, of course, I would go home to Mom and food stamps, which was the total opposite. I remembered that Mom would write a check for the rent and work a double shift that night so it would be good.

I remembered feeling unsure about money a lot. Mom had to hustle to try to make it. But she promised us we would never have to worry as long as she could work. That's how I felt, too. As long as I could play shows, I could support my family and all the people who depend on me. And like Mom, if I needed more money, I would work a double-show week!

Mom called the way we lived "genteel poverty." We were poor but creative. She did a fabulous job of covering up ugly old sofas with tapestries, and hanging just the right picture on the wall. And even if we could only eat at a restaurant every once in a while, she made it memorable. What I had learned was a blurring between reality and fantasy.

Another powerful memory that was prominent during that workshop involved the days when Mom, Ashley and I lived on Del Rio. The closets were tiny in that house, so Mom packed our off-season clothes in trash bags and stowed them away somewhere, usually at Pop's apartment. But we also put trash bags full of trash in the trunk of the car and took them to a Dumpster, since we had no trash pickup. One day, when I came home, I thought the bags in the trunk were filled with trash, and hauled them off to Kroger to dump them in the trash bins out behind the store.

I didn't even realize my mistake until Mom came home from work the next morning. All our winter clothes had been in those bags. We went to Kroger, but the trash had already been picked up. I made a lot of mistakes like that when I was a teenager. One of my life scripts was:

You are so stupid!

I read this story in one of Suze Orman's financial

books. A man says that as a boy, his mom gave him five dollars and sent him to the store alone to buy bread for the family dinner. He somehow lost the money on his way to the store, and had to come home and tell his entire family what had happened. Everyone stared at him, and he felt humiliated. *Fast forward:* the man was in his late forties, and he still didn't trust himself with his own money. He didn't have a relationship with his own money. He turned everything he earned over to others, afraid to trust himself to make any decisions.

Things that happen to you as a child definitely set you up for what you do as an adult. I thought I was stupid about money as a child, and I continued to think I couldn't get involved or make decisions as an adult. No one ever taught me to have a relationship with money. I went from poor to rich and my attitude was that I could always work more to make more money. Onsite gives you the tools to help you understand why you are the way you are.

One of the next steps was to go over all the financial mistakes I had made. I would rather have run naked through church than to have to face the truth about my money missteps. In fact, during one of the first sessions, I had to go back to my room, where I proceeded to have a panic attack. I truly felt that I was going to have a nervous breakdown. The feeling is as intense, I think, as when a longtime spouse comes home and asks for a divorce. It is that much of a personal blow. You feel like you are dying, a 100 percent failure.

You start out feeling guilty. But you have to work past that. Then you have to get to the place where you feel real remorse for what you've done. Only after you get to the remorse stage can you begin to change the behavior. That was such an important step for me. I had often felt guilty about the way I spent money, about not paying attention to my finances like I should. But I would continue to spend the way I did. I felt incredibly sad that I wanted to be living in my own house on my farm, yet I still lived in a rental in 2003. I said, "I don't want to be renting a house in ten years."

In the beginning, I was unable to allow Roach in to help me deal with my embarrassment. I truly was like a deer stranded out on the ice. I couldn't make a move without slipping and falling. It was the most difficult, helpless feeling in the world to sit next to Roach, drowning in grief, and be unable to ask for his help. I felt it was too late. What was done was done. Roach couldn't save me. The coaches pointed out that as a consequence, Roach felt helpless.

During some of the early sessions, when Roach or I became too emotional during our work, one or the other of us would crack a joke. The life coaches made us both aware that what we were doing was trying to get out of the pain by distracting ourselves with humor. We had to learn that true healing involves pain. And when we did allow ourselves to go deeper into the feeling we would come out of the pain with some clarity.

It took a while before Roach would cry. As he said, most of our lives we're taught not to do that, not to *feel* too much, and certainly not to do it in public. It's the *you'll be just fine* syndrome. Don't do anything to make people feel uncomfortable. Don't get too emotional. Don't be too sentimental. Just get over it. And *whatever* you do, don't cry because—especially if you are a man—someone might laugh at you and think you are weak.

Roach felt he really had to get over those old perceptions and to *learn* intimacy. I remember that during one workshop, we both looked in each other's eyes and felt real pain for the first time. Standing there together, instead of looking down, we stayed in the moment. We continued to look deeper and deeper. No one cracked a joke. I felt closer to Roach than I ever have. I have to say, if you can look someone in the eye for two minutes without taking your eyes off them, without laughing or saying anything— good luck! But we did, and I wouldn't have traded that moment for anything in the world.

That night Roach said, "I can't believe that people don't put in this kind of time and effort on their marriages. You have to be willing to continue to show up and do the work."

And then he said the one thing I needed to hear: "I love you. I'm not going anywhere. Together we'll work it out."

I finally understood that I had a partner. I knew that if I heard him say those words long enough, they would replace the old negative life scripts. I felt I could do anything as long as Roach and I stood together. That didn't mean we were finished, that we had learned all we needed to know. Not by a long shot.

They say that change is the most constant force in the universe, but the most difficult to embrace. It was frightening for me in the past. I still sometimes had the deep feeling that I had to "fix" things myself. At other times, in other relationships, I would have thought to myself, "It's nice to have him along, but I'm the one carrying the load." Roach said that he, too, had that feeling, taught to him from the time that he was a little boy. Men *fix* things for their families. We had to learn to share the answers.

Our life coaches liked to teach with physical illustrations. For example, they took us into a room where there were stacks of oversized pillows, and one of the coaches told me to lie down on the floor. I was looking over at Roach the whole time, because I felt really vulnerable.

The life coaches put one of the large pillows on top of me and one said, "You sure are a great singer." Another life coach said, "You know, if you keep singing you're really gonna make it." Then another pillow was placed on my chest: "I'm sure glad I have you in my life." And more comments, and more pillows. The pile started to get more and more uncomfortable. Then another life coach handed me a wad of play money. I had to extricate my arm from the pillows to take it.

"It's getting kind of hot and claustrophobic under here," I said.

"Okay, we'll fix that," a life coach said. He took a couple of pillows off, but at the same time, asked for part of the money back. Then he would throw another pillow on me:

"You sure are a good girl to take care of me."

After a while one asked me how I liked the experience.

"I'm really hot and I'm starting to get irritated," I said truthfully.

"Good. That's what we want."

But the process continued and when I became really angry, one of the coaches said:

"I'll help you." And then he placed another pillow on my chest! This went on and on. Finally, when there were twenty pillows on top of me, I started hyperventilating.

"I don't want to do this anymore!" I yelled.

"My little girl needs some braces. Can I have a loan?" Another pillow.

"Will you do all these benefit concerts?" Another pillow.

"Can you keep the band on salary whether you work or not?" One more.

As long as I took on these burdens without complaining, I believed that people would say I was a good girl, worthy of love. The thing is, burdens don't always involve things you don't want to do. I love to help people whether it is through a loan or a benefit concert or a hospital visit. But when those things get stacked up too high, they can start to smother you. And when you try to remove the burdens, it can cost you financially—that's why the coach kept taking from my wad of play money.

The life coaches told Roach that he was a part of this dynamic. They asked him to crawl under the five-foot-high pile of pillows and lay down next to me. He did, laughing all the way. Until he was half smothered, too.

"I don't like this," I said. "This is crap!" I was hot, angry and starting to panic.

"What did you say?" the coach yelled. "I can't hear you." Then they started leaning on the pillows and I felt the pressure increase. My claustrophobia zoomed.

"What kind of work are you doing up there at Onsite?" a life coach yelled down. "Is that a cult or something? You don't need to change. Everything is just fine the way it is. We don't want you to change."

Some people won't want you to change, especially if it isn't in their best interest. What if I told my staff I had to take six months off to get healthy? What would most managers do?

You can't do that! You have families to feed. If Wy don't work, the people don't eat. Those statements had become life scripts.

I was starting to hyperventilate. When I wanted to get up, I found I could not do so from my prone position on the floor, with two life coaches leaning on the pillows. One of them yelled down:

"If you want out, you and Roach are going to have to fight your way out."

Boy, did we! Both of us together, pushing away one pillow at a time, fought our way out from underneath the pile. The life coaches didn't make it easy on us. As we knocked three or four off, they threw three or four back on. It was one of the wildest things I ever experienced in my life. But I learned that if I wanted to reclaim my own life, I would have to fight for it with my husband by my side.

The coaches could have simply told us all this. They could have sat us down and talked about burdens and getting fed up and fighting for freedom. But I don't think the lesson would have come through quite so loud and clear as it did that day.

One of the most informative exercises we did was when we wrote down some of our desires and dreams on more Post-it notes. I was stunned when I realized that only one of my dreams was professional. The rest were personal.

I didn't list a lot of the things people might think I would dream about—another sold-out tour or having another string of #1 singles. When it was all said and done, I listed one career goal: to again sell five million copies of one CD someday before I retired (at the age of seventy-five), as I had done with my self-titled solo debut. Years ago, when John Unger was still my manager, he told me that he knew I could sell *ten million* CDs, and the idea has never left me.

Aside from that, I had listed things like growing a garden and taking long walks with Roach. I said I wanted a child with Roach. I said I would like to eat out of my own refrigerator for a month, and never have to go to a restaurant or order room service. I wanted to be able to wear clothes that didn't match and go without makeup for a month (sorry, husband). Most of my desires dealt with having more time to devote to home and to my family. Some were large and small fantasies, others were lifelong hopes and desires. But if you'll notice, my dreams had little to do with money or material things.

And while I didn't know it, the life coaches already understood that it was hard for me to ever ask for help—not from them and not from my husband. One day they brought me to a rock-climbing room.

"How high up do you think you could climb blind-folded?" I was asked.

I wasn't sure how to react to the idea of climbing up a wall. First, I felt self-conscious about my weight. I didn't want to look foolish to the men below. Still, being an over-achiever, I said, "I can probably get to the second-to-the-top ledge."

They put the blindfold on me and I was instantly nervous. Without being able to see anything, I had the feeling I was falling even before I started. I was told that someone would always catch me, but it didn't reassure me. I like being in control, and I wasn't sure I *trusted* anyone to catch me.

I know this sounds juvenile, but in addition to the worry of actually falling, I was convinced that the rock climber would leave the workshop saying something like "Man! You should have seen how stupid Wynonna Judd looked today. She was a loser." When I thought about those concerns, it made me realize that I am too worried about being strong for other people, that I am really pained if I look stupid. I suppose we all are, but I think I was overly sensitive to it. Even when I have a really bad day, I am ready to give my best parade wave. But not on that day.

I didn't make it any higher than the second row of ledges at first. I was frightened, dizzy and felt *so* uncoordinated. I could not make it up another level. I couldn't see so I didn't know where to put my feet or where the ledges were for my hands. I called out, "Falling!" The man below responded with an okay. He released the pulley and I was brought back down. I was so embarrassed, but I wouldn't let them see me cry. The life coach asked if I wanted to try again, and I said yes. I ended up trying to climb that wall three more times and failed. I felt scared, lost and incompetent.

Finally I got fired up and mad.

"I want to try again," I said.

And again I tried and failed, even with that *I'm gonna do this* attitude. I was *so* pissed at myself! Have you ever been so angry, but didn't know what to do because people were watching you?

"Are you open for a comment?" the life coach asked.

"Sure."

"You didn't ask for help."

"Well—what are you talking about?" I asked with a shrug.

"Don't feel bad," he said. "Nobody ever asks for help at first."

"I don't understand," I said.

"You never asked, 'Is there anything anyone can tell me that might help me to climb better?' You never asked, 'Would you help me climb higher—to the top?' "

I wanted to scream! I was beginning to see what this exercise was about. My mind was racing! When I went solo, I had a difficult time asking anyone to help me figure things out. Even if I did it the wrong way, I was hell-bent on doing it by myself. I would have never thought to ask how I might watch my career or my money. So I just kept trying to climb to the top, blindfolded and without any information at all that could have helped make the climb easier.

I started thinking about the fellow with the pulley, and it made me think about God. The Lord has always been there when I fell. Yet how many times had I tried to do it without Him? How many times did I crash and burn?

The life coach then pointed to the rock-climbing guy. "Have you thought about the fact that this guy is an expert? It's his job to help you, to give you directions." I hadn't thought about asking for directions!

"Can you help me?" I asked. The rock climber gave me

some tips, and the next time I tried, I quickly ma[...]
the wall two additional levels. The life coach called:

"Okay, Wynonna, hand to the left, up, up, up."

Me, following directions? One hand after the other, up I
climbed. My feet were being firmly planted on each ledge.
I wasn't dizzy, and even if a part of me was afraid, I wasn't
paralyzed.

Then it happened. I made it to the second row from the
top. It was one of the proudest moments of my life! I mean
as proud as when I won awards or was presented with platinum records. I realized that this had been about pride,
about being afraid. But not knowing is not less. You are not
responsible for what you don't know! Only when you are
completely informed are you accountable and then responsible for making a change.

Bottom line: I had always thought of myself as a team
player both in my life and career. But because I didn't ask
for help, I saw that I was trying to carry the ball alone, and
it hadn't always worked. There is a time to lead and a time
to follow, a time to speak and a time to listen. There's a
time to be solo, and a time to be a team. And with what was
in store, Roach and I had to operate as a team!

12

THE OTHER SIDE

One morning one of our workshop leaders started the morning by presenting Roach and me with a chart that he had made. It showed my financial history from 1997 to 2004. He hung it up on the wall and stepped back for us to see. I stared at it for a few minutes. When I realized that I didn't get it, I asked him for an explanation. As he began to share the details, I understood the enormity of my mistakes. I started shaking. I wanted to flee. I wanted to go to sleep for a long time.

"I need a time-out!" I cried, and excused myself. I hurried back to the cabin, lay on the bed and sobbed. I had nothing financial to show for twenty years of hard work! I had no savings. Only debt. How had I allowed this to happen?

When lunchtime came, I didn't go to eat. Instead, I walked back over to the classroom alone and sat looking at the details of every choice I had made for the past five years. I couldn't even imagine what the last *twenty* years would look like! Like the man in Suze Orman's book, I had never had a relationship with my money. A half an hour later Roach and the life coaches walked in the room. I couldn't even look at them.

I was so ashamed that Roach now knew all my mistakes. I truly felt that Roach must have been disappointed in me. He had always worked so hard for everything he had. I could picture him thinking, *How could she have made so much money and gotten rid of it so fast?* And I will never forget him sitting there, staring at the chart as if to say, "Oh, my God! What can I do?" I can imagine that Roach wanted to help me, to save me. But the problem was too enormous.

"I feel helpless," he said.

I hope that someday I can truly forgive myself for the mistakes I have made. What helps me now is sharing what I've learned with others. If this book helps one person to take their life back, to face an addiction, to heal a broken relationship, then this book has been worth writing indeed.

When I first signed my record deal, I didn't have a clue about business. Having a manager is necessary, but you should work alongside of the manager and let them know your wishes. I didn't even know what questions to ask, or what opinions to give. Being eighteen years old, all I cared about was singing.

"I should have gotten more involved," I now say to myself over and over. But back then I simply trusted and let go of the day-to-day details. I was so naive. I felt like the luckiest girl in the world! I felt grateful, like everyone around me was doing me a favor. I truly didn't understand that I paid for everything: the recordings, the videos, my hair and makeup costs, the bus, the *gas* in the bus, the equipment to do a show. (I thought the venue we played paid for the equipment!)

I didn't understand the word *recoupable* as it related to my career. I borrowed money from the record label to make a record, or a video, and then I had to pay that money back from my record sales before I made a dime. Wow! I didn't know that! My manager took his percentage off the top, not after taxes. I wouldn't have known to renegotiate that arrangement after I became more successful. (I'm surprised I even thought to try and change the percentage when I went from being part of a duo to a solo artist!) I didn't know what it had taken to get me where I was. I was young and strong and rocking the country.

I didn't pay attention to what I paid my band. My priority was making music and the people involved in helping me do it. I had no experience on how to negotiate with anyone over a salary. In the beginning, my manager did that, and later, when I finally did understand the concept, I was so concerned about keeping my team together that I instructed management to "Do whatever it takes to keep everyone happy." One year I earned exactly the same money as my bass player. I can laugh about it now. Really! As years passed, I started paying a *huge* overhead—more than I brought in.

In addition to my business losses, by the time I divorced my first husband, my life savings were gone. I never paid attention to what was being spent. We both had credit cards, but I don't ever remember looking at a statement. I was on the road a lot, and my mind was on kids, not cash flow.

Perhaps the biggest revelation came when I saw that my feelings about money were so much like my love affair with food. I ate when I was lonely, and I spent money when I was lonely. We looked at my expenses, month by month. When I wasn't working, I spent more. When I was alone, I tended to gather people around me and spend money on them, whether it was going out to dinner or buying expensive presents. I was an addict.

When I would get home from the road, one of the first

things I did was start going through all the catalogues that had arrived while I was gone. I know they released serotonin into my brain. I would circle items in the catalogues and have Jane, my house manager, order them. There were months when the UPS or FedEx drivers were at my house three or four times a week! I was rewarding myself, giving myself presents. I didn't need a husband to buy me presents. The deliveryman was bringing me packages all the time.

There were trips to New York and Los Angeles where all I did was run from one store to the next buying presents for people. There were big parties for my kids and for other people where I spent thousands of dollars. It had to be coming from an overwhelming sense of wanting to be loved. *I'll pay you so much money and buy you so many gifts that you'll never leave me.*

It has always been hard for me to say no to people. I remember once, as I was being prepped for my gynecological exam, the technician asked if I would sign her guitar. I have had so few boundaries! I had a woman start talking about my music while I was getting a mammogram, and when I was in the stall of a women's restroom. When I got my DUI, the police officer sang country songs all the way to police headquarters. When I was looking at Mamaw Ciminella in her coffin, leaning over to tell her goodbye, someone I didn't know asked me for an autograph. And if someone on the street asks for cash, I'm usually pulling money out of my pocket before they finish explaining.

You're supposed to love your neighbor as you love yourself, not more than you love yourself! Mom and Pop owned a house and were well-off. I had helped Dad buy a house. I had given Ashley a house. I had had to sell my house, and if I wasn't careful, I was going to lose my farm-land. Sitting there at Onsite, I thought to myself, *If I had kept even half of what I earned these past twenty years, I could work when I wanted to, not because I had to.*

Guilt! And more guilt!

When I went back and finished the workshop, Roach and I were given three scenarios.

- Sell the farm now, continue current monthly spending, at age fifty-two be completely bankrupt.
- Reduce spending by fifty percent, bankrupt at age fifty-seven, and have to sell part of the farm.
- Reduce monthly spending by seventy percent, get to keep the farm.

It was like hearing the doctor say, "Miss Judd, you have only a few years to live."

It was like hearing, at age thirty, that Michael Ciminella was not my biological father.

It was like the counselor was saying, "I have some bad news, and some more bad news. And then I have some *more* bad news."

I kept sitting there, looking at that chart.

"So this is my life?" I asked, tears flowing down my face. *Choices are sacred.* The thought flashed through my mind. And I knew that for me, the third scenario was the only choice. The first two were not options. I *couldn't* lose my farm. So I had to cut spending by seventy percent.

Roach and I and the coaches began to discuss what it would take to make the changes. We began making a "to-do" list. I had a difficult time letting go of the control. I had been so used to being in charge, with Roach working for me, that we'd developed a routine. I brought that boss role into the marriage. It extended to other parts of our life, too. Whether it was picking a restaurant, playing a board game, or spending money, I felt the need to lead. I was Mama, the Alpha!

Several times I got so agitated when Roach tried to offer suggestions, that the coaches had to step in. Once, a coach said, "If you are going to let him in the boat, you're going to have to let him help row."

Another time they asked Roach how he was feeling.

Roach got very emotional, and finally said with shattering honesty, "I'm terrified. I don't know what to do."

"What do you want to do?" the coach asked.

"I want to help her any way I can," Roach said softly.

He was so willing to be humble, to admit vulnerability, that it broke my defenses down. When I saw how scared he was that we couldn't get past this barrier, how soft he got, and how he didn't judge me, I fell apart. What he gave to me that day was a true gift. I saw in that moment why we can stay married. Roach never looked at me in judgment, or with an agenda. I turned a corner. For the first time in my life, I was able to feel sad, and even scared, but not that my husband might abandon me. Roach would say, "I'm not going anywhere." I had certainly never felt that feeling before, as a lover and partner.

My husband was willing to come in the muck and try to pull me out. If I asked my husband, "Do you want to run?" he would say NO.

For me it was like looking through life with glasses of a different color. It was the understanding that when a husband and wife have differences, you must ask, *How do you feel?* and want an honest answer.

I had never had a relationship where I had shared my financial details. I always kept personal and business separate. But after Roach and I really started working together on the to-do list, it started to feel like a true partnership. As frightening as it was to face in the beginning, we started to walk through the fire. As we worked, I started to feel like we were coming out on the other side. I still had a chance. (Like my song says, *There really is a place like this where the sun is shining for you.*)

When we left Onsite after that first workshop, it took three and a half hours for us to find our way home. We felt like we were floating, on a spiritual high. I felt light—and believe me, I haven't felt light in a long time! We were so alive, and in the moment, we didn't even pay attention to where we were going. Our life coach later told us that it happens to a lot of people when they leave.

The next morning Roach and I got up and went to work. We knew we had to make the changes immediately. My survival skills kicked in. I became fierce! I had never before been ready to make such a drastic change in my business dealings and personal lifestyle, but I was ready now!

The first task was to separate the household, farm, personal and business accounts for the Judd/Roach family. It was my job to reduce spending to the amount that we had agreed on at Onsite. It was only through doing this that we could realize our dream—to one day build a home on our farm.

One of the most interesting parts of our work is what we're doing with Grace, Elijah and Zac. At the beginning of each month, they get a certain amount of money in an envelope. They are responsible for their food and entertainment anytime they are outside the home. (Unless it's Mama and Papa Roach's treat, of course!) Imagine the look on the waitress' face when she has to write out separate checks for each child! And the children are learning about making responsible choices.

"I wanna go eat at P. F. Chang's," Grace said the other day.

"No, it's too expensive," Elijah answered. "Let's eat at Moe's."

I had to laugh. If they don't spend all their money in a given month, the remainder goes into the bank. At the end of the year, they can save it or spend it. They are starting to get it. Hallelujah!

That was just the beginning.

For the past three years, ever since I sold my house on Old Hillsboro Road, I had been boarding a lot of my animals. The house I am renting has no facilities for horses or my deer or buffalo. I have less room for my large outside dogs. Boarding was costing me approximately the amount of one person's full-time salary. I had some dogs that I thought I was just keeping temporarily for other people, but who ended up not being able to take them back. At first I thought I might be able to find homes for them. I soon realized that the dogs had bonded, and unless I could find homes for a dog duo, I wasn't willing to give them up.

I've always had animals in pairs through the years, so much so that a lot of my friends call me Wy-Noah. And I often end up with dogs that have been abused or abandoned—they find me. And I think when people knew where I lived, they dropped off animals, knowing they'd be taken care of. I can usually integrate a new animal into the group. (I am a dog whisperer!)

One of the best examples is my little rat terrier Pixie. I first met her when I was involved in a public-awareness campaign regarding new medications that help older dogs in pain. (I used to say that I was the spokeswoman for the Elderly Dogs of America.) I did a satellite broadcast from New York, spotlighting various facilities and talking about how to care for your older pets. It was connected to arthritis medication, so on the very first day, the organizers asked if I would be willing to adopt an older dog suffering from arthritis. I cringed when they said they'd show me pictures of some in animal shelters across the country via satellite. I can't take seeing animals in facilities where I know they will be put to sleep if not adopted. Happily, the pictures came from no-kill shelters.

One of the dogs was the skinniest, saddest little terrier with the biggest ears I had ever seen on such a tiny dog. Her ears took up the whole picture. "That's the one," I immediately said, thinking she looked like a refugee from the Island of Misfit Toys.

"Well." The woman hesitated. "She's having some problems. It's a bad case. She's been abused and has a pin in her leg. Someone must have kicked her or thrown her against a wall."

Of course, that meant she was going to come home with me. I know that people usually want to adopt the prettiest dog, the one that's fluffy and looks like a stuffed toy. I've never been that way. The organization flew her in that night from Los Angeles, and when I arrived the following day, there was Pixie, eyes downcast and trembling. I took her home and kept her wrapped up inside my robe for several days. She slept in my bathroom, separate from the rest of the dogs. One by one, I introduced the other nine dogs to this little one. It took about two months before she came trotting out of her room one morning, and took a look around as if to say, "Okay. I'm here and I'm in charge." Pixie is my littlest dog, and the one with the biggest bark. She is also my biggest success when it comes to integrating an abused dog into our household.

We put up fencing and brought the rest of my dogs home. We did some research and found a dog food that was nutritional, but less expensive. That made a big difference, since so many dogs were involved! I had to sell the horses, and the woman who boarded the animals wanted to keep the deer. Before we made the move, we lost twenty-one outdoor cats in a barn fire. (I'll *never* get over that.)

Of all that I did, dealing with my animals was the hardest. There have been times, especially before my children were born, that I felt my dogs and my two indoor cats were the only things keeping me sane. I still end up on the couch with six or seven of them piled on top of me.

I cut out two cell phones and a landline at the house. I made a new grocery budget. I had always done the grocery shopping. I love to grocery shop, and ended up filling two carts even though we didn't need it! (I'm addicted to the snack aisle.) I paid little or no attention to what I was spending at the store. Our chef, Cathy, has a budget each month, and if we run out, I have to dip into my personal allowance.

Looking at the money spent on the children was just mortifying. For one thing, the amount of money I often spent on them was to make up for all the times their visits with their dad got canceled. Once again, I used food as a way to soothe and comfort. Also, as parents, we fall into the trap of buying into all the latest and greatest gadgets to keep our children happy. Feeling guilt because I had been gone, I always brought gifts with me when I came home from the road.

Guilt accounts for a lot of parental spending. But what children really need is more time and less money. Before I started homeschooling, I tried to get up every morning to get them to school on time. But when I had been in the studio until midnight, I just couldn't do it. I tried too hard to do everything, be all things to all people, that I failed at a lot of it. I had to have a come-to-Jesus meeting with myself about what kids really need. I asked the kids to make a list of their wishes, of things we could do together.

We don't go to as many movies. Instead, Roach put up a

tent and at nights or on weekends we roast marshmallows and camp out. I read to the kids at night instead of taking them to the arcade and letting them blow money on video games. Just a few weeks ago, I gave Grace her allowance and then took her to a bookstore. Of *course*, she thought that Chuck E. Cheese's would be better than any bookstore. *Where's the lights? Where's the action? Where's the pizza?* On the way there, in the car, Grace acted like I was punishing her, even though she loves going to the library. But once she got to the bookstore, I almost couldn't get her to leave. That's where she wanted to spend all her money—and she even found a couple of books on sale!

At Christmas I had a bad habit of waiting until the last minute to buy presents, then spending several hundred dollars on overnight shipping. It was a lack of organization, plus the fear that I hadn't bought enough *stuff*. At the last minute, I would think of someone else. I wanted to give presents to everyone! I felt it had to be something spectacular. God forbid if somebody thought that I couldn't afford that extra special something.

Birthdays were worse. One year Grace commented on a huge cake she saw in a magazine, so I had a bakery duplicate it. Fine, except that it cost a hundred dollars and the kids didn't eat much of it anyway. (You know they'd rather eat the Kroger birthday cake.)

I couldn't keep myself from turning their parties into extravaganzas. I would invite fifty, a hundred, sometimes more. We'd rent roller rinks, boats. We even had Santa Claus come to one party! At Grace's parties, I would hire clowns and get tons of expensive decorations. Then I would spend even more on presents. In the end, I would sometimes spend over a thousand dollars on a child's birthday party! I wasn't even aware of the fact that I was spending so much. I just did it. I justified it by saying, "I'm giving the children what I didn't have." Now they get a set amount and they can either spend it on the party or keep the money and order pizzas. They get presents, but now I save for them and appreciate giving them more.

I thought a lot about the difference between Roach and me when it came to gift giving. In the past, I might have spent a thousand dollars on his present, while he spent a few hundred on mine. But because he couldn't pay as much for his gift, he made the presentation something special. It's rare for someone to put the thought and energy into gift giving like Roach does. No one in my life had ever done that. Times that he has blessed me with a gift, even before we were dating, he might have spent six months planning or preparing it. It came from the heart.

The gifts he has given me have been wonderful. One time after we were dating, he asked me to come to his condo for dinner. When I arrived, he did a Chippendale-style strip dance for me to one of my songs! He had on the tie and the hat cocked to the side. He even had a G-string on! He is such a great dancer—astonishingly professional!

"Are you sure you haven't been moonlighting???" I laughed.

What I learned is that you can make changes in many areas of your life when you are trying to cut down on spending. They don't even have to be extreme changes. You don't have to cut off an arm. It can be as simple as staying away from temptation. I've cut back on going to the mall with the children. They see things they want, and it's hard for me to say no. So we decide what we're buying before we go, and we stick to the plan. I don't even take them with me if I'm just shopping for myself.

It was a major revelation for me when I understood that the children can pitch in and help much more than they ever have. That's not to say that the shift in our way of life was easy for them. I had taken on too much for them. They were raised in hotels and on the road. They'd say, *What do you mean I have to clean my room?* You should have seen Jane and me trying to teach them how to make their beds!

I made lists of everything they were to do before school, from brushing their teeth to putting away toys. We had to get very specific with the list, since they are young. They had to understand that putting away their stuff didn't mean shoving it into a closet or under the bed. They also had lists of chores for during the day, and at night before bedtime. That was hard for me, because I remember how I used to feel when Mom made her lists for me! If they don't get their chores done, they get one demerit for each thing not done. They can work it off here at home, or they can work it off at the thrift store. A man from our church started the store, and young people volunteer daily to help keep the store organized, clean and running smoothly. It's good for kids to work or to volunteer their time, no matter what their financial status is. And if they do come from a family that has money, they need to keep it in perspective.

I remember an episode of *The Cosby Show* where Theo is complaining that the kids at school treated him differently because he was rich. Theo says, "Dad, I don't want to be rich. I want to be like everyone else and be treated like everyone else."

Bill Cosby answers, "You're not rich, Theo. I'm rich. You're poor. *You* don't have any money!"

I laughed out loud when he said that.

Saving money was an even bigger challenge than cutting back on spending. If we had money left over from our budget, we were trying to save it. That was a tremendous challenge. I have a tendency to spend what money I have left over from anything, rather than saving it for a rainy day. I tended to say, "I might not be here by the time it rains!"

The biggest fear I had was in cutting my tour expenses. I didn't want to look cheap. I really had to think about it from a production standpoint—what is essential, what can go without hurting the quality of the show. For my next tour I came up with a musical autobiography format, where I relied more on my gift than on elaborate production. We also played smaller venues, so it was an intimate show. That 2004 tour ended up being one of my all-time favorite tours. I learned that less really is more!

Another change Roach and I made was flying Southwest. No first-class tickets or sitting around in a VIP lounge awaiting takeoff. It was humbling because I had flown first class since I was eighteen years old. The truth is, when you're used to something, you get set in your ways. I have traveled so much and spent so much time getting to a gig—sometimes four or five flights a week—and first class was a blessing. Sometimes it was the only downtime that I would have in a day. (Of course, first class *was* where I met my first husband.)

I have to be honest about this: flying economy can get strange. It's a cattle call every time! For some reason, it seemed like I was always flying with large groups of crazy people on their way to Las Vegas. I would end up taking pictures with everyone while standing in line to get on board. I've gotten standing ovations on sold-out flights! It was great! Someone actually offered to pay me to sing to him over the intercom once.

Roach and I really kept our hearts open to what cool things might happen when we were even more accessible than ever before. We have heard some awesome stories from people we sat with. (People will tell me anything.)

There were days when I was so tired that I thought I would cry; then somehow the flight worked out to be a positive experience. Bottom line: it was a pain in the butt getting to the airport two to three hours early when I was used to one. But when I'm ninety years old, I'll still remember some of my fellow passengers and their stories.

I stopped checking into hotels when I'm on tour. I just stay on the bus now. In the past, I had a tendency to slip into a depression when I spent so much time alone on the bus, so I have to guard against it. I know myself well enough to know that if I start to feel lonely, I'll look for something to eat. So times when Roach is busy with post-show business, I light my candles, play music or listen to books on CD. I've started answering my fan mail again. I try to look at it as solitude, not isolation. People were shocked when I started spending more time at sound checks with the band and crew. That's become another positive.

One of the things that has really excited me is seeing how all the changes add up at the end of the month. I'm tightening the spending even more now. When I'm not working, I get my hair touched up twice a month instead of three times. My roots grow so fast, but by doing this I save a few hundred dollars a month. I know that I have to save now to be able to buy something I want in the future. If I don't, I won't even be able to keep what I have!

Some people will find this hard to believe but changing my spending habits was life altering. I love using cash instead of credit cards! I love knowing exactly how much money I have left. I've even got to the point where if I have a hundred-dollar bill, I will wait longer to break it than I would a ten or twenty.

Making these outward changes required a lot of looking inward. I have always believed in meditation. Even Jesus meditated. And I've learned through my workshops that much of what I do daily is a form of meditation. It's also about praise and worship. Getting out of bed in the morning can be a form of praise and worship. Instead of saying, "Oh, God, it's morning," I say, "Good morning, God!"

I learned at Onsite how to slow down everything I normally do fast—walking, talking, chewing, showering. It's hard and I have to *practice* doing things slowly. And I've spent so much time distracted that I needed to be able to focus. As I wrote in a song, *God whispers*. The world yells, but God whispers.

I realized that I had spent a lot of my life pissed-off because I couldn't say a simple no. I would come in off the road and be exhausted, wanting to do nothing more than rest or play or do absolutely nothing. Then a manager would call and say, "Look, I know you're tired, but we have this great opportunity . . ." It might be a big arena show, or it might be a White House performance. So sure, I understood that it was a great opportunity. But I needed rest more than I needed another gig. A part of me needed to be home. But there was also that part of me that wanted to be loved and needed.

After I would agree to the show, I would hang up the phone with a sinking heart. I had done it again! I would get mad at myself for sabotaging my personal plans for the sake of the team. I spent too much time *reacting* to my career. When I am *proactive*, I make clear choices from within. Being *reactive* means the power behind the choices comes from outside forces.

The Onsite process opened my peripheral vision. Even in the dark night of the soul, in the saddest part of sad, I felt a sense of hope. Usually when I would get that depressed, I would feel hopeless. But at Onsite I felt I wasn't alone. I would still freak out, but I learned the Serenity

Prayer. *God grant me the serenity to accept the things I cannot change, courage to change the things I can, and wisdom to know the difference.* God says in the Bible: *in your weakness, I am strong.* I don't know if I understood those words before I started through the work at Onsite, but they have changed the way I look at everything—my own life, my relationships with others and my understanding of the world.

13

NEW DAY DAWNING

I t seems incredible that so much had happened in such a short time. After the day I first met with Oprah to talk about my struggles, I had started a journey toward a healthier life, then was derailed with a DUI, had married the man I loved, was confronted with potential financial disaster and began working on my life at Onsite.

Finally, on February 11, 2004, I went on *Oprah* to talk publicly for the first time. I prayed for two things before that show. First, I prayed that I would remain real even if people thought I was whining and complaining. Second, I also prayed that I would have the courage to be vulnerable even if people saw it as a weakness.

I shouldn't have worried about showing my emotions. The minute Oprah told the audience that they would see raw, emotional moments on the show, my eyes filled with tears. I talked about my deepest fears, about feeling inadequate when I tried to balance a career with taking care of my children and devoting time to my husband. I said I had to face the fact that I couldn't do it all.

Oprah showed clips of Mom and Ashley. Ashley appeared angry about the "thirty-year lie," and said she had known for years that Charlie Jordan was my father. Mom said that Charlie had left town when he learned she was pregnant, and that she married Michael to give me a name and a home. I admitted that only in the past few years had I started realizing "just how stinkin' mad" I am about the big lie.

Ashley added that both of us had talked about feeling lonely while we were growing up. She said that all she really cared about was my health and the problems carrying around extra pounds can cause. Mom also said that I hadn't been overweight as a teen. "It was called *chunky*," she said.

I told the audience, "I finally looked in the mirror and said, 'You're not immortal. This is going to kill me.'"

Bob Greene said that my marriage might face some challenges during this process. Oprah asked Roach if he could comment. "I see the challenge as a positive thing," he said. "I see it as a new beginning, as living longer. I see it as Wy caring about herself and the family." He paused, and added: "Because, without her, there is no family."

Bob also told Oprah that after listening to me talk that day, he predicted that I would have *many* more challenges ahead of me. When Oprah had asked if I was planning to work out that day after the taping, I immediately started finding reasons why I might not have time. Bob reminded me that by doing that, I was putting off the commitment. Oprah said it was all about being disciplined, something she had to force herself to become. "I say, 'Lord! Please send me discipline!'" she laughed. "I didn't realize that I had to do it!"

One of the most poignant times during the show came when Mom was interviewed on tape, and said that she just wanted me to know that she knew I had potential, and that she was there for me. I admitted to Oprah that I feared there was something else on Mom's mind. I was afraid that she secretly believed I would fail and do it in front of millions of people. Failing isn't something the Judd women do.

I sincerely hoped I wouldn't fail. But as we wrapped the show, Bob Greene had a warning for me. "Everyone hopes for a happy ending," he said. "But remember, there's a lot of tough work to do." (I remember looking at him and wanting to mess up his perfect hair!)

When I got back from *Oprah*, I worked even harder with Cathy to learn how to eat a variety of foods every day so I wouldn't feel "cheated" and start to binge. I know that it's important to satisfy your taste buds, and reserved one day a week for my old favorites. You shouldn't take away everything you love just because you are trying to get healthy! The key, of course, is moderation, and that was something I had to teach myself.

I was raised on comfort food—soup beans and corn bread, fried bologna sandwiches, chicken potpie and mashed potatoes. So Cathy started developing recipes for healthier potpies, and making mashed sweet potatoes. I started eating more salads, but with additions like dried fruits and nuts.

I started eating about every three hours. I drank hot tea, either herbal or green, to help calm my body and mind. It also gives you a chance to take a time-out! I didn't eat two to four hours before bedtime, and was amazed at the difference in the way I felt because of it! In fact, when I broke that rule, I realized just how sluggish those late-night meals had been making me. I could wake up earlier, and with far more energy.

One thing I did not do was start buying those low-carb foods that have flooded the market. So many of them have junk in the ingredients. Here's a good rule—the more ingredients listed, the worse it probably is for you. Also, I started paying attention to how many calories and fat grams some of those low-carb products have in them. You'd be amazed. I always look at the nutritional information now. I've learned that if you see something that's marked fat-free it will usually have more sugar added for taste. Diet drinks have aspartame as an ingredient, which turns to wood alcohol—basically, it's formaldehyde. I only drink Diet Rite, and in moderation, because carbonation is not good for our bones! I now look for Stevia, which is the only sweetener I use.

In a very short time, I could feel myself losing weight. I say "feel" because one of the things Dominick kept reminding me was that the journey was not about weight. It isn't about numbers on a scale because muscle weighs more than fat. It's about inches lost. Instead of being consumed with my weight, I'm making lifestyle changes and taking better care of myself. What a concept!

I decided to not be defined by a number because it just might ruin my day! Feeling good in clothes was going to be my barometer. I measured myself every four weeks, and got very excited as the inches came off.

I also wanted to continue working with Onsite about health issues, and signed up for another workshop.

One of the things I was asked to do was to write a letter describing my feelings and thoughts about my relationship with food. At first I thought it was a really weird assignment. But I started thinking about the fact that food is just as much an addiction as alcohol or drugs or gambling. I first had to admit the addiction, and then admit what an important role it had played in my life. I started writing, wanting to try to understand.

The more time I spent on this love letter—and that's

just what it is—the more clearly I saw that food had b̶
an integral part of it all, my successes and my failures. If you've never faced a food addiction, this letter may sound strange. But I believe that those of you who have will find the sentiments eerily familiar.

A letter to food . . .

I have loved you for 40 years. You have been such a blessing to me. You've comforted me in my darkest nights, and celebrated with me on my brightest days. You've been the one true and constant friend in my life.

You have never judged me. You have always lifted me up when I was down. You've given me the energy to do the work I had to do, and the love to keep me going when I thought I could not. I couldn't have made it this far if not for you.

You never talk back! I can call on you at all hours of the day and night. You're 24/7/365. I've never had a problem reaching you when I needed you most.

You soothe me, and you love me unconditionally. You always fill me up! When I feel hurt, angry, lonely, tired or stressed, you are the perfect ending to a crappy day.

I could not ask for a better nurturer when I am sick. When I'm with you, it reminds me of when I was little and didn't have to go to school. I could have all the 7-Up I wanted! I long to be taken care of that way again.

Each day you remind me that to be fully in the moment and to appreciate all that God has to give. And I know He has given me so much.

Rosie O'Donnell once told me, "Bone is for the dog, meat is for the man."

"Some men like some meat with their potatoes," I often say.

Food, I've always made jokes about you and me. But there's been a lot of pain right under the surface of my humor.

All the times I wake up in the middle of the night you've called to me, and you've brought me back to a place of belonging. I was lost but now I'm found has been our song. You and I play when everyone else is asleep. I am like a child sneaking that extra piece of candy—I get away with it and you laugh with me. You never slap my hand when I reach for you. There is no shame. Thank you for not judging me when the world did.

You have always been the centerpiece of all my parties. You don't go home early. You stay late and you're even willing to go home with me. In the end, when everyone else is gone, and I feel blue, the party continues with us. I'm the guest of honor. You're loyal and dedicated to making me happy.

When I'm in the studio and sing well, you cater to my every need. When I'm a lonesome, weary traveler out on the road, you remind me of where I come from. When you are with me I always feel at home.

You have always been my reward at the end of a long day, and you've always been there to greet me when I walk in the door. I can always count on you. What would I have done without you when the show was over, the lights were dimmed, my fans had all gone home and I was in that hotel room alone?

When I am with Roach, you bring us closer. We

are intimate once more. You are like a mediator. We plan all of our celebrations around you. After all, it was the crème brûlée kiss that changed our relationship forever. You were there when we got engaged, when we got married and for our anniversaries.

Family is everything to me. Thank you for bringing us together each day. It is the most sacred part of my day.

Food is love. To eat is to live.

Thank you for being there for all those late night visits with my mamaw. Thank you for being there when Ashley and I were young. Thank you for staying with me all those nights when I waited and waited for someone to come home.

Thank you for being there each time I made a terrible mistake in my life and felt like a failure.

When I feel fat, ugly and unwanted, you remind me of what I AM, not what I am NOT.

Thank you for being my best friend all these years. Thank you for helping me survive the pain. You saved my life.

Wy

Writing that letter became the first time I fully understood the enormity of the challenge I faced with food and health issues. I didn't have one negative thing to say about food. I have a friend who tried to quit smoking, and said she felt like she had abandoned her best friend. And it is how I view food, as my friend and confidant. That is addiction. What I am trying to do now is to see eating *healthy* as my friend!

One day Roach and I sat on the floor of our classroom at Onsite. Our life coach handed both of us a dried cranberry. "Eat this the way you normally would."

I popped it in my mouth, chewed it once or twice and swallowed.

Then he handed us each another cranberry. "Roll this one around in your mouths a minute before chewing. I want you to notice the texture, and how it feels on your tongue."

We did this for about a minute before he said we could chew and swallow.

He handed us a third cranberry, and said:

"Before you put this in your mouth, look at it, smell it—*then* put it in your mouth and chew it until it is almost liquid."

I chewed sixty-five times. I counted.

I felt like a little girl! I looked at Roach and laughed. "Now what?" I asked.

"The first cranberry represents the way most of us eat," the life coach said.

It was true. The first cranberry was Wynonna personified. At a buffet I don't even taste the food on my first plateful! I am going back for seconds before I actually take the time to taste anything. I'm so embarrassed to admit that!

"I want you to start using your senses," the coach said.

Roach and I said we were going to start paying attention to the way we approached our meals both at home and when we dined out. Our coach laughed and warned that other diners might stare at us when we started passing the plate under our noses for a good sniff.

"No, they'll probably just think it's some religious thing," Roach said with a grin.

Then we were served a meal. We sat with our eyes closed and absorbed the wonderful aroma for about thirty seconds. We ate for the first ten minutes without saying a word.

"How do you feel about this?" the coach asked.

"I feel pretty weird," I admitted. "In my world, when no one says anything at the table, it means people are upset."

I'm not one who would ever go out to eat alone. I see dining as a celebratory thing: talking, laughing and cutting up. I want company and conversation. But the whole time we stayed at Onsite, we spent the first ten minutes of each meal in silence. The second time we did it, it didn't feel exactly weird, just odd. But as we went through the week, it became a meditation and the meal a much more fulfilling event.

It was hilarious when we came home and involved the children in this new way of eating. The first few times they ate in silence, they twitched, glanced at each other uncomfortably, moved around in the chair and could *barely* keep from blurting out a comment. But in about a week, they, too, started enjoying it.

Between the help I had received from Oprah and the work I had done at Onsite, I was doing a pretty good job with my program—with some slips. It was hard for me to keep to my schedule when I went out on the road. And impulse eating is one of the biggest temptations when the bus is rolling along or you are sitting in a hotel room at midnight, with room service just a phone call away. As I had grown smaller, I had started giving away some of my bigger clothes. I bought a pair of smaller pants and hung them in my closet. I decided that my goal would be to wear the smaller pants and to be able to breathe when I bent over to tie my shoes.

I get frustrated with the quick-fix mentality when it comes to getting healthy. I saw a television show where they sent two teams of people to a weight-loss "contest" at a mountain camp. Well, if you put me on a mountaintop, I would probably lose weight, too. It's the same with these programs where prepackaged meals are supplied. What happens when you come off the mountain or go off the program? Many people regain the weight and more. I wanted a program that I was willing to do for the rest of my life. I want to change my life, not just lose thirty pounds for this year's Country Music Awards.

The things that were the most difficult for me in the beginning were still the hardest: not eating at night, portion control and keeping a strict exercise schedule. I really felt like I had to deprogram myself. Controlling my portions was probably the biggest hurdle. One of my most prominent memories of childhood involves running out of food when Mom was gone. Ashley and I would be hungry and stay that way until Mom returned. Then I would eat as much as I possibly could. Also, restaurants now serve such huge portions! It really is a supersized society.

But I knew that Oprah had been right. The bottom line is—why are we eating? In my case, I understand that it is because somewhere deep down, despite all the #1 records, the awards and applause, I have a self-loathing. It has nothing to do with success. It has to do with the self-image developed during childhood. Were you taught to believe in yourself when you were a small child? How did you view yourself when you were in high school? What was your experience with your first boyfriend? Did your parents say things like *You'd be so pretty if* . . .

I felt I had made a great deal of progress in working my way out of self-loathing. But I was about to see just how fragile that progress was.

14

ROCK BOTTOM

I n May of 2004 I returned for a second appearance on *Oprah*. It was three months after my first meeting with her, and at this point my journey wasn't about losing pounds. As Oprah has said, "It's not about weight—weight is a symptom, not the problem. It's about caring for yourself on a daily basis." The plan I agreed to with Bob Greene was that I wouldn't eat two to four hours before bedtime, and that I would work out thirty minutes a day, five days a week. It wasn't about *what* I was eating. More importantly, I was beginning to make significant personal and professional life changes. During my first meeting with Oprah, I had told her that when it came to priorities, I had forgotten to put myself on the list. By the time I returned, I felt I had begun to change that.

Even though I felt good about the progress I was making with my eating and workout schedule, I was nervous because I had been asked to sing on the show. Initially I declined because I didn't want people to think I was coming on the show to sell CDs. The appearance was about my personal life, not about my career.

After a great deal of internal debate, I eventually agreed to the performance. I soon realized that I would have to face another fear. I had been asked to sing alone to tracks, without the band or backup singers. I have struggled with performer's anxiety for twenty years now, especially in a situation where I have to stand alone onstage, without my guitar in front of a microphone. Some artists may be used to singing to tracks, but I had only done it a few times. I've always performed with my guitar, the musicians and the singers. However, I decided that my journey was about, in great part, being open to change. It was time to face the music, literally.

I was anxious about Mom and Ashley coming to this show, even though it was me who had asked them. I told them I needed their support personally this time, but I was especially nervous about Mom coming, because I had some things I wanted to say to her. I knew I would be emotional. I wanted my mom there, not my singing partner. What I needed most that day was for my mom to show up and just be my mom.

Even though we stopped touring together twelve years ago, it has continued to be a challenge for me to separate from Mom at times. I still worry about making sure Mom is taken care of at my shows and appearances. I want to honor her and treat her like a queen. All moms deserve that! But despite wanting a close connection, I didn't want to lose myself, either. I had made a promise to myself that on *Oprah* I wouldn't try to mediate between Ashley and Mom, or get caught up in saying the right thing instead of the real thing.

I was concerned, though, that as three Alpha females, we might air too much dirty laundry. I wanted the show to stay focused on my journey, and not get off into details that might muddy the waters. I had asked Mom and Ashley to come to *Oprah*, not to *Family Feud*.

I didn't want people to think that I went on *Oprah* to complain about my life. I did go on *Oprah* to share my personal journey. I didn't want to be perceived as being disrespectful to Mom or selling her out. In the past I had to be careful about what I said about our relationship, but there were some things that I felt I could now say that were real about how hard it is to be family.

One of our issues was my openness. I wear my heart on my sleeve and it often causes me to be too free with my words. Over the years my spontaneity has been a source of concern to Mom. Even though she says that she wears her heart on her mouth, she is often more scripted. I felt like Mom saw me as the heart and her as the head. I often feel, too, that Mom views me as someone so free and in the moment that I appear too vulnerable or too weak.

I think one of my biggest concerns was that if I said too much, Mom would feel I had abandoned her and leave the show angry. But I was even more afraid that I would not express my true feelings. Which is worse, the pain of speaking your truth or the pain of not speaking your truth?

I ultimately decided that no matter what, it was time for me to communicate my struggles to my fans and not just talk about my life as if it were perfect. Too many artists hide behind a mask. It's not real. I wanted them to know that even though I love my life, and know that it has been a tremendous blessing, being so successful so young has been difficult at times. I made a pact with God and myself that I would try to be even more real about my life: the good, the bad *and* the ugly.

That's the reason I was so open to talking about my DUI arrest during my first appearance. I had the option to stay away from that subject. But I wanted to address it and talk about what I was doing to get on with my life. I wanted people to understand that I made the mistake and that I took responsibility for it, that I held myself accountable.

Believe it or not, I felt that being honest with my fans was going to be easier than opening up to Mom and telling her what was in my heart that day. There were many things I wished I could tell her. If I had written about my feelings in a letter, it would probably have begun:

I love you, Mom. I know that professionally we had it all, but in our personal relationship there were things I feel we never got right. We've both been through so much, and I've tried to be there for you when you needed me. I've done my best to never abandon you or be disloyal to you or intentionally hurt you. I've been going through some life changes, to be healthier, to be proactive, to not place blame on you. It's important that you hear me. I wish you would put your arms around me and hug me, to tell me you're proud of what I'm doing right now.

I needed to say:

I know that as a parent you did the best you could, but there were some things that I needed as a child that I didn't get. Mom, I feel that it has been my role for most of my life to take care of you. There were so many times when I was so mad at you that I couldn't look at you on the stage, when it seemed as though we were miles apart, yet I still did my best to put our relationship in a good light, to be the good daughter, to put my feelings away. I feel like I was often the butt of your jokes. Both of us have used jokes to cover up our hostility, and I would like for it to change. I want to have a healthier relationship with you.

There was another point that needed addressing:

Mom, I feel our relationship has often been too code-pendent. I'm understanding more and more that in the past my feelings toward you have been resentful, that it was un-healthy. I'm forty years old and it's only been in the past few years that I felt as though I could make a decision on my own, without asking for your approval—that if you dis-agree I won't change my mind to please you. My biggest fear now is that you will feel that as I begin to find myself, that you will see this as my rejecting you. But I just want our relationship to be healthier, to begin to rebuild.

In my heart I knew I wasn't far enough into my journey to say all that in public. But I also knew if Mom and I were to have a new and different relationship, one day I would need to say it.

Oprah had once explained to me that people have to write out a new contract with each other for a relationship to change. Mom and I would need to do just that. Also, a new contract was in order between my sister and me. Because of what I call *the incident*, I had been afraid that Ashley wouldn't come to the show at all, and was relieved when she said she would. I hoped that the show would be a positive step in our relationship. It had been almost a year that Ashley and I had been disconnected.

The *incident* happened one night when Mom, Pop and I went to a dinner at Ashley's house. Anytime the three Judd women get together, there is the distinct possibility for fireworks. In many families what would be normal talk at the dinner table, for us would end up becoming a summit. A wonderful conversation could easily go to hell, and that night that's exactly what happened.

When I arrived at Ashley's after a long day in the stu-dio, Mom and Pop were already there and the mood was

276 · WYNONNA JUDD

cheerful. The three of them were discussing current events, which can often be dangerous in our family. For most of Ashley's adult life, Mom and Ashley have had intense differences in how they view the world. For years I have taken on the role of standing between them as the mediator.

By the time we were getting our coats to leave, Mom had disagreed with Ashley, and Ashley aggressively defended her position. Ashley has always felt the need to stand up for the underdog, and she is fiercely passionate about her feelings. She doesn't let go easily. There are many times when I have disagreed with her positions, but I know her heart is good and she is coming from an honest place of caring. So I understood *why* Ashley became so passionate. She and Mom are so much alike, even more than Mom and I are.

As happens in many family arguments, the person who gets his or her feelings hurt often takes on the role of "victim." This time Mom got very quiet, and I know when that happens she feels victimized.

I had worked for years trying to take myself out of the middle of the two of them. No matter whose side you take, it's a lose-lose situation. *Nobody wins.* However, looking back on that night, the word FOOL must have been written across my forehead because I made the mistake of defending Mom in Ashley's home and not letting them work it out themselves.

In the past I had often taken Mom's side, judging Ashley and asking, "Why are you doing this to Mom?" I've always been protective of Mom and that role expanded after her illness. It often put me at odds with my sister. Additionally, I think Ashley has long believed that she hasn't been heard or understood, and that Mom, Pop and I gang up on her. She's probably right in some instances.

I call what happens to me in these confrontations "the

setup." My mother and my sister are engaged. I see the problem, believe I have the answer, and I insert myself, thinking I will solve the problem. Since I'm very emotional, I get very animated about my "solution" to their differences. I become convinced that if I can stand in the gap between them, I can help bridge their differences and help each to have compassion for the other. But what usually ends up happening is that because their direct connection isn't working, they connect through me. I end up getting zapped by their anger and frustration, and I become highly charged. When the two of them look at me with *what's with her?* expressions, I end up feeling like I'm wearing a dunce cap.

I did not handle myself well that night, to say the least. I wanted Mom and Ashley to stop, but I ended up throwing fuel on the fire. Ashley is so good with words that I knew I couldn't keep up with her verbally. Unfortunately, I tried. The two of us went at it with words. We got louder and louder. Mom and Pop just stood there while Ashley and I went on and on. Ashley knew all the right buttons to push, and push she did until I snapped.

I grabbed Ashley's shoulders, pushed her onto the daybed on her screened-in porch. I held her down and screamed, "STOP IT!" She kept yelling back at me, then kicked me. Pop jumped in the middle of it just as I was getting ready to hit her.

Ashley was stunned, and rightfully furious. There I stood in her home, shouting at her and physically restraining her. I was so upset that I had started having an asthma attack. I left trembling, barely able to breathe.

The next day I got a phone call from our family counselor, who said Ashley requested a meeting with me. Once there, I was asked if I was willing to listen to what Ashley had to say without saying anything back. I agreed, feeling I owed her that.

It was as if all the pain and frustration that had built up for Ashley's whole life came tumbling out. She said that she would no longer allow me to bully her. In effect, she was saying, *I'm grown up, I'm here, and I'm not afraid to stand up to you. I'm not going to take your crap anymore.*

I know Ashley has long felt that I try to dominate her, that I often act more like a mother than a sister. I'm four years older, and have reminded her many times that *I'm the big sister*. I wonder what she must have felt, having such a strong mother, and then a bossy older sister who said things like, "Do my chores or I won't take you to cheerleading practice." Or worse, an older sister who held her down and licked her face until she peed her pants, which was shamefully similar to what I had done the night before.

I can only begin to imagine the resentment that had built up over the years, too, because Mom was at work so much that I was all Ashley had. Though she loved me and depended on me, I'm feeling that she resented me as well.

That day with the counselor, I remember thinking, *This is one of those life-changing moments when you get to tell someone everything and anything you've ever felt about her in your whole life.* I also thought she must love and trust me a lot to feel safe enough to say such horrible things, to take that chance of losing me. When she stopped talking, I asked her if she was finished. She said that she was, and without saying a word, I left. I wept all the way home.

God must have been in the room that day. Under any other circumstances, I would have had to defend myself. But I realized that during this particular appointment, it would have been wrong. I hadn't really heard her the previous night, so it was her turn.

It reminded me of a story about a man who is walking along a path and sees a butterfly trying to break free from its cocoon. He continues to watch the struggle, and when he can't stand it any longer, he breaks open the cocoon so the butterfly can emerge quicker. With a clumsy flutter, the butterfly takes flight for a brief moment, only to spiral down to the ground and die. Because, you see, it is in the struggle of breaking free from its cocoon that blood goes to the wings and gives them strength. It is in that one solitary effort that the butterfly learns to fly.

Ashley was freeing herself from me on her own terms. It was painful to watch.

I still have a hard time thinking about that day with Ashley. A part of me shut down when I heard those words that came from my sister. Whoever wrote *Sticks and stones can break my bones but words can never hurt me* was wrong. Words do hurt. Those words continue to echo in my head.

The very next week I went back to Ashley's house to celebrate her birthday. We didn't say a word about our fight. An outsider would never have guessed that we had ever had a harsh word with each other. One thing about us, we may not agree with or support what the other one is doing, but we accept who we are. That night was about Ashley, and I wasn't going to miss out on an opportunity to celebrate my sister.

Yet something had changed. I carried the conversation around like a sack of *@!* bricks. From that day on, it seemed as though there was a sadness in me, and since that day I had been waiting for that joy to come back in. I so wanted to have a conversation with Ashley about the incident, wanted to be forgiven, so I could be loved again. Backing down first in order to regain love seems to be a pattern with me. But given our professional schedules, our time together had been minimal and nothing was ever resolved for me.

And so, as we all prepared to appear together on *Oprah*,

and as I continued thinking about the incident, and what she had said to me at our counselor's, I wondered how she truly felt about me now and about appearing on the show. I hoped this day would help the two of us reconnect. I didn't want us to wake up in our sixties or seventies and say, "Wow, we missed out on a relationship all those years."

All of us were very quiet before the show started taping. I had watched my mother get ready for stage and television shows so many times before, yet as she was having her makeup done on this day I felt as if she was putting up a protective wall. I felt a distinct sense of fear coming from her. When the stage manager gave us the ten-minute warning before showtime, I went in the bathroom to focus and pray as I always do before going onstage.

I thought about family, and how wonderful it would be to offer love without strings—or stings. I thought that "family" should be a safe place to go where all you had to do was show up and just *be* yourself and that was enough. It should be a place where no one criticizes your clothes or your hair or suggests that your boyfriend is a loser and you could have done much better or that you spent too much for the car you just bought. It should be a peaceful place where you don't feel the need to please all of the people all of the time.

When I was finally called to the stage, I felt intense emotions boiling up inside. I stood alone and watched the intro of the show on one of the stage monitors. When Oprah walked out onto the set, the audience went berserk. A wave of adrenaline shot through my body. I felt the same intense feeling that I had experienced back in 1984 at the Judds' first show in Omaha. Even twenty years later, I was still looking for exits. But I had come too far to turn back. So I took the deepest breath and held it in. As I exhaled, I pushed off with my left foot and walked out to meet Oprah. It was a defining moment in my life.

Oprah asked about the fact that Mom and I had not talked about my weight, and I said, "I would rather go to the gynecologist." *There I go again, hiding my feelings of sadness behind humor!*

What Oprah meant was that Mom and I had not addressed the how or why I had come to this point in my life. Mom had made comments about my health along the way. She had said that she was worried, but there had been no real dialogue about my weight.

I think most mothers have the tendency to believe they know their daughters better than their daughters know themselves. During the first part of the show, Oprah asked Mom how she felt about my journey, and Mom went into a free-flow talk about how she knew me inside and out, how she had been in the delivery room with me and seen my uterus. *What the heck?*

After she mentioned my uterus, Mom looked at me and asked, "Does that make sense?"

"No," I said. *My uterus?*

Oprah asked Ashley if she ever felt guilt over being the skinny sister. Ashley's answer was like her: healthy and honest. She said she had no guilt feelings because our love for each other was strong enough to survive us being different sizes. We talked about body types, and Mom said *she* struggled with *her* weight. Oprah and I looked at each other like *huh?* Oprah said she hoped Mom wasn't offended if the two of us didn't sympathize with her over a few pounds.

At one point Oprah asked me if there was anything I wanted to say to my mother that I hadn't said. That would have been the time to come forward with some of the things in my heart, but again, I grinned and shrugged.

"Oh! How much time have you got?" I joked, once again, *Miss Hilarious*.

Mom stood up, legs wide apart in a defiant stance, and with both hands, she motioned for me. "Bring it on," she said.

I thought, *Hmm, that's such an unfeminine pose for Mom.* It was as if she was preparing for a fight.

"I just want you to know how hard I'm trying," I said.

"I know you are," Mom answered.

At one point I was choking back tears. "The hardest part of this is just being honest. I have to be honest and admit that I don't love myself enough. I love what I *do*, but not *me*." That is what so much of my unhappiness stemmed from, not loving myself. I knew it. Everyone watching knew it. But I still didn't know what to do about it.

When the televised portion of the show wrapped, the cameras kept rolling while Mom, Ashley and I talked on during Oprah's *After Show*. I think that it is possible that the postshow conversation lulled me into a false sense of security, because we did get down to some issues.

As she talked, I realized that although Mom is convinced she is being pro-me, what I end up feeling is that she is diagnosing me, and this is not always helpful. She said I had to get in touch with my emotions, that I seemed to only be actualized when I was singing. She said the whole family had been praying for me. She suggested I had a "disconnect," that something must be going on with a girl who could "talk the talk" like a Ph.D. psychologist, implying that I couldn't make it work in my life, I guess. My reality was that on both of Oprah's shows I was simply trying to share my emotions, not trying to sound like an expert.

When Mom said, "I knew Wynonna had a problem. I used to see the room service trays outside her hotel suite,"

I felt humiliated. It felt like she was telling on me, and I remember wanting to ask, "Mom, was that helpful?" But I didn't want to appear defensive, so I once again resorted to a joke and called myself a *road scholar*. It is one of Mom's favorite old sayings about herself.

Then Mom sighed. "I can't figure out for the life of me what is missing."

Ashley jumped in then, telling Mom that the point was, she didn't *have* to get it. "We understand how you feel, Mom," she said. "But you don't have to figure it out. Relieve yourself of that job, 'cause if you don't, *I'll* fire you. It ain't your business."

I was shocked. Ashley has such a way with words.

"I resign," Mom said quickly. "There's a whole chapter in my book, 'Resign as General Manager of the Universe.'"

She was talking about *Naomi's Breakthrough Guide: 20 Choices to Transform Your Life*, which she had published a few months earlier. I hadn't started reading it yet, and it bothered her.

I tried to get Mom off the book pitch and back to finding a way around the problem: "I know how to give love," I said. "Most women are raised to give. I know I'm a giving singer, a mother, a wife, and a lover. What I don't know how to do is to receive."

Mom seemed a little defensive. "But we all give to you!"

It reminded me of something I had heard often happens when men and women come in for counseling. The woman will say what she needs. The man will immediately counter: "Look, I work my butt off. You have a nice house and a new car. I support you and the kids. I don't hit you. What's *wrong* with you?" It's such a disconnect.

At that point Ashley rolled her eyes and said she was glad she was in the middle between Mom and me. That was my cue to say that I felt I was the one who'd always stood in the middle between them. But I felt too vulnerable, and let it go.

"For what it's worth," Ashley said to me, "I think you're doing great. I want you to be happy. I want you to be healthy. And I think this is an incredible odyssey. You're excavating in a way you've not had to do. Keep your elbows out sharp—remember that boundaries are good. Sometimes you've resented that mine are so strong. I'll give them to you willingly. You have to have them to survive."

"Keep your elbows out sharp." I think that was Ashley telling me to fight for my own space. She had become better at doing that at a younger age, and I was just beginning to learn how.

I told her that I was working on it, and that I knew this journey was in part about the self that falls into bed and worries about the two or three things left undone that day.

"Why can't we celebrate the ten things we *did* do?" I asked. "Why don't we throw a party and celebrate ourselves more often?"

Then I turned to Mom. "You say you give to me. I know you do."

"Then what else can I do?" she asked.

I wasn't sure how to put it. Talk about a long story! It all had to do with the sound bite wisdom and advice that so often seemed like criticism.

"It's just—you feel the need to give me some piece of advice, when sometimes I just need you to sit and listen." That's the number one thing kids say about their parents: I just wish you'd listen. They want to be heard.

At that point my husband spoke up from the audience. "I think what would help is if you wait until Wy *asks* for the advice," he told Mom.

"Mom, what you can do is back off," Ashley said more bluntly.

Mom looked at me and in a particularly "instructive" manner asked: "What do I say I try to be?" When I didn't answer right away, she reiterated:

"What do I say I try to be like? The—"

I thought, *Uh-oh—here we go again!*

"Fireman," I said wearily.

"That's right," she said. "I only come when I'm called. Am I improving?"

"Yes, you are," I said. What I didn't say was: "I wish we didn't have to play these games." Believe it or not, I didn't feel like being funny.

Mom then insisted I read her book. I think she feels she has to promote herself, because she had been on her own for so long. For most of her life it was her against the world. I don't criticize her for it. I actually feel for her. She has often said, "I have to do it myself!"

That's the survivor in Mom, and it kept all of us alive many times. It's that same determination that she used to keep persevering until somebody in Nashville listened to our music. But what had worked for her for so many years was now beginning to affect our relationship in a way that wasn't working for me.

Mom explained that her book was about healing and it was helping thousands of people. Surely it wouldn't hurt me to read it.

"It's helping me," Ashley interjected. "It's a good book. And I'm a tough customer when it comes to my mother."

Mom gasped, and started to cry. She had had no idea Ashley was reading it.

"It's amazing that all that corny stuff you pull at the dinner table really works in print," Ashley added with a smile.

"I worked on this book for three years, and this is the

first time Ashley's ever mentioned it," Mom said to the audience. That didn't help.

At this point I was beginning to think Mom was being Naomi Judd promoting a product. But I decided not to point that out. I felt like it was important for Mom to feel validated. It was a rare exchange between her and Ashley. But Ashley did point it out. She told Mom that she had mentioned that she was reading *Naomi's Breakthrough Guide* so that Mom didn't have to sit there and try to sell it herself. "Of course, *you* think it's good," she said to Mom. "But *I* can vouch for it."

Wow, I thought. *Ashley isn't cutting Mom much slack!*

Ashley doesn't often offer much about her personal relationship with Mom. It's a very private subject. And she was right when she said she could be a tough customer when it came to our mom. It seems to me that her childhood sense of abandonment is still formidable. I think it took a lot for Ashley to talk about Mom's book on television.

At the end of the *After Show*, when Mom and I sang, both Ashley and Oprah had tears in their eyes. Music really is healing.

I often feel like we all wear masks, afraid of people finding out who we *really* are. It feels to me like people seldom quite get a true picture of us. I feel really frustrated that for a great deal of my life I've been portrayed as the one who was the overly emotional, rebellious Judd. Because of her political involvement, Ashley is often seen as a strong, literate leader, and she *is*. But to me she's more, too. She can be vulnerable, as we all can be. During the appearance I realized that as sisters, there were times when I felt like I led and provided strength, and other times when Ashley stepped into that role. On *Oprah* that day, I felt good that the three of us were not just labeled as professionals, as two singers and an actress. I felt that we were all seen as women, with the many dynamics of our family—all the strengths and vulnerabilities. That thrilled me.

Ashley left for the airport immediately after the show, and I felt an intense sadness. My heart ached. I realized how much I had missed her. We had just reconnected, and she was gone again. But I still felt that I had my sister back. And I felt incredibly grateful.

After the show Roach and I hugged everyone, said goodbye and got into our limousine. For me, the ride back to the hotel was bittersweet. I felt so many different emotions. By the time Roach and I got to our suite, I was so exhausted that I went straight to bed.

I lay there with all my makeup on, still fully dressed, recalling all the things that Mom, Ashley and I had said. I felt that for the most part the show went really well. (*At least no one lost a limb!* I silently joked.) I had not yet won the race, but I would run as long and as hard as I could. I was able to say some things that had been in my heart and I had survived the experience.

By the time I got home to Nashville, I had convinced myself that the experience had gone well for me and for our family. Roach, Mom, Ashley, Nana and I had all come together and I felt it was healing for each one of us.

A day later I called to make an appointment with one of my Onsite life coaches.

"How do you think the show went?" he asked.

"I thought it went great," I said.

Long pause, then: *"Really?"*

"Yeah."

"Have you watched the show on tape?"

"No, I haven't seen it."

Another pause. "If you're open to it, let's watch the show together."

I love that about my life coaches. They ask for permission.

They even suggest that people ask permission to hug a child. After all, the child might not *at that moment* be open to one. This also applies to adults. Allow the individual time to invite you in.

We put the tape in the VCR, and watching it became one of the most eye-opening experiences of my life.

What happened on the day I saw the second *Oprah* show is a good example of why I like to call the people at Onsite "life coaches" instead of therapists. They stand on the sidelines, not doing the work for you, but guiding you through the process. They help to interpret when there's a communications breakdown, but they won't give you the answer.

My life coach fast-forwarded the tape to the scene where Mom stood and said, "Bring it on."

"What do you think of this?" he asked.

"Well, that's Mom," I said with a shrug.

But I noticed that she seemed tense from start to end. For the first time, I started to have compassion for how fearful she must have been that day.

"Do you feel the tension building between the two of you?" the life coach asked.

Yes, I did. The show was filled with interactions where I thought, *What was that?!* and *Why the heck did she say that?!*

One significant moment was when, out of nowhere, Mom brought up my DUI, saying that my mug shot had been shown in *Time*, right next to a picture of Saddam Hussein. I was mortified! And before I had a chance to say, *What was that?!* she mentioned that she was the spokeswoman for M.A.D.D., Mothers Against Drunk Drivers. That was one moment when I became very defensive.

"Thanks for bringing that up," I said.

"Well," she said with a shrug. "They showed it."

Then she was off and running. "It's so bizarre. There are three hundred sixty-five days in a year, and that day after your DUI was a national vigil for M.A.D.D."

I wanted to run to the bathroom!

I do want to acknowledge that Mom then mentioned my community service, and that I had just received a humanitarian award from the country music industry. Is that called a bait and switch? Or a slap and hug?

The part of the show that affected me the most was when Mom was filmed with Elijah. Again, in the intensity of the moment, I wasn't awake to what had really happened.

On a B-roll tape that had been filmed in Tennessee, I was showing Oprah how growing a garden was part of my food recovery, as well as inspiring my children to work with me as part of our homeschooling. When we were filming in the greenhouse, Elijah and Grace hovered nearby, watching. Mom grabbed Elijah by the arm and pulled him into the shot with her. When he tried to pull away, Mom reached around and got him in a headlock.

My life coach pushed the PAUSE button on the remote.

"Wynonna, do you have any feelings about what is happening here?" he asked.

It hit me right in the face. Elijah is ten years old and at this point in his life dislikes being on television or having people stare at him. He's camera shy. Sometimes he'll agree to be part of the show, but most of the time he would rather play and be a kid. At this age in Elijah's life, it even embarrasses him when I kiss him in public! I think that's normal and I try to respect his wishes. We even made an agreement that he doesn't have to participate in tapings if he doesn't want to. On that particular day, we all knew he didn't want to be filmed.

While watching the tape, I noticed that after Mom got Elijah in a headlock, I walked over and instinctively put my hand on his head. Watching that scene, I realized that I must have subconsciously felt his misery, but I didn't stop the cameras and ask Mom to let go. I was too caught up in the moment and didn't act in the best interests of my son. *I had not lived up to my promise to honor his request to be asked before being on television.* Even one time is too many. Watching his face was all I needed to understand how he felt.

"There are no boundaries," I said, trembling. Both Ashley and I had issues with our mother about boundaries. Ashley had dealt with it, elbows out sharp. I had not. And now I had allowed my children to be put in the same predicament.

On Oprah's *After Show*, Ashley had pointed out Mom's tendency to say things about her daughters (like any mother would) on national television. She said she was still haunted by one experience back in 1995. Mom announced to the studio audience (and the world!) that Ashley wasn't wearing panties. Ashley was twenty-six years old at the time, and Mom was talking about her underwear!

"I've had flight attendants comment on that, Mom!" Ashley said.

Mom looked out at the audience and said: "She's wearing a *thong* today."

Ashley's jaw dropped. "I AM NOT. I think thongs are unhygienic, nasty things and I would NEVER wear one."

Mom had been saying inappropriate things in public about me for years, and I had never called her on it the way Ashley does. I remembered a time when Mom was on the Larry King show and started talking about my attention deficit disorder. I will tell anyone that I have ADD. But I don't necessarily want my mom talking about it. Not only did she have her say about *my* ADD, but she then started talking about my husband, Roach (without permission), indicating that he had the same condition. I sat and watched in disbelief. I said to myself, *This has to stop. You cannot do this to me! You cannot do this to my husband!*

I don't believe it is usually a parent's intention to shame or humiliate a child. It certainly isn't Mom's. But there is this sickness called *It's my right to say anything I want about you*. It may sound funny or even charming at the time, but it can still be hurtful or embarrassing. I think Mom feels a sense of entitlement when it comes to me. She not only raised me from birth but has continued to parent me privately and publicly in my profession. Mom still pinches my cheeks and pats me like a child in front of anyone from the next-door neighbor to the President of the United States. *Isn't she cute?* When it comes to my children, I've also had feelings of entitlement, of ownership. But as our children get older, it's no longer appropriate.

One of the toughest clips for me to watch was when Mom and I were at the Opry House and Mom introduced me to some fans as "Sweet Tater."

"A sweet tater is a big fat carb, Mom!" I had protested.

When the Opry clip was over, Oprah asked Mom if she always knew how to push my buttons. Mom's face froze. Oprah was *questioning* her. And in that frozen snapshot moment, I saw what was happening. I sometimes see my mother as two people—Diana Judd, the young woman who had me when she was only eighteen. That's the mom side that I love the most, the woman who is tenderhearted, soft and likes to laugh. She has enormous love for her family, friends and community. She is real. I had prayed for that part of her to show up.

Instead, I felt like the woman who showed up was Naomi Judd—the professional, the survivor, the part of Mom who feels she is on trial for her life. There is a judge and jury and she is the only one who can be her lawyer, the only one who will defend her. On top of that, this was all being done in the public eye. I felt incredibly sad and abandoned, in that moment, for the sake of television entertainment.

I thought a lot about what Oprah said about redefining relationships, and realized something important. This was not just about Mom. It was about all my relationships, the way I related to people in the past, in the present, and in the future. It was about me learning to *not be reactive*. How could I ever get to my weight issues if I couldn't get to my family issues and heal them?

Mom and I had a long journey ahead. The work that we had to do both independently and together was going to take time. Mom and I were on different paths, and had different information. I prayed that someday we'd make it together.

Hope didn't stop me from suffering a setback after watching that tape, though. I felt completely bewildered, was shaken to the core; just recognizing the difficulties ahead for Mom and me was overwhelming. Huge waves of sadness washed over me. I fell into a depression. I headed right back down the wrong road, the one filled with detours and dead ends. I wandered away from the light. I broke my promise to myself. I found it hard to work out and eat properly. I began using food for comfort again and canceled my workouts more. I gained weight. I felt bloated and sluggish. It's hard to know which I avoided more, my trainer or my mirrors.

I went back out on the road for the summer and had a successful tour. But at the same time, I felt such a sense of personal failure. I abandoned myself. I became more introverted with people again, and I lost my focus. I was so scattered that I was leaving messages at work for the wrong people. I literally had to look at a piece of paper to see what I was supposed to be doing every minute.

Professionally, it dimmed my light. It felt like such a letdown, like every day was the day after Christmas. I didn't let the people I love down, but I had abandoned myself. I continued to fulfill my obligations, even when I ended up crying all the way home. Once I got to my house I'd put on my depression clothes, the big-butt pants with no elastic, big shirts, putting my hair back in a ponytail, no makeup.

How many times had I sung these lines with confidence: *A dead end street's just a place to turn around.* Well, easier sung than done. It would be December 31 of 2004 before I got so sick and tired of being sick and tired that I put myself back on the list.

15

PEACE IN THIS HOUSE

It was a cold, dark and rainy day in New York. Roach, Kerry and I headed back to our hotel after a stressful day out. It was the 2004 Christmas season, and the streets of the city were in complete chaos. During the holidays, chaos can be good or bad. When it's good, the holiday hustle and bustle feels wonderful. People rush from store to store carrying packages, appearing confident that they've found that perfect gift for their loved one. The salesclerks smile and wish you a Merry Christmas. Joy is in the air.

But our shopping excursion had not been one of those times. Maybe it was because of the relentlessly cold rain, but people seemed to be in such a bad mood. Everywhere we went was overcrowded—the stores, the restaurants, the streets. Traffic was in gridlock. In all the years I've been to New York, I had never seen so many people in the streets. And every one of them seemed to be wearing black. I held my umbrella up as high as I could, yet I was still bumping into other people and their umbrellas. It was a parade of angry people—absolute madness.

Kerry, Roach and I hadn't been together on a trip like this for quite a while, and the three of us had been so looking forward to taking in the holiday cheer. Instead, people got meaner and meaner. I remember walking into one of the major department stores and it felt like a sauna. I said, "Merry Christmas," to the security guard standing at the entrance. He frowned at me and said, "Yeah, right!"

My heart sank. I turned to Roach and said, "I can't stay in here." Too many people seemed too unhappy. It felt toxic. So as we left the store I smiled at the security guy and said, "Don't forget the reason for the season." I laughed to myself and thought, *That sounds like something Mom would say*. It made me smile. She's a good teacher.

When we got back to the hotel on that cold rainy New York day, Kerry suggested we all go up to my room and order lunch together.

"I have something I want you to hear," she said. "I have found an incredible song for you!"

"A song?" I asked. Kerry had given me songs before, but she was practically glowing about this one.

"Yes," she said. "And I'm telling you, you're really going to love it!"

I was inspired and curious. Kerry gets excited about business deals. I had never seen her get so excited about a specific song! So for her to get this animated made me *really* interested. And when she spoke her next words, I couldn't wait to get to my room and listen!

"Wy, this song affected me deeply every time I listened to it."

We sat down in the room, and she put the CD in the player.

Hey you kids turn off the TV
No, I don't want to watch the evening news
So come over here and sit down next to me
And let your mama look at you, and you, and you,
*   and you*

*And your beautiful faces that I want to keep safe as
long as I have anything to say
I'm tellin' you right now*

As soon as I heard *and your beautiful faces*, I began to
cry. I could immediately see Grace, Elijah and Zac in my
mind's eye. I looked at Kerry. She had tears in her eyes.
Roach was emotional, too. Of course, Roach and I are already so emotional that we cry at stoplights! The moment
was so sweet, so personal. It didn't even feel like a commercial hit being pitched to me. It felt more like a love
song being played *for* me. Love permeated that room. It
was a beautiful, magnificent moment.

Then Kerry told me that the name of the song was
"Peace in This House." I smiled and said, "It's perfect."

The chorus played.

*There's gonna be peace in this house
Gonna be peace in this house
Gonna be some tender talkin'
And some sweet little nothings
That add up to the somethings we can't live without
There's gonna be peace in this house
Some belief in this house
And every good thing that ever happens
Starts from the inside out
I'm tellin' you now
There's gonna be peace in this house*

My soul opened up, and I felt an ache in my heart. Those
words confirmed what I want more than anything—peace
in my house. It's what I long for in my life and I believed
that the song had been written just for me. I felt the same

way as when I first heard "Only Love." It immediately became a *heart piece*. I called Angela Kaset, one of the song's writers, and told her that the song read like a beautiful prayer. The chorus draws you in and you can't help singing along. It was almost like singing a familiar hymn.

"Dear sweet child of God, what have you done?" I asked Angela.

I didn't do what I usually do when I want to record—call and ask to put the song on hold so that the publisher won't pitch it to anyone else. I just called to say how much the words and music spoke to me and how much I loved listening to such an incredible piece of music. Angela and I instantly connected and when I hung up I sat in amazement once again at God's timing.

I felt like this moment in time was a divine appointment. I don't find myself singing my own songs offstage very often. But the melody is so infectious that once I had listened to "Peace in This House" several times I found myself singing the chorus again and again. Then I began to hear Grace and Elijah and even Roach singing the song. This song set the tone for our family and it became the first song chosen for my next record. It also set the tone to begin the process of my healing—from personal and professional bankruptcy.

After months of feeling depressed, I turned a corner as I went through the rest of the holiday season. It is our family tradition to begin each new year with a theme. And by December 31, 2004, I had decided that the Judd/Roach family theme for 2005 was going to be Peace in This House.

In 2005, I was going to be back on the list!

One of the things that the second appearance on Oprah's show taught me was that even with all the work I had done at Onsite and in my other therapeutic experiences, I had not seriously dealt with certain parts of my childhood, with some of my family's dynamics. And so I took an individual workshop called Learning to Love Yourself, where I learned to separate the good from the bad, how to celebrate the good and heal the bad. It was one of the loneliest six days I could have imagined. I felt separated from everything and everyone except for God. I was told that many strong, successful businesspeople come to these workshops and truly experience for the first time deep feelings of pain and sadness. They arrive with a reservoir filled with tears, and sometimes end up crying the whole time they're at Onsite.

On the very first day of my workshop, my life coach and I constructed my family tree on the classroom board. Beside each family member I had to put a letter that represented various afflictions: for example, A for addiction; I for illness; D for drugs; S for suicide. After I constructed my coded genealogy, I stepped back and stood looking at my family history. My life coach said, "Well, they say that stuff trickles downhill."

I suddenly realized that there had been addiction, illness and abuse generation after generation. And unless the cycle was broken, unless I worked hard at learning how not to repeat history, but to live differently, that some of those dynamics could possibly be handed down to our children and the cycle would continue.

One of the things that I had not understood was that addiction takes so many forms—chemical addictions, pornography, gambling. *Anything* that separates you from your family or loved ones for unhealthy periods of time can be an addiction—work, for example. (There's a reason some people are called workaholics.) We are now discovering that some people are on the Internet up to fifteen hours a day. Technology has a place, but it cannot take the place of relationships.

I was shocked when I realized just how much addiction of one kind or another runs through my legacy. So many family members on my list had been affected by some kind of illness or addiction. That goes for most families. No one is exempt. And it affects you even more than you realize. If you put your own family tree on paper and code it, I can imagine that you would be surprised at all the addictions and illness that has affected the past and present. Nobody gets out of this world without some wounds.

I think that one of the most valuable things I have learned through my workshops is that if I want to change the world I must first change myself. I have to start with me. It's the Serenity Prayer, indeed! *God grant me the serenity to accept the things I cannot change.* I can go back in the past, draw from my experience and the reality of various family members, and get to my reality, find my own truth. One of my truths involved this thought: some people would rather be right than be loved. *I want to be loved.* No wonder I learned to put on shows and tell funny stories and jokes to get love and attention. I didn't have boundaries because I didn't want to say "no." I didn't want to disappoint. I wanted to be a mediator more than I wanted to be separated from family in a conflict.

As we worked at Onsite that week, I understood that a lot of what happened to me as a child and as an adult was a result of simply being at the right or wrong place at the right or wrong time. What family members and friends did to me was not about them not loving me or wanting to hurt me. What I realize now is that it didn't have anything to do with me. Those people were having life experiences, and I happened to be there. All of the things that I thought my mom and dad did *to* me were not about me. It finally set me free when I realized that they were just trying to survive, with too few tools. However it was important for me to acknowledge that there were many times during my childhood when I didn't get what I needed, physically, emotionally or spiritually. There were times when I felt unloved and insecure. I truly believe that if my mom and dad had known that a decision would affect me in a negative way, they would have done what they could to keep it from happening. But, as is so true in this life, things did happen.

Each day during my workshop we began peeling away the layers, like you would peel back an onion. On the third day of my workshop, I began feeling so many intense emotions that I worried if I could take it in. I started to feel more and more apprehensive about peeling away so many layers—it meant going back to my birth, to get to the smallest of small, to conception, the atom that is the beginning, the soul. It would mean getting down to the core of who I truly am. Finally, at the end of that third day, Wynonna Ellen came face-to-face with Christina Claire and it was in that small—almost microcosmic—moment, that I saw the vastness of what was happening in my journey home to myself.

I *knew* Christina. I went back in time and remembered that small innocent child. I had left her behind—I had abandoned her years ago. I had forgotten how it felt to be so young, so happy, so full of joy. I had grown up too fast and had learned to distract myself from my deepest feelings. We all use different distractions—food, alcohol, drugs, sex—to help dull the pain, to cope. But when you show up at Onsite, distractions are removed. The days and nights are spent in a quiet, serene setting, and you find yourself alone, able just to *be*. Once I began to understand that everything we were doing was a form of meditation, an act of kindness or love, I began to feel myself changing. I began to slow down. My blood pressure even slowed! I noticed that when I sat down to eat, I took the time to enjoy each portion of God's bounty instead of eating a whole plate of food without even tasting it. I started to hear and appreciate the birds singing on my daily walks. I began noticing the smallest flower. And it was in those quiet moments that I discovered that for years I had been carrying around the belief that *I'm not lovable*, that I'm not worthy of the incredible success I've had. It took me going through some difficult and painful therapy sessions to begin to understand that this philosophy was a lie that I had begun telling myself years ago—that there were things wrong with me, that I was the problem.

Only recently have I begun to fully understand the connection between my food addiction and my emotions. Mom has often said that she thinks my weight issues are because of my troubled relationship with my dad, Michael. I believe now that my relationships with both parents have a lot to do with my feelings about myself. My parents were so young when I was born, and spent so many years in survival mode, that they simply could not always meet my emotional needs.

I can remember being nineteen years old and craving a more intimate relationship with Mom that was not based on a successful career and hit records. I can remember yearning for time spent with her just talking and sharing stories about life instead of planning what we were going to wear on the *Tonight Show*. A lot of our personal mother/daughter relationship was lost to show business. And I spent years distracting myself from those intense feelings of loneliness with food. She and I missed out on a lot of opportunities to connect with one another from the heart.

While I did more work, I often thought back to that videotape from *Oprah*, to Mom being so aggressive with Elijah. I'm sure it was not Mom's intention to scare or embarrass Elijah and I believe that she would not have done it if she had known he was uncomfortable. But sometimes adults forget that they are so big and children are so small. They forget just *how* little children are—they already feel powerless with an adult.

I was brought up to be nice even when adults were not. Most of us were brought up that way. We were never taught to have healthy boundaries. We were told that it is even okay to tell a little white lie to keep from hurting someone's feelings. We were sent mixed signals. Onsite workshops have taught me to say what I mean, to mean what I say when I'm ready to say it. But the workshops have also taught me to not say things to shame or guilt someone.

Another moment on *Oprah* that kept coming back to me was when Mom had called me "Sweet Tater." I'm so sensitive about nicknames. If you label children, it can be damaging. I know so many adults who still *feel* like "the ditzy one" or "the clumsy one" or whatever they were labeled in the family. Words either encourage or discourage. I would NEVER say to a young girl, "You are getting *so* big!" Big represents weight. When someone says to Grace that she's getting *so big*, I immediately step in and say, "So Grace has really gotten *taller* since the last time you saw her." *No girl ever wants to hear that they're getting big, no matter how young or old they are!*

Another hot button for me was when Mom said something about me wearing a pair of jeans. I know she meant no harm, but I was still so embarrassed! I hardly ever wear jeans because I'm so self-conscious. Mom has been saying things that embarrass me for years. I thought that I had grown used to it, and I guess I had gotten to a point where

I even expected it and learned to play off of her, to say something funny in response.

In addition to the importance of *what is said*, I also learned how to understand *why* parents do and say things. What experiences in their own lives might contribute to their actions? For example, I thought about Mom's constant habit of checking my moles to see if they were any bigger. A good friend asked me if I thought that it had anything to do with the fact that Mom had been the one who discovered the lump on her brother Brian's back. It had never even occurred to me to think that this was the reason why she continues to check on me.

Most parents do not deliberately intend to ever break a child's spirit or to steal their joy. It certainly wasn't Mom's intention. I believe that in the past she has been real hard on me to try to kick my butt into gear. But there's also a feeling that I think most parents have called *It's my right to say anything I want to about you because I gave life to you*! It may sound funny or even charming at the time, but it can still be hurtful and embarrassing to the child. I think Mom feels a sense of entitlement when it comes to me. She not only raised me from birth, but she has continued to parent me privately as well as publicly into my adult life. It's sweet that Mom still pats me like I'm her little girl. But I'm forty-one years old and the other day she licked her finger and wiped something off of my cheek! She sometimes tells people stories about me not realizing that I might be embarrassed. I believe with all my heart that Mom will continue to see me as that eighteen-year-old girl standing next to her onstage until the day she goes to meet Jesus. She will always be my mom and I will always be her child.

When it comes to my children, I, too, have struggled with feelings of entitlement and ownership. It was so important for me to see that and to break the cycle! The other day, when Grace came downstairs, I started to say something about her hair and how I thought she should fix it. I stopped myself. The way Grace feels about herself and about the way she looks is so personal. I must admit that before I went to Onsite, I felt that the way my children looked was a reflection on me. I went through a time where I was *very* concerned about how Grace's hair looked. I have now learned to choose my battles. It's my job to teach her to take care of herself and not to make her dependent on me. I allow her the freedom to do her own hair, to decide on what she wants to wear. She has to learn to make good choices.

I have told all three of our children that unless I see that their behavior is unhealthy or unsafe, I will give them space—I will wait for them to ask my opinion before giving it unsolicited. I am enjoying watching them make healthy choices, and when they do make an unhealthy one, I'm there to redirect.

I also struggled with my way of handling day-to-day discipline and setting boundaries when I was a single parent. When they would fail to please, I felt the need to let them know how upset I was, how disappointed I was that they had not lived up to my expectations. I tried to get them to change their behavior by shaming or guilting them into doing something different. For example, before I did the work at Onsite, I might have said to Zac that I was disappointed that his grade had gone down from a B to a C. I might have said, "I expect better of you and if I see that your grade doesn't come up it's going to threaten your ability to get into a good college."

It always felt so hopeless. I thought that by talking so much I could get Zac to see into the future—to think like I did—but we would end with him feeling down and me continuing to be angry. I now keep it short and sweet. I remind him what the rules are and that I know he can do better. I now have the tools to do things differently and I feel calmer and more in control.

I'm enjoying learning to coparent. Roach and I first have meetings with each other, away from the children. We decide what the objectives are and how to discipline together. We then give information to the children without emotion. It has saved our relationship. We spend less time and energy on going over things again and again. We have learned how to cut the amount of words we use in half. Before the Onsite experience, we would have communicated on a case-by-case basis. Now we establish all the rules in advance. The children know what is expected regarding their grades and behavior, their chores and how they treat one another—it's all written down and posted. That takes the anger and the drama out of our day. As parents we often take our children's mistakes so personally that we actually think the child is doing it to us—and on purpose. Roach and I list our rules and the children can continue to see what it is that we want them to do—on paper. If the checklist doesn't get done, there is a consequence. The rules are written and we all know how to play the game.

We examine our role in the process, too. If we see that Zac's grades have come down, we first try to see what is distracting him from his schoolwork. If needed, we can possibly lighten the load, in an effort to keep him healthy and safe. There is no more shame or guilt—just results.

Before Onsite, if Elijah or Grace left out their belongings, it would really upset me and I would end up in an ongoing battle, trying to remind them how lucky they were. I would raise my voice, thinking they would see that I meant what I said.

"How many times do I have to tell you to put up your

...rt when you're done riding it for the day? When I was your age we couldn't afford go-karts! You're lucky to have such nice things!"

Now they know if they leave it out, they lose it for a week. All I have to do is say, "Your go-kart was out last night." I use fewer words and I don't have to lose my mind trying to encourage them to take care of their things.

Presetting guidelines has saved our family. For example, when we used to go to Disney World, everyone would be mad by the second day. Now, before we even get on the plane, we all write down two or three things that each of us wants to do when we get there. Each child knows what to expect and they can look forward to having their expectations met. Each person feels like they matter. There's no room for manipulation. Nobody is going to feel left out or forgotten. It has made a huge difference in the dynamics of our family.

When dealing with the children, Roach and I have also learned to mirror—the wonderful technique that we learned at Onsite. It takes extra time and energy but the return is worth every minute. Who doesn't want to feel heard?

I had a moment with Grace once when she said: "I don't want to live with you and Papa Roach anymore! I want to go live with my dad!"

I was so hurt and angry. What I wanted to say was "Your dad has never paid any child support or taken care of you for more than a few days since you were born! Go live with him and see how long it lasts."

But I remembered what I had learned about feelings—that they are not wrong. What Grace feels is not about punishing me. She must feel lonely and left out. She must want attention. Her wanting to live with her dad does not make me a bad parent. And so, even though I was truly emotional, I sat down and mirrored her:

"You sound really upset, Grace."

"I am really mad at you!" Grace cried.

At that point I was almost ready to go off—but I stayed with it. I allowed myself and Grace the chance to work through the problem and stay connected during conflict.

"What I hear you saying, Grace, is that you're really mad at me."

The key words are *what I hear you saying*. When children feel you're really hearing them, that they are safe to truly share with you their honest opinions, they will continue to sit with you and communicate. If they feel that you are judging them in that moment, or showing emotion about whether or not you agree or disagree with them, then they will shut down. The key is to hear them, and when they are done talking, your job is to validate them. I continued to tell myself that this wasn't about me.

"Is there more?" I asked.

"Yes!" Grace said.

I paused again, and waited. This is the hard part—to wait, to listen, to allow her to keep going without saying anything back.

"I don't want you to be married to Papa Roach!"

(We were starting to get to the bottom line. So I felt inspired.)

"You don't want me to be married to Papa."

"No! I wish it could be just us again. You, me and Elijah. I don't like you sleeping with Papa. I want to sleep with you."

(I call this the payoff—when your child begins to truly become vulnerable and shoot straight from the heart.)

"I want to sleep with you, Mom!" she cried again.

Then I summarized everything Grace had said.

"So what you're saying is that you're really mad at me and that you don't want me to be married to Papa, and that you wish it could just be me, you and Elijah again. You don't like me sleeping with Papa and you want to sleep with me instead. Is there more?"

"No," Grace said calmly.

I said: "Grace, I can imagine that you feel really lonesome for me right now, and that you wish I could spend more time with just you. I can also understand that you miss sleeping with me. Now that Papa and Zac have moved in, I can imagine that you feel left out. You don't want Papa to try and be your dad because you already have a dad. Did I get it all?"

"Yes," she said.

That seemed to satisfy her—just to be heard. So at this particular time, I decided not to try and change her mind or to fix the situation. I felt that the gift I could give both of us during that conflict was to continue to stay focused on Grace and allow her to be heard. Sometimes that's all the other person wants—to be heard and validated. Grace has not brought up wanting to go live with her dad again, but if she does, I'll be there for her once again.

I hope that one day Mom and I will go to Onsite for workshops together because then we, too, could feel heard in such a safe environment. If we could work on communicating using techniques like mirroring, I believe she and I could eventually be able to drop our defenses and begin to fully understand who we are as individuals. We could avoid so many misunderstandings.

For example, when I think back to *Oprah*, and Mom saying, "Bring it on," I can imagine that she felt that she was getting ready to have to defend herself in front of Oprah and everyone. It made sense that she might react that way because she could have thought that I was getting ready to blast her, as I have many times in the past. Mirroring, and getting deeper into our real feelings, our deepest ears, allowing ourselves to be vulnerable to one another will be a wonderful experience because it is then that I can ee her as Diana Ellen Judd, the child of God, not Naomi Ellen Judd, my mother.

I now understand that during the taping of *Oprah*, I was o busy reacting to what Mom was saying to me, thinking of what I was going to say back to her, that it was hard for ne to notice the dynamics of what was going on. In the heat of the moment, my emotions were running too high or any objectivity. But sitting quietly, viewing the tape, I was able to step back from the intensity. I had backed down from Mom at the show, even though I had intense feelings and opinions about what she had said, because I had learned not to be disrespectful.

And thus began a great discovery about my relationship with my mom. Once, when Mom had deeply hurt my feelings, I struggled with the relationship, and felt hurt that she had not apologized to me. My counselor reminded me to "continue honoring what is honorable." When Mom guilts or shames me, she may not even know she is doing it. I don't have to accept what she has done, but it's important o accept who she is, to honor her for the many honorable things she *is*. I remember saying the Serenity Prayer at On-ite, the way *they* say it: *God grant me the serenity to ac-ept the things I cannot change* (which is Mom), *the courage to change the things I can* (which is me) *and the wisdom to know the difference* (which is hard!).

I now feel that when Mom started talking about my DUI and Mothers Against Drunk Drivers, she might have elt a need to be looked upon as an authority on the sub-ject. She might have felt the need to defend me but at the same time to remind me of where she stands on the issue. Yes, she is so bright, and has had so much life experience. But we must be careful when talking about our children as if they are not in the room. We also must keep in mind that we sometimes say things because we are trying to be cool or show just how brilliant a parent we are. (We all love to be geniuses and impress others, don't we?!)

I also thought about the dynamic between my manager, Ken, and me during both the Judds' career and my early solo career. When I was a new artist, I believed that Ken discovered us—that he was doing me a favor by managing me. I will always appreciate what he did for me over a decade. However, I was so naive. I continued to believe for such a long time that if not for Ken I would be singing in a hotel lounge still today! When he called me *shit-for-brains*, I believed him.

Being raised in a home and business where the expectations were so high and the words said were often harsh, I developed such a criticism of my own abilities. It has taken me years to reprogram my thoughts and feelings about SELF. I have had to relearn a new and different way of communicating to the people I love, work and live with.

In writing this book, and examining my family and career, I have now changed the way I do business. For example, Kerry, my manager, who stands in the gap between the business and me, sometimes has to come to me and say, "You are not going to like the choices, but I need to give you the facts." There was a time when, if I *didn't* like what I heard, I would get defensive and feel like she was on their side and not mine. I would go into a siege mentality. Now that Kerry and I have both gone to Onsite, and we *hear* each other, our communication is healthier than ever. We are able to validate feelings and at the same time face the reality.

Prior to doing this life-changing work, if I was shooting a video, and the director suggested doing something I didn't want to do or was uncomfortable trying, I would

ave gotten scared and become negative about whether or
ot I was capable of doing it. These directors are powerful
eople, and sometimes they have completely different
deas of what I should do or how I should present myself. I
ave finally learned how to be a cocreator without being
mbattled. Now I have learned how to dialogue. It's a big
ing to be able to say, "I hear what you are saying, but I
isagree."

Recently I had a situation with one of my longtime
and members. During a meeting about the tour, this indi-
idual seemed uninterested in being a part of our group.
he meeting was ending and this person asked, "What
me is dinner? When are we going to eat?" I was so of-
nded. My feelings were really hurt—I was in need of
reative input about the show and was asking everyone for
eir help. I was really counting on everyone, yet this per-
on seemed distracted and in a hurry. The next day I asked
or a private meeting. I was concerned that our words
ight lead to a hurtful separation. It had only happened a
w times in my life, because when it comes to people I try
hang on for good!

In the past I would have felt the need to be heard first.
ut instead of getting all worked up and telling the person
ow upset I was, how emotional I felt (yada, yada, yada), I
mply asked a question:

"Is there something going on with you that you want to
ll me about?"

I learned that the person was very ill, had in fact received the bad news the day of the meeting and was strug-
ling not to cry in front of everyone. *Thank God I had
one the work on developing new communication skills!*
ometimes when you have some success, you start to think
ou are *so* fabulous that you automatically deserve to be
eard *first*. I now try harder to wait to be invited in. It has

been one of the hardest parts of my journey—to listen when I have a strong opinion, and to not interrupt when I disagree.

The work I continue to do has changed the way I give interviews, too. In the past, my tendency was to interrupt the interviewers, to cut them off before they had even finished asking the question because I get so excited. I now know that I had the habit of answering without really listening to what was first being asked. Now I listen more carefully to what the other person has to say, then pause before I speak. I have finally developed a healthy way to carry on a conversation in both interview situations, and with my friends and acquaintances. (If you want a friend, you have to *be* one.)

I have had good results from traditional therapy, but I have to admit that after a while I get so weary of going in, stirring the pot of emotions, feeling them and then going home. It's like taking a box down off the shelf, opening it up, looking through it, crying, then closing it and putting it back on the shelf.

What Onsite did was give me new tools that help me to change the behavior. Onsite workshops have given me the information I need, the "why" and the "how" of understanding the choices I have made. For the first time in my life, I'm examining my habits and the reasons I do the things I do. The workshops have given me the tools so that I will not allow myself to get lost in emotionally unsafe conflicts with people. I have learned how to take care of myself in many different kinds of relationships, long before you might say, *Uh-oh, this situation is really going to hell!* I now know who I feel safe with and who I don't. I know how to limit my time with these people before things become unhealthy.

I have also come to understand the effects of my

engthy separations from Ashley. Ever since I went out on the road, I have pined for my little sister—even if there were times that I was so involved in my career that I didn't fully grasp how much I missed her. Since the day Ashley hitched that U-Haul to the back of her car and drove herself to Hollywood, I've pined for her even more.

I have always wanted to have a big family—I think that's why I kept so many people on yearly salaries even when I wasn't working. I want the people I love close to me. I have missed out on having those daily sisterly talks about life. Sometimes I sit alone thinking that someday when Ashley and I are sixty and sixty-four, we'll be living close to each other on the farm, where we can walk and talk in her flower gardens and the only thing that matters is what we're having for dinner. There was a time when I couldn't even think about that dream without crying. I have been so hungry for a deeper connection with Ashley that I know I wore her out at times. When we were together, I would get so emotional that I can imagine that I used up most of the oxygen in the room. I was so manic about wanting to be with her that she must have felt smothered. I have had to relax and try to breathe through all those desperate memories.

I also spent so much time and energy thinking I had to take care of Ashley and Mom. Ashley witnessed my struggle to be loyal to both of them. I wasn't healthy enough to tell Mom that I didn't want to be in the middle anymore. I was too busy doing my best to survive, living with Mom 24/7 and failing miserably at being a big sister so far away.

Ashley was recently quoted in *Ladies' Home Journal* saying that her relationship with me was getting better because I was getting healthier. I think she knows that I am now able to take myself out from the middle between my mom and my sister and say, "Mom, you need to go talk to

Ashley about that yourself." I finally realized that I canno force one to have compassion for the other. I've finall learned how to *let go, and let God*. That knowledge ha added a few years onto my life, I'm sure!

I have also learned a tremendous amount about forgive ness. One of my dearest and oldest friends, Bryce Edgar, i one of the greatest examples of unconditional love an loyalty that I have ever experienced. We dated early in m career, and at times I wasn't honest in my relationship wit him. I even abandoned the relationship, yet he never gav up on me or cast blame. Bryce stayed humble and real, tol me how he felt and said that he would never abandon m It has been my experience that most people stick aroun until something doesn't go their way, then it's *Well, I'll se ya*. But between us, it was never just about something on or the other did. It has always been about who we are t each other. I have always known that if I was ever in trou ble and called Bryce, there would be no hesitation. So if have any piece of advice to offer you when it comes to tak ing stock: look around and see if you can identify th keepers—the lifers. Then hang on to them.

Even with all the work dealing with everything fro family to forgiveness, I knew there was something left— still had to deal with my *past trauma*. To do that work, contacted Dr. Janis Christenson in Nashville. Dr. Christen son uses EMDR (Eye Movement Desensitization an Reprocessing), which some professionals say is the mo important treatment involving trauma. It was first used o war veterans who suffered from combat-related post traumatic stress syndrome.

Traumatic memories are so powerful and easily trig gered that they continue to echo in your brain. EMD works by changing the way traumatic memories are store in your memory, giving you more control over them. Whe the memory doesn't get triggered as easily, you don't have to relive the event over and over. I knew, for example, that my early sexual traumas continued to affect my relationships with men even into adulthood. I worked with Dr. Christenson to "refile" those memories, as well as other traumas—like learning that my dad, Michael Ciminella, was not my biological father. I still have some memories that I continue to work through. The time when I was stuck in Atlanta and Mom didn't come for me is one of those memories. Another is when I left my manager, Ken Stilts, after twelve years. On a Monday he was still my manager, but come Friday I never saw him again. There was no closure. I still have dreams about him and wake up crying. Despite all the turmoil, he meant a lot to me. We *never* forget someone we have loved! And so I continue to do work at Onsite, to work with Dr. Christenson on past trauma. I continue to work on my weight and health issues. It's not over!

I almost couldn't write this last chapter. I felt like I hadn't made enough progress to make this a success story (by the world's standards). After all, I still don't wear a size eight. I realize more than ever that we live in a society that is consumed with being younger and thinner. Every time you watch television, you see younger models, more advertisements for products like Viagra. The Internet is bombarded with e-mails promoting breast and penis enlargements. Knowing that so many of us struggle to find peace in the physical world makes me very sad.

It has taken me forty-one years to come to terms with the fact that for so much of my life I have forgotten to put myself on the list. I did not take care of me. I loved my neighbors not *as* myself, but *more than* myself. I am still on my way to the top of the mountain. I am working harder than I ever have at learning to do a "little bit" some of the time instead of a "lot" all of the time when it comes to food and spending. I still face crises, and have to regroup. So I am certainly a work in progress.

But in talking with Kerry, I was reminded of the real steps I have taken. Since that day when I called her and said I had hit a wall, Roach and I have been on a cash budget (no personal credit cards) and cut our family and individual spending by 30 percent; we've cut concert expenses by running a leaner, more cost-effective and efficient tour. Roach and I are much healthier mentally, spiritually and physically. Just last week I got the numbers from my doctor. I was ecstatic! My cholesterol is down from 274 to 198. (200 is considered normal.) My triglyceride numbers are down as well, and now sit at 165. That's down from 274. (Normal is 150.)

I know that the next stage of my journey is getting real about food portions and my commitment to working out on a consistent basis. I have been eating healthier food— the numbers show that—but I have had to be honest about *how much* I eat and *how little* I exercise. I know that even when I feel out of control in my life, I can control what I put in my body. I not only eat meals when I am hungry, I continue to use food to soothe throughout the day. In my life, food has provided insulation; it has grounded and protected me. All you need do to see just how much it has meant is to reread my letter to food!

It's time to find other ways to be fed—to feel full—to comfort and heal my life and my body!

When I first went to Chicago to meet with Oprah, weight was just one of my concerns. So when Bob Greene and Oprah talked with me about my weight, though I was grateful, I felt like there was so much more I had to face. I knew in my heart that I had a lot of emotional and spiritual work to do as well. It wasn't as simple for me as eating less and exercising. I knew I was a food addict and I wanted to succeed. I tried to follow Bob Greene's instructions—I wanted so much to be "that girl." I failed. I started out with great enthusiasm, but after the second *Oprah* appearance I found myself in a depressed state, feeling defeated.

This I know: weight isn't the problem. It's a symptom. Now dig that! I know that I have to better understand how I got to where I am today and what emotions cause me to continue to use food to distract from the pain. I also know that the more I communicate, the more I cry and laugh from the depths of my soul, the happier and healthier I'll be. If I don't go within, I go without.

I have become a student of change. Today I am grateful that my first meeting with Oprah and Bob Greene was where it all began. I stepped out on faith and allowed myself to open up my spirit, mind and body to what the universe had in store for me. But as time went on, I learned that there was so much more that I had to deal with than just the physical. Then the question was, where to begin? I realized that weight was the window that I had to go through first to begin the process of my healing. It was tough squeezing through!

Once inside, I began to look around my "house"—which represents *my life*. Every room was in complete disorder. It was time to clear the clutter—to change my lifestyle. I started with the kitchen (my relationship with food), the living room (family counseling), and my office (time management, organizing my finances). I'm still working on completing the renovation. (The dictionary defines "renovation" this way: restore to good condition; renew; repair.) Then I guess I'll have to redecorate! (I'll have time to get that extreme makeover—a lift, a suck and a tuck . . . NOT!)

I just want to be healthy. Can I get an Amen?

* * *

Turning forty and taking stock of my life gave me permission to allow myself to stop worrying about being defined by the world outside and start enjoying being defined from within. I had used the idea of looking back on my life—the colorful musical journey I have had both personally and professionally—to create my 2004 concert tour. I took the word "History" and changed it to "Herstory" (I live for creative moments like this) because during the show I tell my story—a *woman's* story—by singing the music that I loved growing up, the hits I made, and the songs I have continued to listen to while traveling down the road to my dreams. The tour, titled "Herstory: Scenes from a Lifetime," was one of the highlights of my life. It gave me the chance, after twenty years of working hard to create a foundation in country music, to take a musical vacation— to enjoy singing bluegrass, pop, rock, blues and gospel. I traveled beyond the musical boundaries. I drove to the very edge, stood there and sang at the top of my lungs, free to be me.

This tour was planned differently than any I had done. Usually you hire a coordinator, and they help plan your material around what they think the audience wants. But I planned this tour—for me.

The tour was so loved by the critics and the fans that my record label, Curb, decided to film a DVD of the two hour show and release it this year. What a celebration that night was! I felt like I was being given a Lifetime Achievement Award for having survived twenty years of living on the road. I felt like I was being given the key to the universe, the key to starting on the next chapter of my life—which is what writing this book represents to me.

Everyone I care so much about was coming to the show that night. I was overcome with feelings of love and support. The backstage vibe was electric! There was so much joy—

and I had a true sense of this night being magical. In a setting like this, it's easy for an entertainer to start to feel arrogant. You can start to feel full of yourself. But after all these years, I felt like that night was not about ego; it was about spirit. I told myself, "Tonight I'm going to sing like I never have before. I'm going to celebrate *what I am* instead of being consumed with *what I'm not*. I'm going to show up and wait for God to walk through the room."

My Onsite workshops taught me how to slow down and appreciate every moment. Those tools came in handy on the day of the DVD taping. I approached the day of the show the same way that I would if I were at Onsite, slowing things down, appreciating and savoring every moment. I remember walking down several flights of back steps at the Opryland Hotel listening to how my shoes sounded as they hit the concrete. I paused when I stepped outside the hotel. I found myself constantly stopping to take a mental snapshot of each experience.

If you knew that you only had so much time on this earth, you would see everything differently. That's how I looked at things that night. I was keenly aware that this was a once-in-a-lifetime night. I couldn't believe that I wasn't sick to my stomach over being on camera! I didn't have that *I'm going to throw up* stage fright.

I had insisted that the show be taped from beginning to end—no stopping for mistakes. I wanted the show to be real. In an interview prior to the taping, I was asked, "What can we expect to see when you perform on the night of your DVD taping?"

"Imperfection!" I said, laughing. "I'm going to dare to allow myself the opportunity to make mistakes and experience real life as it happens." What a concept!

As I sat alone in my dressing room for a few minutes before I started my hair and makeup, scenes from my life kept flashing before me. I looked in the mirror. "You've come a long way, girl," I said aloud. Then I thought of my mamaw and papaw. I always miss them at these big events. I would have given anything if they could have been there with me.

"Hello, Christina," a voice said.

I looked up and smiled. "I love you, Don Potter," I said, and started crying.

"I see a little girl named Christina," he said, and walked over to hug me.

"Do not worry tonight," he continued. "You are the instrument. Let the Lord play you."

Don confirmed what I had felt in my heart all day. I felt safe and loved.

When Don left, I got ready. I teased the roots of my hair, broke out the jumbo-sized hair spray. (I planned on breakin' a serious sweat that night!) I lined my lips and slapped on the shine. As I put my stage clothes on, my heart opened up and it felt like someone had poured warm honey down my body. I walked out of the dressing room and down the hall to the "circle of life," where Don led the band, crew, family and office staff in prayer. We all held hands and I squeezed Grace's hand. She looked up at me and said, "Mommy, you look so pretty."

"Thank you, my sweet girl," I said. My eyes welled up. All the crap we go through in life—it's all worth it when you share moments like this with your children.

I stepped into my quick-change booth and put on my ear monitors. They fit way down into my ears and allow me to hear the audience. That really gets me activated! I listened as a young girl said she'd driven almost ten hours to be there to hear the show. My heart started racing! No matter what is going on in my life, I know that when I walk onstage, the most important thing for me to do is to light a fire underneath that girl's butt—and everyone else's! I want them to experience emotion. Music prepares the heart, opens us up so that we can begin to heal.

I sprayed sparkles in my hair and walked to center stage. Standing behind the red velvet curtains, I could feel the energy from the audience, and even though I felt no stage fright, my knees were weak with emotion. The lights dimmed and the audience erupted with applause. A lightning bolt of energy shot through my body. It was a feeling of total bliss—a heaven on earth moment. I had come home, to my music, and to myself.

As the curtain started to rise, I took a long, deep breath and held it in. "This is it," I said aloud. All of a sudden I was aware of my body, and I thought, *I may not be exactly where I want to be—but I'm sure as heck not where I was!*

The audience rose to give me a standing ovation and I stepped into the light.

Penguin Group (USA) Online

What will you be reading tomorrow?

Tom Clancy, Patricia Cornwell, W.E.B. Griffin,
Nora Roberts, William Gibson, Robin Cook,
Brian Jacques, Catherine Coulter, Stephen King,
Dean Koontz, Ken Follett, Clive Cussler,
Eric Jerome Dickey, John Sandford,
Terry McMillan, Sue Monk Kidd, Amy Tan,
John Berendt...

You'll find them all at
penguin.com

*Read excerpts and newsletters,
find tour schedules and reading group guides,
and enter contests.*

Subscribe to Penguin Group (USA) newsletters
and get an exclusive inside look
at exciting new titles and the authors you love
long before everyone else does.

PENGUIN GROUP (USA)
us.penguingroup.com